'This is really an amazing book . . .; it is life-threatening to forget, and life-threatening to give such interpretation before we are mature to receive it.'

Prof. Dr. Yolanda Gampel, *professor in Advanced Psychotherapy, Sackler Medical School, Tel-Aviv University, Israel; training, supervising and past president of the Israel Psychoanalytic Society and Institute; vice-president of the European Federation of Psychoanalysis (2001–2005); representative for Europe on the board of the IPA (2007–2011); recipient, Hayman International Prize and the Mary S. Sigourney Award, 2006*

'I was greatly honoured to be able to read such a brilliant and excellent work. The author succeeds in re-creating and condensing what is best in Bion in such a brilliant way. This makes him a remarkable thinker in psychoanalysis. This book should absolutely be read.'

Prof. Dr. David Rosenfeld, *M.D., professor of psychiatry and mental health at the medical faculty of the University of Buenos Ayres; training and supervising psychoanalyst at the Buenos Aires Psychoanalytic Association. He was awarded the 1996 Sigourney Prize*

'Monteiro takes psychoanalysis out of the dogmatism in which it locked itself up to make it rediscover all the freshness of its beginnings. Freud's *interpretation of dreams* has marked its emergence; the *dream functions* (Bion) raise a corner of the veil of the mysterious process of transformation of the physiological into the psychic. Monteiro brings together Bion's *dream functions* and Meltzer's *theory of intimacy*. A big step in the understanding of the analytical work. Nothing more mechanical, systematic, forced in the analytical work, but the emergence from the depths of the unknown, the unknowable and the unthinkable (*dream's navel*) of a sense that never exhausts the living forces of the human soul, but which gradually reveals to our amazed eyes the beauty of the inner world.'

Prof. Dr. Didier Houzel, *M.D., emeritus professor at Caen University (France); training and supervising analyst at the French Psychoanalytic Association*

'As I became increasingly engaged in Monteiro's rigorous and yet passionate book, I experienced it as a genuinely artistic (master)piece.

The way the author has read Bion led him to formulate the ground-breaking thesis that psychoanalysis is essentially about the *unknown, the unknowable* and *the unthinkable.*

The conclusion of this astonishing book speaks for the whole book in an inextinguishable moment of emotional beauty: Meltzer's "(. . .) strenuous and astonishingly powerful clamour: 'NOOO!!. . . You *always* have to be *beyond* the breaking-point!!'" resonates in this book from beginning to end. *We can read this book, hear it, feel it, dream it all along Monteiro's poetic and passionate voyage to the realm of the unknown, the unknowable and the unthinkable; to the very heart and soul of psychoanalysis, to the unending mystery of psychoanalysis and the psychoanalytic praxis.*'

Prof. Dr. Carlos Farate, *M.D., training and supervising analyst at the Portuguese Psychoanalytic Society; Editor-in-Chief of the* Revista Portuguesa de Psicanálise (Portuguese Journal of Psychoanalysis)

T0386459

'Monteiro takes us to the edge of that which is essential to our analytic work: "the unknown, the unknowable, and the unthinkable". He reveals another level of understanding of Bion's theory of dreaming. While we accompany him on this journey, he poses questions about Bion's theory of dreaming, then circles back to answer them, always taking us to a level of understanding beyond what we knew about Bion's model of the mind, and the ever-deepening perplexity and mystery of dreams and dreaming. The mind continuously creates itself into existence through dreaming.

Monteiro expands our thinking about the process of dreaming. Rather than something to be avoided by the analyst, uncertainty becomes a precious guiding light in our analytic thinking and work.'

Dr. John A. Schneider, Ph.D., personal and supervising analyst, Psychoanalytic Institute of Northern California

'This is not just a book on Bion's theories but a text that investigates the psychic functions that lie beyond the dynamic unconscious and that concerns the great terrain of unknowable and unrepresentable mental functions that are the basis of our existence. Written in a clear and compelling way, this book is a strong stimulus for future psychoanalytic thinking.'

Dr. Franco De Masi, M.D., training and supervising analyst at the Italian Psychoanalytical Society; former President of the Psychoanalytic Centre of Milan; author of nine books with Karnac/Routledge

'Monteiro's book is nothing short of a work of genius. It touches on the mechanism of unearthing and enveloping in the psyche much of what lives beyond the edge of the unthinkable, revealing for the reader, with the delicate manner of an artist, additional lay-ers. As Meltzer's student, Monteiro directs us to work with the primal, chaotic and psy-chotic areas within the psyche and proposes an analytic attentiveness similar to that of a musician. Additionally, he suggests that it is in these areas that the patient listens to the analyst's interpretation in a manner akin to the way one listens to music, or to the manner in which a baby perceives his mother's language.'

Dr. Hilit Brodsky, Ph.D., training and supervising analyst at the Israel Psychoanalytic Society; lecturer at the Tel Aviv Institute of psychoanalysis and university; awarded the Psychoanalytic Training Today Award (2015) and the Hayman Prize (2021)

'In this carefully reasoned book about the functions of dreaming, Monteiro puts us in touch with the passion and the awe of meaning making. His creative and inspiring interpretation of Bion's dream work describes the ongoing development of our minds as a deeply uncon-scious process of contact with that which is unknown, unknowable and unthinkable. The book is a disciplined study and an intuitive original exploration of the process of dreaming. Indeed, the book is even more than that: it explores what it is to be human.'

Dr. Judy K. Eekhoff, Ph.D., training and supervising analyst and a full faculty member of Seattle Psychoanalytic Society and Institute; former president of Northwestern Psychoanalytic Society & Institute. Author of Trauma and Primitive Mental States, An Object Relations Perspective *and* Bion and Primitive Mental States, Trauma and the Symbiotic Link

'This is a deeply stimulating, enriching and extremely well-written book. The author believes the mind is continually dreaming the unthinkable. He provides many thought-stimulating and interesting ideas, such as the significance of the analyst's kindness and sustained sensitivity to uncertainty and complexity. A significant contribution of Monteiro's reading of Bion is the implications it has for the analyst. By conceptualizing the mind as dependent on dreaming, he explores how the human mind is endlessly mysterious, evoking awe and humility. The challenge of the analyst is to be sensitive to this creative and mysterious dreaming function in himself and in his patient. The analyst's role is not first to interpret, but to be passionately interested and in wonder of the patient's unconscious.'

Prof. Erik Stänicke, *Ph.D., former President of The Norwegian Psychoanalytic Society; member of the Research Committee, Norwegian Psychoanalytic Society; Associate Professor of clinical psychology at the University of Oslo*

Bion's Theory of Dreams

Through a richly detailed close reading of Wilfred R. Bion's work on dreaming, as scattered across multifarious and largely unworked texts, this book argues that Bion's thinking can form a unified theory of dreams which extends and has further implications as a visionary model of the mind.

The central quality of Bion's visionary model of the mind is the belief that all that is interesting in the human mind pulsates with an unreadably complex dynamic beyond the unknown, the unknowable and the unthinkable. However, rather than interpreting this negatively, the author understands the inevitable unknowability of the human mind as a call to perplexity and wonder which actively encourages the intuition of fundamental insights into who and what determines our internal lives. A major implication of this belief is that psychoanalysis is itself essentially about the unknown, and Monteiro generates informed observations about how this may influence psychoanalytical work.

Providing renewed insight into psychoanalytical understandings of dreams, this book is essential reading for any psychoanalyst wishing to broaden their knowledge of the importance of Wilfred R. Bion's dream work.

João Sousa Monteiro has been a psychoanalyst in private practice in Lisbon. He has worked under the supervision of Donald Meltzer, meeting him in Oxford every month for 13 years, and twice monthly for the last few years. Meltzer supervised all his clinical cases during these years. He authored *Long-term Psychoanalytic Supervision with Donald Meltzer: The Tragedy of Triumph* (Routledge, 2019), which describes in great detail the supervision of a particularly demanding analysis over 12 years. João has made five radio programmes on psychoanalysis, four of which are in conversation with distinguished analysts, including a co-founder and former president of the Portuguese Psychoanalytic Society. Four books came from these programmes, one of which he authored, and the other three he edited.

Bion's Theory of Dreams

A Visionary Model of the Mind

João Sousa Monteiro

Routledge
Taylor & Francis Group

LONDON AND NEW YORK

Designed cover image: 'Durante o Sono' by Rui Chafes, 2002;
photograph: Paulo Costa. Centro de Arte Moderna –
F Gulbenkian.

First published 2023
by Routledge
4 Park Square, Milton Park, Abingdon, Oxon OX14 4RN

and by Routledge
605 Third Avenue, New York, NY 10158

*Routledge is an imprint of the Taylor & Francis Group, an informa
business*

British Library Cataloguing-in-Publication Data
A catalogue record for this book is available from the British
Library

ISBN: 978-1-032-45053-7 (hbk)
ISBN: 978-1-032-45051-3 (pbk)
ISBN: 978-1-003-37515-9 (ebk)

DOI: 10.4324/9781003375159

Typeset in Times New Roman
by Apex CoVantage, LLC

To Carmo

Contents

10   Bion's Theory of Dream-Work-Alpha: Part II   88

11   The Enigmatic Fabric of Mental Life   104

12   The Dreaming Ego   115

13   How Conscious Is Conscious and Unconscious Unconscious?   121

14   Freud's Wrestling With "The Fact of Consciousness"   129

15   What, Then, Is a Dream?   133

16   The Soul and the Stone   140

17   Still Unregistered Disorders   143

18   I Don't Know   148

19   What Is *Hearing*?   152

PART 2
The Human Mind as the Celebration of Unmeasure   179

20   The Fundamental Basic Assumption of Psychoanalysis   181

21   The Myth of Interpretation and the Role of the Ineffable   191

22   The Slippery Word *Understanding*   200

23   Knowledge as a Privileged Path to Intimacy   208

24   Passion and the Wonder of Unmeasure   216

25   The Misfortune of Explanation   225

26   "Thinking With Passion Is the Unconscious Thing"   229

27   The Inspiring Light of Perplexity and the Emerging
     Experience of Mystery: A Note   243

     Conclusion   245

     Bibliography   246
     Index   252

Acknowledgements

I am deeply grateful to Prof. Dr. Yolanda Gambel, Prof. Dr. David Rosenfeld, Prof. Dr. Dider Houzel, Prof. Dr. Carlos Farate, Dr. Franco De Masi, Dr. John Schneider, Dr. Bernd Nissen, Dr. Hilit Brodsky, Dr. Judy K. Eekhoff and Prof. Erik Stänicke – for their touching generosity, for the warmth, even often keenness and inspiring depth of so many of their remarks. I am also so grateful to them for the correspondence I was so privileged to have exchanged with many of them. Many of their words will remain with me for a very long time as a source of gratitude and of a deeper source of understanding.

I am also deeply indebted to Georgina Clutterbuck, Editorial Assistant at Routledge, for her so rare kindness and care at every single step of the demanding process of editing this manuscript.

Presentation of the Book

Most of Bion's deeply inspiring insights and thoughts on dreams and dreaming still live today in the printed page in the form of widely scattered, unconnected and unworked pieces.

This book argues that most of these deeply inspiring pieces can, however, be worked out into the relatively unified form of a theory. This theory is called, in this book, *Bion's Theory of Dreams*. This theory is shown to branch out into *a visionary model of the mind*.

The most crucial quality of this model of the mind is the belief that all that is interesting in the human mind intensely pulsates in an unreadably complex creative dynamic beyond the edge of the unknown, the unknowable and the unthinkable. So in whatever way we may try to very deeply look into the human mind, we are promised to be soon lost in both perplexity and wonder. A major implication of this belief is that psychoanalysis is itself essentially about the unknown, the unknowable and the unthinkable.

This book comes out not exactly of Bion's words themselves but of the inspiring depth of his own perplexity and wonder that his words are believed to speak so deeply of as he struggles with the unending much he is so unprepared to see through the host of enigmas and mysteries tightly weaving the human mind, or rather *being* the human mind. An equally crucial source of inspiration guiding us to closely follow Bion's visionary model is his feeling so often so deeply lost before all he could not read in the human mind.

Bion's perplexity itself, together with his feeling so often so deeply lost, speak in an odd voice. The inspiring light of uncertainty, which we all owe Bion to have first brought to the heart of psychoanalysis, still joins this voice. This voice can very attentively be heard in his written words. This book is an attempt to read some of the immensely much this voice has to tell us.

Foreword

The characteristic of a genius is his ability to discover new horizons on the physical or psychical world, changing our view of the reality that surrounds us or inhabits us. At each stage of this discovery, however, there is the risk of freezing this view, forgetting the very movement of the discovery, carrier of creativity. Everything, then, seems to happen as if the audacity which had pushed the discoverer towards those new horizons had led him to a vertigo that it is urgent to control by stopping this progression of the mind.

Freud had opened the black box of our inner world and embarked on a meticulous exploration of every corner to which he had access. His legacy is impressive, almost staggering, to the point of giving rise to quarrels over orthodoxy that tend to freeze metapsychology in an intangible dogmatic. Wilfred Bion wanted to escape this rigidity, whether it comes from the legacy of Freud or that of Melanie Klein. Perched on the shoulders of these giants,[1] he has adopted a whole new vertex by being less interested in the content of the psychic world than in the functions that animate it. Bion's metapsychology is a theory of psychic functions, but the extreme conciseness of his writings makes it difficult to apprehend this change of vertex. The author deploys entire areas of Bionian metapsychology, centring his study on the functions of the contact barrier, functions of differentiation between the two spheres of the inner world: the conscious mind and the unconscious mind – and on the dreaming functions, functions of transformation of sensory excitations into psychic elements and of making sense. His deciphering of Bion's thought is based on Meltzer's contributions, which give abstract concepts the weight of lived experience.

---

1 In a letter to Robert Hooke dated 5 February 1675, Isaac Newton wrote, "If I have seen farther, it is by standing on the shoulders of giants." (*discover.hsp.org*)

At the school of Bion and Meltzer, Monteiro takes psychoanalysis out of the dogmatic shackles in which it tended to lock itself up to make it rediscover all the freshness of its first steps. Freud's *Interpretation of Dreams* marked the beginning. The *functions of the dream* described by Wilfred Bion renew the method, lifting a corner of the great veil[2] of the mysterious transformation of the physiological into the psychic. The position of the psychoanalyst is profoundly modified: he is no longer the hieratic character, sheltered behind his silence and his theory, to modestly endorse a capacity for *rêverie* which puts him in contact with his own internal characters, settling himself down to *hearing* the analysand's internal characters. Monteiro then connects, in a fascinating way, Bion's *dream functions* to Meltzer's *theory of intimacy*. A big step in the understanding of the analytical work. Nothing more mechanical, systematic, forced in the analytic work, but the emergence from the depths of the unknown, the unknowable, the unthinkable (the *dream's navel*) of a sense that never exhausts the living forces of the human soul, but which gradually reveals to our amazed eyes the beauty of the internal world.

Prof. Dr. Didier Houzel, M.D., Emeritus Professor at the Caen University (France); training and supervising of the French Psychoanalytic Association

---

2 Reading Louis de Broglie's thesis, Einstein remarked, "He lifted a corner of the great veil."

Preface I

This book is really amazing. . . . It's life-threatening to forget and life-threatening to give such interpretation before we are mature to receive it.

Prof. Dr. Yolanda Gampel, Professor in Advanced Psychotherapy, Sackler Medical School, Tel-Aviv University, Israel; Training, Supervising and Past President of the Israel Psychoanalytic Society and Institute; Vice President of the European Federation of Psychoanalysis (2001–2005); representative for Europe in the board of the IPA (2007–2011); recipient, Hayman International Prize and the Mary S. Sigourney Award, 2006

Preface II

As I became increasingly engaged in Monteiro's rigorous and yet passionate book, I experienced it as a genuinely artistic (master)piece. The way the author has read Bion led him to formulate the ground-breaking thesis that psychoanalysis is essentially about the *unknown, the unknowable* and *the unthinkable*. The conclusion of this astonishing book speaks for the whole book in an inextinguishable moment of emotional beauty: Meltzer's "strenuous and astonishingly powerful clamour: 'NOOO!! You *always* have to be *beyond* the breaking point!!'" resonates in this book from beginning to end. *We can read this book, hear it, feel it, dream it all along Monteiro's poetic and passionate voyage to the realm of the unknown, the unknowable and the unthinkable; to the very heart and soul of psychoanalysis, to the unending mystery of psychoanalysis and the psychoanalytic praxis.*

Prof. Dr. Carlos Farate, M.D., Training and Supervising
Analyst of the Portuguese Psychoanalytic Society;
Editor-in-Chief of the *Revista Portuguesa de
Psicanálise* (*Portuguese Journal of Psychoanalysis*)

Introduction

Many of Bion's more inspiring insights and thoughts on dreams and dreaming still live today in the printed page in the form of widely scattered, unconnected and largely unworked pieces. Many of these pieces were left behind Bion in the form of posthumous fragments, which were eventually brought together into a single collection entitled *Cogitations* (1992). Many other illuminating lines on dreams and dreaming still live today largely in the same condition of scattered, unconnected and unworked pieces.

This book extensively argues that most of these inspiring lines can, however, be worked out into the relatively unified form of a theory. This theory is called in this book *Bion's Theory of Dreams*.

Bion's theory of dreams is shown to branch out into a visionary model of the mind.

At the centre of Bion's visionary model of the mind is the belief that all that is interesting in the human mind pulsates with life beyond the edge of the unknown, the unknowable and the unthinkable. An immediate implication of this belief is that psychoanalysis is itself essentially about the unknown, the unknowable and the unthinkable.

Also quite crucial in *Bion's visionary model of the mind* is that the human mind is believed to unendingly *dream* itself into the awestruck complexity and beauty of its structure, its ever-changing qualities, and its defeatingly complex workings.

Although much of this book comes out from Bion's many inspiring lines on dreams and dreaming, not very much of it comes *directly* from the words themselves through which Bion had first shared with history so many of his breaking-through intuitions. The book comes out, more precisely, directly from the inspiring depth of perplexity and wonder that Bion's words and lines speak of as he keeps struggling with the unending

DOI: 10.4324/9781003375159-1

much he is unprepared to see of the overwhelming complexity, and yet awestruck beauty of the human mind.

Another key source of inspiration guiding the writing of this book is Bion's feeling so often so deeply lost before all that he could not read in the host of enigmas and mysteries that tightly weave the human mind, making it such an unending source of wonder.

So in whatever way we may attempt to closely look into the human mind, we are promised to be soon lost in both perplexity and yet in wonder.

The depth of Bion's perplexity as well as of his feeling so deeply lost speak in his words and lines in an odd voice. This book is an attempt to read what this odd voice tells us.

Much of Bion's undelivered meaning is believed to be eventually revealed in the depth of his perplexity, in his feeling so often so lost, in the inspiring strength of his uncertainty, and in the unwritten strength of his wonder, rather than in what his words may immediately yield.

His perplexity, together with his courage to remain deeply lost before the much he is not prepared to see, his unvoiced passion for the unending enigmas and mysteries that make the human mind so awestruck, so profoundly beautiful and so profoundly human, is what I believe have most crucially guided him in opening such illuminating new unseen view of the human mind. This seems why perplexity stirs up in so many of his words and lines. This is also why dilemma so often recurs on his hand, being heard in his odd words and lines.

Donald Meltzer is argued to play a critically important role in branching out Bion's theory of dreams into his visionary model of the mind. This is evident all through the whole book but particularly so in Part 2, in which the helm of the argument is smoothly handed over to Meltzer himself. Meltzer is argued to have lent a whole new dimension to many key areas of Bion's thought. This had a key role in enriching the reading of the odd voice that Bion's perplexity and feeling so deeply lost in which most of his words speak to us. The close reading of this voice is what this book is about.

. . .

While working on this book, I gave much thought to the question of the clarity of the argument. I particularly considered whether repetitions – of views, thoughts, even quotes – should be avoided in points where they would evidently assist the clarity of the argument. Finally, I have decided to always favour the clarity of the argument rather than the common canon of presentation. So every time a conflict between both these qualities threatened to emerge, I always leaned towards the former – the clarity of the argument – even if this would imply calling back the same pieces, whatever they are, and no matter how often.

Part 1

On the Unknown, the Unknowable and the Unthinkable

King

... Can you devise me?

Laertes

I am lost in it, my lord
(*Ham*. IV. vii. 52–53)

Introduction

Ogden rewords one of Bion's many thoughts on dreams and dreaming into the line:

> "the work of dreaming *creates* the conscious and unconscious mind (and not the other way around)."

> (2003, p. 17)

Ogden's line raises at least two questions: (1) what *the conscious mind* and *the unconscious mind* are exactly supposed to consist of, and (2) how exactly is it that, through the workings of what Ogden calls "dreaming," we may create both these two minds.

This book is largely a detailed investigation into both these two questions. Question (2) may be rewritten:

> "*Freud* says Aristotle states that a dream is the way the mind works in sleep: *I* say it is the way it works when awake."
> (Bion 1992, p. 43 [cf. Freud 1933a, S.E. 22, p. 16])[1]

This book extensively argues that the dream is the way the human mind continuously creates itself into existence in its awestruck complex

DOI: 10.4324/9781003375159-2

structure, its ever-changing qualities and its defeatingly complex workings. In this book this enigmatic way is called *dreaming*. What precise way is, then, this way?

Note

1 An equivalent statement closes a longer passage of Freud's concerning Aristotle's thought on dreams in Freud 1900a, S.E. 4, p. 2.

Chapter 1

Freud's Dream-Thoughts

An Uninvited Step Into the Unknown, the Unknowable and the Unthinkable

1 Introduction

All Freud's allusions to dream-thoughts I am aware of show him converging on the same view concerning their role in the structure of dreams. What exactly dream-thoughts consist of was soon established in Freud's historic page in which he first described his view of both the structure and the fundamental workings of dreams (1900a, S.E. 4, p. 277). Throughout his entire working days, Freud remained firm and final on his understanding of dream-thoughts. And yet a few times in his celebrated book on dreams we surprise him feeling unexpectedly puzzled by some of the qualities of dream-thoughts that he himself had first described. In some passages of his great book Freud shared with history the exact cause of his bewilderment. I will next argue that the qualities of dream-thoughts that have led to Freud's *malaise* may raise a puzzling question on the consistency of his theory of dreams. The following is a particularly important passage of Freud's showing what exactly, in these qualities, bewildered Freud himself:

> There is often a passage in even the most thoroughly interpreted dream which has to be left obscure; this is because we become aware during the work of interpretation that at that point there is a tangle of dream-thoughts that cannot be unravelled and which moreover adds nothing to our knowledge of the content of the dream. This is the dream's navel, the spot where it reaches down into the unknown. The dream-thoughts to which we are led by interpretation cannot, by the nature of things, have any definite endings; they already bound to branch out in every direction into the intricate network of our world of thought. It is at some point where this meshwork is particularly close where that the dream-wish grows up like a mushroom out of its mycelium.
>
> (Freud 1900b, S.E. 5, p. 525)

DOI: 10.4324/9781003375159-3

No less than four insights into the odd qualities of dream-thoughts are discernible in Freud's lines. Moreover, Freud himself seems to have responded puzzlingly to each of them. I will next examine each of these oddities as well as Freud's responses to each of them.

2 Freud's First Insight Into the Puzzling Qualities of Dream-Thoughts

The first of these four insights shows Freud believing that at some point in the course of his interpretative journey of dreams he would find himself lost in an obscure tangle of dream-thoughts. Eventually, this tangle of dream-thoughts would defeat him in his own key purpose to completely read the meaning of dreams. Freud's meeting with this unyielding unreadable lump of dream-thoughts would even force him into an experience which he particularly unwelcomed: the experience, that is, of the unknown. Soon Freud has realized that although he could evade this experience, he could never avoid facing it, still less resolve it. On the contrary: the experience of the unknown swelled into an experience of the unknowable and even the unthinkable.

Quite disconcertingly, therefore, the dynamic of dream-thoughts would itself stop Freud in his own way to eventually reveal to the patient the hidden meaning of his dreams. Freud called this unreadable tangle of dream-thoughts the *dream's navel*. While discussing Irma's dream, Freud had already surprised us with the finding that has surprised himself: "There is at least one spot in every dream which is unplumbable, a navel, as it were, which is its point of contact with the unknown" (Freud 1900a, S.E. 4, p. 111).

To Freud's purposes, and indeed to his theory of dreams, the dynamic of dream-thoughts could hardly be a more unwelcome finding and a more disconcerting turn of things. And yet Freud puzzled us by unexpectedly seeing no merits in attempting to investigate this odd quality of dream-thoughts – a quality which, once again, would threaten him never to reach the full meaning of a dream, of *any* dream. These, again, are Freud's words: "At that point there is a tangle of dream-thoughts that cannot be unravelled and *which moreover adds nothing to our knowledge of the [latent] content of the dream*" (my emphasis). One would wonder what exact grounds support Freud? What exactly upholds his disconcerting claim? How can he know anything about the latent content of any dream if not by going down the chain of dream-thoughts engendered by the dream-work with no purpose other than ensure the dreamer the cunning satisfaction of his forbidden wish? Even more surprising is that Freud's unexpected claim seems to have opened for him an undue door legitimating him to just ignore the threatening impact of such extraordinary quality on his entire theory of dreams, as this discussion suggests.

It may puzzle us even more as we realize that the dynamic of the dream-thoughts reaches down not only into the unknown but indeed also into the unknowable – into the *unplumbable*, as Freud himself described it in his footnote on Irma's dream, that is, into the *unknowable*, and even the *unthinkable* in the basic sense that we do not seem equipped to represent this odd unreadably lump of dream-thoughts within any rationally intelligible model.

Freud's description of the "tangle of dream-thoughts that cannot be unravelled" and, therefore, in his own words, "has to be left obscure" comes as a warning. It warns us that, in light of Freud's theory of dreams, dreams themselves seem to prevent us from ever succeeding to fully know, understand and even think of both the internal structure and the dynamic of dreams themselves.

It may, therefore, come as a rather disconcerting surprise that Freud had decided never to investigate that which seems to disturb his own theory of dreams.

3 Freud's Second Insight Into the Qualities of Dream-Thoughts

Closely related to Freud's first insight into the qualities of dream-thoughts, the second such insight surfacing in his lines seems to reveal a still unknown quality not only of dream-thoughts, and therefore not only about the structure and the workings of dreams, but even about the structure of the human mind. For now Freud claims that dream-thoughts "are bound to branch out in every direction into the intricate network of our world of thought." Apparently, it is this extraordinary quality of dream-thoughts that creates the *dream's navel* – that creates, in every dream, that which remains unplumbable, in Freud's own word, and therefore, pulsating with life, at the core of each dream, within the mental realm of the unknown, the unknowable and the unthinkable.

The *dream's navel*, then, is the point beyond which Freud's methods of investigating dreams can no longer be of any assistance. And yet what psychical functions are exactly those which have both triggered and governed the dynamic of all these bewildering qualities of dream-thoughts? With what exact purpose has the human mind created them? With what exact role in the human mind have we entrusted them with? Freud's insight would seem full of promise. And yet Freud had never been driven to examine the psychical role of their extraordinary dynamic or workings, leaving behind him the promising strength of his own insight and what appears might have turned out to be yet another new encouraging line of research into the human mind. It seems even more puzzling that classical psychoanalysis has allowed the question to slide into inattention.

4   Freud's Third Insight Into the Qualities of Dream-Thoughts

Slightly different from, though again closely connected with this group of extraordinary qualities of dream-thoughts that Freud himself had first unveiled is what I take for Freud's third insight into these remarkable qualities: that dream-thoughts do not, and indeed *cannot*, "by the nature of things," have any definite endings. This other quality of dream-thoughts seems to threaten still further all Freud's efforts to ever unveil the meaning of dreams – of *every* dream. The dreamer's forbidden wishes, the plain description of which dream-thoughts should cloak away from the dreamer's consciousness together with their cunning satisfaction, now appear to splinter in a dust of scattered thoughts, carrying it further away from Freud's reach. This new extraordinary quality of dream-thoughts makes it even more surprising Freud's claim that the fact that he will always be stopped, however short of reaching the plain meaning of dreams, has nothing to teach him about dreams or indeed the human mind.

5   Freud's Fourth Bewildering Insight Into the Workings of Dream-Thoughts

But our bewilderment before Freud's responses to his own illuminating findings concerning the odd and yet fascinating qualities of dream-thoughts swells still further when we meet yet another insight of his – the fourth I read in his key page. This new insight showed Freud claiming that it is precisely at the point where the meshwork of dream-thoughts reaches its most unreadable stage that he sees the very wish, so far so cunningly hidden from everyone's eyes, suddenly springing forth fully formed and fully readable. This other insight joins the previous three in their puzzling fate. For quite paradoxically, this new quality of dream-thoughts would, once again, exclude Freud himself from the full access to the meaning of dreams. It would once again seem that the dynamic of dream-thoughts shows him how unequipped he himself seems to be to carry out his much desired end. That this dynamic comes between the meaning of dreams and Freud's struggle to fully read them, defeating his efforts. What most stands between himself and his own most cherished aims seems to be his inability to deal with the unknown, the unknowable and the unthinkable that seems inherent in the core of dream-thoughts.

These four extraordinary qualities of dream-thoughts might conceivably have led Freud to once again step beyond the edge of history should he have investigated them. But he has turned the same unpromising eye on all of them, choosing not to offer history the potentially illuminating fruits of his research into them.

6 Further Remarks on the Dynamic of Dream-Thoughts

In section 2 of this chapter, when I discussed Freud's first insight into the odd qualities of dream-thoughts, we met Freud's two consecutive claims: "We become aware during the work of interpretation that at that point there is a tangle of dream-thoughts that cannot be unravelled and which moreover adds nothing to our knowledge of the content of the dream." In this section I will try to look in closer detail to the latter: "[This] adds nothing to our knowledge of the content of the dream." The point I propose to briefly discuss in this section is the legitimacy of Freud's latter claim. I will go back to Freud's historic page in which he first shared with history the core of his own view of dreams.

> Every attempt that has hitherto been made to solve the problem of dreams has dealt directly with their *manifest* content as it is presented in our memory. All these attempts have endeavoured to arrive at an interpretation of dreams from their manifest content or . . . to form a judgement as to their nature on the basis of that same manifest content. We are alone in taking something else into account. We have introduced a new class of psychical material between the manifest content of dreams and the conclusions of our enquiry: namely, their *latent* content, or (as we say) the "dream-thoughts," arrived at by means of our procedure. *It is from these dream-thoughts and not from a dream's*

manifest content that we disentangle its meaning. We are thus presented with a new task which had no previous existence: the task, that is, of investigating the relations between the manifest content of dreams and the latent dream-thoughts, and of tracing out the processes by which the latter have been changed into the former. The dream-thoughts and the dream [manifest] content are presented to us like two versions of the same subject-matter in two different languages. Or, more precisely, the dream content seems like a transcript of the dream-thoughts into another mode of expression, whose characters and syntactic laws is our business to discover by comparing the original and the translation. The dream-thoughts are immediately comprehensible, as soon as we have learnt them.

(Freud 1900b, S.E. IV, p. 277; my emphasis)

We all know well the name of this translator. It is called *dream*-work. Analysts are therefore expected to attempt to fully decode it, hoping to eventually reach the plain text of the analysand's hidden wishes having them at last fully revealed to him. The process of decoding is called interpretation. The interpretation of dreams should then unveil the dream-thoughts that have been bluffing the truth of the dreamer's disguised wish or wishes that have alone pressed the dreamer into concocting a dream. The following claim closes Freud's historic page: "The dream-thoughts are immediately comprehensible, as soon as we have learnt them." How could we ever come to "learn them" if we are all promised to meet "at least one spot in every dream which is unplumbable, a navel, as it were, which is its point of contact with the unknown"? How could we ever be urged to fully read all that pulsates with life beyond that point where the dream-thought leads us into the unknown, the unknowable and the unthinkable? How could we possibly continue to go down the chain of dream-thoughts towards the plain text of the forbidden wish, and the new fact that these forbidden wishes have all been deviously satisfied throughout the dream, this being, in Freud's understanding, the only reason to concoct dreams, if we are promised to hurt ourselves against "a tangle of dream-thoughts that cannot be unravelled and that, by the nature of things, do not have any definite endings"? How, furthermore, could we ever decode it if this unreadable lump of dream-thoughts are, again, "bound to branch out in every direction into the intricate network of our world of thought"? We may really wonder, how could Freud believe that this unreadable tangle of dream-thoughts do not have anything to teach him – and us – about both the structure and the qualities of dreams, and even about both the structure and the qualities of the human mind?

One might wonder, why was it that Freud had never felt the urgency to research into the extraordinary dynamic of dream-thoughts? How many possibly fascinating qualities of the human mind are carried away by the dream-navel into our unawareness?

7 An Undocumented Conjecture

Although I cannot explicitly document the conjecture, I nevertheless take the view all along this book that Bion's most illuminating and far-reaching intuition was that all that is really interesting in the human mind essentially pulsates beyond the edge of the unknown, the unknowable and the unthinkable. This view is quite central in Bion's visionary model of the mind. This extraordinary intuition is believed to have pointed to Bion a whole uncharted field of psychical life, crowded with enigmas, perhaps even with mysteries leaving to the care of his most insightful eyes countless untried directions of research into the human mind.

Freud's unexpected meeting with the unwelcome experience of something in the human mind, which seemed to him essentially unknown, unknowable and even unthinkable draws a line beyond which Freud showed no will to step. Freud seems to have always assumed that we are equipped to both fully know and understand the human mind. Bion has soon intuited that we are not. Bion and, soon after him, Meltzer have both extensively questioned the adequacy of Freud's unexamined concepts of knowledge, understanding and thinking to get us any near the truth of psychic reality and indeed any near of the meaning of *being human*.

Even if Bion had never converted this extraordinary intuition into any clear claim, I believe that we can see it coming fully alive in the creative strength of so many of his most promising ideas and views, as well as in guiding most of his clinical hours and researching pages.

This book is about what I believe is Bion's most illuminating and far-reaching intuition: that the most fundamental quality of the human mind is that it essentially pulsates with unreadably complex and yet overwhelming awestruck life beyond the edge of the unknown, the unknowable and the unthinkable. So the book is also about the psychical functions entrusted with continuously *dreaming* the human mind into its awestruck structure, its ever-changing qualities and its defeatingly complex workings and about these unending *dreaming* processes which constantly creates the enigmas and even the mysteries believed to tightly weave the human mind, even to *be* the essential of the human mind.

Chapter 2

Bion's Theory of Contact-Barrier

A Winding Road Into the Mysteries of the Human Mind

1 Introduction

It may perhaps assist the argument in this chapter if I would briefly recall the two aims of this book.

The book will first argue that Bion's many lines on dreams and dreaming that survived in his published pages mostly in the form of unworked and scattered pieces may nevertheless be worked out into the relatively unified form of a theory. This is called *Bion's Theory of Dreams*.

The second, and main aim of the book, is to argue that the human mind continuously *dreams* itself into existence in its overwhelmingly complex and awestruck structure, its ever-changing qualities and in its defeatingly complex workings.

Bion's theory of contact-barrier is believed to play a key role in both Bion's theory of dreams and his visionary model of the mind. This theory will next be argued to play a key role in continuously *dreaming* the human mind into existence.

A stepping stone crucially assists this end. This is Bion's odd figure "dream." I will next briefly describe this figure and then extensively discuss its role in both the structure and the workings of the contact-barrier.

In *Learning from Experience* (1962, p. 15), Bion coined the odd term "dream." This term is printed ten times in pages 15–17 and is then converted into what Bion called *contact-barrier*. I cannot recall this odd figure surfacing in the same odd sense in any of Bion's other published pages.

2 Bion's Theory of Contact-Barrier – Introduction

In spite of the quite central role that his theory will next be extensively argued to play in both his theory of dreams and his visionary model of the

DOI: 10.4324/9781003375159-4

mind, Bion surprisingly forced his presentation of the concept into no more than three hardly readable pages (1962, pp. 15–17). As we first attempt to read these three pages, it immediately becomes clear that Bion had just scribbled a few unworked thoughts into them, hardly suggesting that he was intending to deliver a whole fundamental new theory. The language in which Bion penned down on paper these thoughts strongly suggests that he was far from realizing the key role that his scrawled thoughts were to play in his own theory of dreams and his visionary model of the mind. It very gradually emerged as a real surprise when we gather the first hints that this untidy bunch of unworked lines would seem to be destined to play a key role not only in psychoanalysis but in the history of research into the human mind. But again, Bion seemed too far from hinting at any of these possible fates of his own theory. And indeed, Bion never returned to it (if we disregard a brief line in *Learning,* p. 22, which I, in fact, decided to leave unexamined in this book).

So Bion seems to have just left his theory of the contact-barrier behind him this unworked and indeed this uncared for.

As it so often happened with Bion's writings, here too he left the reader to wrestle with a language dotted with unclear, sometimes contradictory, sometimes even oracular terms and statements, as well as with unfilled hints and gaps. In this and in Chapters 3, 4, 6, 7 and 8, I will strive to unravel some of his opaque lines and fill in most of his hints and gaps, try-ing to perhaps go some distance in nearing Bion's undelivered meaning. In a few points of Bion's theory, I have departed from him. With a few oth-ers, I have tentatively rephrased as well as extended him. And I tentatively introduced no less than four auxiliary concepts in the hope of rescuing the readability of his theory by closing some of the many gaps left to the reader to struggle with. By tentatively proceeding along these lines, I hope I may perhaps have worked out this collection of scribbled thoughts into something more like a unified draft of a theory. By hopefully reading some of his unfinished lines and misleading terms in a way somehow closer to his unclear meaning, I may perhaps have gained some hint at its structure, its workings, its far-reaching implications and its surprising beauty.

3 "Dream" – An Introduction

So exactly what for has Bion called such cumbersome term no less than ten times into his lines only to soon drop it, never to summon it back? What exact psychical functions has Bion entrusted "dream" with?

Bion himself answered the essential part of this question:

> The "dream" has many of the functions of censorship and resistance. These functions are not the product of the unconscious but instruments by which the "dream" creates and differentiates consciousness from unconsciousness.
>
> (Bion 1962, p. 16)

What exactly, then, is this odd figure that is now so unexpectedly entrusted with such momentous task? What psychical entity is exactly this that is now asked to *continuously create* consciousness and unconsciousness? What exactly is it that Bion may have meant by *creating consciousness* and *unconsciousness*? What exactly did Bion mean by *consciousness*? And by *unconsciousness*? How exactly does this implausible figure – "dream" – relate at all to Bion's *contact-barrier*? What exactly is it that is *momentous* and *overwhelming* in the tasks now suddenly asked "dream" to continuously perform?

4 A Meeting

Bion invites us to consider the trivial picture of a man talking to a friend:

> A man talking to a friend converts the sense impressions of emotional experience into alpha-elements, thus becoming capable of dream-thoughts and therefore of undisturbed consciousness of the facts whether the facts are the events in which he participates or his feelings about those events or both.
>
> (Bion 1962, p. 15)

In this quote Bion's *thus* and *therefore* are both *non sequiturs*. These *non sequiturs* are important because they both hide crucial psychical functions operating "dream" that are, therefore, left both unnamed and undescribed. These psychical functions will soon be shown to be central in the structure of the *contact-barrier*.

Although alpha-elements are postulated to be *necessary* psychical elements to ensure the genesis of Bion's *dream-thoughts*, they are certainly not equipped to create dream-thoughts by themselves alone (Bion 1962, p. 6). Some still undescribed psychical functions seem to be requested to continuously create *dream-thoughts*, or more precisely, to convert the sense impressions associated with emotional experiences into dream-thoughts.

At this point of the discussion of Bion's theory of contact-barrier, and for the sake of the consistency of this discussion, I should perhaps resort to a short clarifying note.

5 On Freud's Dream-Thoughts and Bion's Dream-Thoughts

The concept of dream-thought is, of course, quite crucial in Freud's theory of dreams (cf. 1900a, S.E. 4, p. 277; cf. detailed discussion in the previous chapter). Exactly the same term, however, is equally crucial in Bion. It is central in Bion's theory of alpha-function, in his theory of contact-barrier (cf. chapters 2, 3, 4, 6, 7, 8 and 15), in his theory of dream-work-alpha (cf. chapters 10, 11, 12, 13 and 14) and in many other key points in both his theory of dreams and his visionary model of the mind. And yet Freud's *dream-thoughts* and Bion's *dream-thoughts* are quite disparate concepts. Nothing but the name is shared by both. They have nothing else in common. We may, therefore, puzzle over with what exact purpose had Bion borrowed Freud's *term* though not his concept and kept calling it back to his pages time and again without any qualification. It is, indeed, surprising that Freud's *dream-thoughts* and Bion's *dream-thoughts* continue to live happily together in the psycho-analytical literature though standing for quite disparate objects. Freud's term seems to have been smuggled into Bion's language under the unvoiced indulgence of analysts, doubly confusing Bion's thought: it confuses it because the term may lure the reader into wrongly taking it in the same sense as Freud's, thus introducing yet another source of bewilderment into Bion's language already so crowded with puzzling lines; and it may also help muddling up Bion's thought in another, still more unfortunate way, by perhaps inviting readers to remain in ignorance of what Bion may exactly mean by *dream-thoughts* every time he called the term back to his pages. Having been allowed to travel unexamined throughout the psychoanalytical literature, Bion's term may have encouraged readers to half-store it away under the already too large heading of Bion's neglectable oddities.

And yet Bion's *dream-thought*, which he himself has unfortunately allowed to live in his written work in such unworked form, is believed in this book to play a key role in his theory of dreams as well as in his visionary model of the mind.

6 Bion's Theory of Contact-Barrier – Further Notes

I previously suggested that Bion's *thus*, in his earlier quote about a conversation between two friends, is a *non sequitur*. Bion's *therefore*, in the same quote, is another *non-sequitur*. For again, although dream-thoughts seem necessary to ensure this man an undisturbed consciousness of facts and feelings constantly emerging in the course of his conversation with his friend, they in themselves alone do not seem equipped to guarantee that this conversation can proceed undisturbed. Some still undescribed psychical functions would, therefore, seem necessary to ensure that this conversation will not be derailed at any moment. So what exactly are these psychical functions *continuously* operating behind Bion's misleading "thus"? And what are those lining up hidden behind his unsubstantiated "therefore"? Some seem crucial in continuously working out alpha-elements into Bion's *dream-thoughts*, some in operating on these dream-thoughts so as to ensure that both friends' consciousness of facts and feelings remain undisturbed as they go on talking to each other. In a way, Bion's "dream" echoes a key function he has given to alpha-function:

> Alpha-function is needed for conscious thinking and reasoning and for the relegation of thinking to the unconscious.
>
> (Bion 1962, p. 8)

By carefully unfolding the functions hidden behind both Bion's *thus* and *therefore* we may perhaps begin to gain a glimpse at the extreme complexity of both the structure and the workings of the contact-barrier and perhaps get a first tentative hint of its far-reaching consequences.

7 The Dynamic of the Dreaming Functions – A Preliminary Note

Puzzlingly, however, both these groups of still undescribed, even unnamed psychical functions – some hiding behind Bion's "thus," some behind his "therefore" – are believed to essentially operate beyond the edge of the unknown, the unknowable and the unthinkable in the elementary sense that they cannot be represented in a rationally readable model. So if, once again, my tentative reading of Bion's lines leads any closer to his unshared meaning, we do not seem equipped to *directly* observe, still less describe the concrete workings of both these groups of psychical functions and, therefore, not of the contact-barrier. And yet we are believed to observe so many of their effects as they actually operate, these effects hopefully inviting us, even perhaps urging us to postulate a structure endowed with a dynamic that would mature as a model in which one could perhaps be able to read something closer to the truth of psychic reality.

8 "Dream" and the Contact-Barrier – A Preliminary Note

The keyword in Bion's quote describing the meeting of the two friends seems to be *undisturbed*. I will soon argue why. This is the quote again:

> A man talking to a friend converts the sense impressions of emotional experience into alpha-elements, thus becoming capable of dream-thoughts and therefore of undisturbed consciousness of the facts whether the facts are the events in which he participates or his feelings about those events or both.
>
> (Bion 1962, p. 15)

Then Bion enlarges on the previous lines:

> He [the man talking to a friend] is able to remain "asleep" or uncon-scious of certain elements that cannot penetrate the barrier presented by his "dream." Thanks to the "dream" he can continue uninterrupt-edly to be awake, that is, awake to the fact that he is talking to his friend, but asleep to elements which, if they could penetrate the barrier of his "dream," would lead to the domination of his mind by what are ordinarily unconscious ideas and emotions.
>
> (1962, p. 15)

It is in this passage that Bion first brings in both the odd term "dream" and the idea of a "barrier."

Now: how exactly are both these terms connected – "dream" and "barrier" – if indeed they are connected at all? The answer to this ques-tion is believed to largely be the answer to the question: what is the struc-ture of Bion's *contact-barrier*? My tentative answer to both questions is this: "dream" and *contact-barrier* are two different names for exactly the same cluster of *dreaming functions*, the contact-barrier being in itself nothing but a specific cluster of *dreaming functions* obeying a specific set of qualities.

In the preceding passage, Bion's "Thanks to the 'dream'" will now be unfolded in the following longer line: it is the continuous workings of the defeatingly complex cluster of psychical functions operating within "dream" that makes it possible for the man talking to his friend to continue *uninterruptedly* conscious of some of the facts, feelings and thoughts surfacing in their conversation and yet *simultaneously* unconscious of a number of other facts, feelings and thoughts equally being raised by this conversation.

How exactly? How exactly is it that the "dream," that is, the cluster of *dreaming functions* operating within "dream" ensure that the man talking to his friend would continue to be *uninterruptedly* conscious of some of these many elements and yet, *at the same time*, unconscious of a number of other elements emerging along their conversation? Attempts to answer this question is believed to leave us at the door of Bion's theory of the contact-barrier. Nevertheless, what makes it possible for this man to *simultaneously* be active on both mental states is believed to be this specific cluster of *dreaming functions*.

9 "Dream" and the Contact-Barrier – New Notes

How exactly, then, does this particular cluster of *dreaming functions* operating within the "dream," or more precisely, *being* the "dream," relate with the idea of a *"barrier"*? What exact psychical mechanisms form this "barrier"?

To my tentative understanding, this *"barrier"* is created by the concrete workings of this cluster of functions *as they continuously convert each new element surfacing the conversation between both these friends into either new conscious material, or new unconscious material, though not simultaneously, for any single element, both conscious and unconscious,* thus preventing any element from freely travelling through the mind undreamed, that is, unconverted.

So this complex cluster of psychical functions has to *continuously* and *directly* operate on every new element being newly presented to the mind, continuously *dreaming* them all, one by one, into a new psychical element, now endowed with a new condition, namely, again, of being either part of what Bion called *consciousness* or *unconsciousness* though not both, or more precisely, each being *dreamed* into what *will soon call* the conscious mind *or* the unconscious mind.

10   Dreaming Functions and the Contact-Barrier – A Note

A key problem concerning the workings of *any* cluster of *dreaming functions* considered in this book is the problem of the nature of the elements that each of these functions is believed to *directly* operate on. Until this still early point of this discussion of Bion's theory of contact-barrier, the elements that have to be directly operated on and continuously converted into new psychical elements are the facts, thoughts and feelings surfacing the conversation between two friends. So we may perhaps now tentatively formulate a first, rudimentary view of both the structure of the contact-barrier, as well as a still very general view of its workings. We may now perhaps see it to consist of a specific cluster of *dreaming functions* entrusted with two crucial tasks. The first consists in continuously *dreaming* the elements newly presented to the mind into new psychical elements, ensuring each of them, however, to be either conscious, or unconscious but not simultaneously both. So again, no new element would be allowed to travel, unconverted, through the mind. The second task, and indeed the most crucial, is to continuously create the conscious and the unconscious. How exactly, however, are both these two tasks connected to one another? In brief though still unworked words, the process of continuously *dreaming* each element being newly presented to the mind into new psychical elements being either part of consciousness or of unconsciousness is exactly the same by which the human mind *dreams* itself into existence.

This is, again, just a rudimentary view of both the structure and the workings of the contact-barrier. This tentative view will now be examined in much closer detail. I will now return to the main task entrusted by Bion with the contact-barrier: to continuously create what Bion called *consciousness* and *unconsciousness*.

11   The Main Role of the Contact-Barrier – An Introductory Note

At this still early and tentative point of my discussion of Bion's theory of contact-barrier, it would seem fair to think that if some unconscious feelings or thoughts have somehow disrupted the course of this friendly conversation, this may perhaps be usefully seen as a failure in the workings of any of the *dreaming functions* operating the contact-barrier, that is, a failure in *dreaming* some elements newly emerging in the mind of any of these friends into new psychical elements. This is one reason why Bion's theory may be of clinical relevance. Such failure may emerge in many different forms in the sessions. It may surface as a surprising ruffle of the analysand's language, or a fleeting thought disorder, or a weird response to the analyst, or a sudden loss of contact with the analyst, among many other.

But again how exactly do both key tasks Bion entrusted with the contact-barrier relate to one another? The next sections attempts to perhaps answer this question. To assist me in lending both substance and clarity to this tentative answer, I will introduce four auxiliary concepts – *the conscious form of thought, the unconscious form of thought, conscious mind* and *unconscious mind.*

I will next look at the first two of these concepts: *the conscious form of thought* and *the unconscious form of thought.*

12 The Terms "The Conscious" and "The Unconscious" – A Preliminary Note

As Bion hasted himself in leaving with us his sketchy view of the meaning of contact-barrier, he resisted in allowing the terms "*the* conscious" and "*the* unconscious." Indeed, in a long footnote to *Learning*, Bion shared with us what has made him demur at bringing both these two terms to join his three pages:

> This use of terms [*the conscious* and *the unconscious*] is typical of the difficulty of using ambiguous terms when no more precise terms are available. I do not mean "the" conscious or "the" unconscious because that would imply that an observer would be required to differentiate two objects. Yet I do not wish to exclude that shade of meaning because when elements have been differentiated, some becoming conscious and some unconscious, it is reasonable to say that there is an unconscious if such concept is valuable.
>
> (Bion 1962, p. 100)

I would closely share Bion's qualms about the terms *the* conscious and *the* unconscious.

I wonder whether there is, in psychic reality, any substantive elements corresponding to any of these two terms. I would also closely follow Bion in his hesitation in seeing *the unconscious* a valuable concept; the same would hold for *a conscious*. In Chapters 3, 4, 9–16, I extensively argue in favour of both Bion's qualms.

13 On the Genesis and the Dynamic of the Forms of Thought

So once again the first of the two fundamental tasks of contact-barrier consist in *continuously* preventing unconscious elements to disrupt our conscious awareness of facts, feelings and thoughts. This is described by Bion as "penetrating the 'barrier'" (cf. above). By this expression I there-fore tentatively understand that some of the *dreaming functions* operating within the contact-barrier, or again, *being* the contact-barrier must have failed in their key role of continuously *dreaming* every element newly presented to the mind into new psychical elements.

It is, however, at this point that the concept of *forms of thought* may be of special assistance in filling in yet a few other key gaps that Bion has left behind him for us to wrestle with. For how exactly such disrup-tive effects resulting from the interference of unconscious elements may *continuously* be prevented by the contact-barrier? What exact psychical mechanisms, central within the contact-barrier, are continuously called to ward off this uninvited end? Although, once again, this conversion of ele-ments is believed to be carried out by *dreaming functions*, these functions seem to proceed according to two well-defined courses of action, aiming each at its well defined end. These courses of action are determined by both *forms of thought*. These are the *conscious form of thought* and *the unconscious form of thought*. The contact-barrier is believed, more pre-cisely, to *continuously* create *two different forms of thought as it dreams each element newly presented to the mind into new psychical ones*. These forms of thought are defined by (1) their main aims and (2) the *intellectual* qualities best adapted to take us to both their specific aims: the conscious form of thought aiming at ensuring our relationship with the experience of reality defined by sense perceptions, the unconscious form of thought to ensure our relationship with the experience of reality. The conscious form of thought is believed to be ripened into its essential qualities: observation, description, inference, reasoning, knowledge and understanding. It is, therefore, both its main aim together with its corresponding qualities that define *the conscious form of thought*. In my tentative reading of Bion's theory of contact-barrier, it is crucial that the qualities of the conscious form of thought be continuously *created* as the contact-barrier converts ever new elements into ever new psychical elements. More generally, as the contact-barrier creates both forms of thought while continuously converting every element newly presented to the mind into new psychical elements, it is also believed to continuously ripen their qualities.

Similarly, the *unconscious form of thought* refers to the emotional relationship with the world with special emphasis on our faculty of inspiration, insight, imagination, the capacity for emotional synthesis as well as for linking things beyond implausibility all that we are prepared to understand, as Sidney's line puts it: "O how the soule, apt for all impressions transcending reason, can comprehend unapprehensible things!" (*Arcadia*, 1622, p. 333; Sidney 1593, 1987). However, the nub of the contact-barrier is how to continuously bring both forms of thought together so as to ensure our capacity for making life and the world glittering with creative insight and meaning. I would believe, however, that this extraordinary task of contact-barrier, as well as so many of the intricacies of Bion's theory, may not be brought to some light after Chapters 3 and 4.

14 New Notes on the Genesis and the Dynamic of the Forms of Thought

As it was briefly referred in the previous section, a quite crucial difference between both these forms of thought is the nature of the experience of reality each form of thought is believed to tend to continuously create. The experience of reality limited by sense perceptions assisted by the qualities inherent in the conscious form of thought and the experience of reality left to the hands of the unconscious form of thought and its many qualities. The latter, however, is expected to endlessly enliven the former. Quite central in the latter is of course the *concrete reality of unconscious phantasies*.

The cluster of *dreaming functions* called in this book *contact-barrier* must continuously *dream* both forms of experience of reality into one another so as to ensure us full access to the extraordinary experience of reality as an unending source of meaning epitomized in our capacity for keeping making life and the world glittering with creative insight and meaning. It is this *dreaming functions* which allows us to read reality *simultaneously* in both forms of thought; to make it possible for us the awestruck achievement of *continuously* see it with such different eyes.

This cluster of *dreaming functions* must proceed continuously and yet with extreme accuracy so as to make sure that this exceedingly complex conversion of experiences of reality does not allow any disruption of the workings of any of these two forms of thought, thus preventing our relations with the world from collapsing.

The continuous *dreaming* of these two kinds of the experience of reality into one another should, furthermore, unendingly enrich both.

Another important difference between both forms of thought is that the conscious form of thought houses the concept of *fact* as a key piece of its complex structure and group of qualities, while this concept does not seem to have any representation within the unconscious form of thought. So *facts* should also be continuously *dreamed* into new psychical elements, thus bringing them fully alive in the mind, enlivening them into mental life, having them sharing some of the qualities of both forms of thought. This may make Keats' line clearer: "The great beauty of Poetry is that it makes everything every place interesting" (Keats 1970, *Letters of John Keats*, p. 315). As I tentatively see it, the core of the contact-barrier is, to a crucial extent, to both continuously *create* these two forms of thought, and therefore also, these forms of the experience of reality, and *continuously* weave them together into the experience of the creation of meaning. This experience is believed in this book to be foundational of the human mind. I will return to it time and again along the whole book.

This is yet another way how Bion's theory of contact-barrier is also a theory on how the human mind is believed to continuously *dream* itself into its own awestruck structure and qualities and why it has such a key place in both Bion's theory of dreams and his visionary model of the mind.

16 The Dynamic of Dreaming Functions and the Forms of Thought – New Remarks

Suppose that the concrete reality of an unconscious phantasy, or of an emotion triggered by some trivial word, or an image suddenly evoked in the mind of one of the two friends talking to one another. Suppose that the concrete reality of an unconscious phantasy was suddenly allowed to erupt through the conscious awareness of facts, feelings and thoughts of one of the friends, possibly threatening to disrupt their conversation. This threat of disruption may be caused by some failure in *dreaming* both forms of thought together into the experience of meaning, or in *dreaming* the differences between the experiences of reality specific of each form of thought.

As just said, the psychical experience of the concreteness of unconscious phantasies characteristic of the unconscious form of thought and the psychical experience of the concreteness of sense perceptions characteristic of the conscious form of thought must be *dreamed* into a unified psychical experience. This extraordinary process of *continuously dreaming* both forms of thought together into *the same* psychical experience creating yet another experience of meaning, instead of a psychical disruption of our experience of reality seems to demand an extreme accuracy. What, however, seems more puzzling is that the degree of accuracy requested to work this process out may be beyond any rational conception, so complex this process seems to be at the level of psychic reality.

An interesting question concerning the differences between the different nature of the experiences of reality is that while the concrete reality of unconscious phantasy is not known to the conscious form of thought, and the concrete reality of sense perceptions is also not known to the unconscious form of thought, both these unknowns must be continuously *dreamed* into the new psychical elements. The remarkable problem is how exactly do we *dream* two entirely different experiences of reality and two entirely different forms of knowledge into *the same* psychical experience integrating both.

This is crucial in both the structure and the workings of the contact-barrier.

17 A Short Unsubstantiated Claim

To Bion's view of the importance of preventing unconscious elements to disrupt our conscious awareness of facts, feelings and thoughts, I now add its reciprocal: the importance of continuously preventing conscious elements from seriously disturbing our unconscious awareness of facts, feelings and thoughts in ways that may disrupt either its qualities or its workings or by variously inhibiting or derailing its dynamic. This also demands the continuous works of some of the *dreaming functions* operating the contact-barrier and carefully monitoring every new step in this defeatingly complex process of continuously creating the consciousness and unconsciousness or, more precisely, *the conscious mind* and *the unconscious mind*.

Chapter 3

New Remarks on the Structure

And the Workings of the Contact-Barrier

1 Introduction

This is how Bion introduces his notion of the contact-barrier:

> My statement that a man has to 'dream' a current emotional experience whether it occurs in sleep or in waking life is reformulated thus: the man's alpha-function whether in sleeping or waking transforms sense impressions related to an emotional experience into alpha-elements, which cohere as they proliferate to form the contact-barrier. This contact-barrier, thus in continuous process of formation, marks the point of contact between the conscious and the unconscious elements and originates the distinction between them.
>
> (1962, p. 17)

This occurrence of the term "dream" is the tenth and last in the three pages in which Bion has penned down on paper the fundamentals of his theory the contact-barrier. I am not aware that Bion has ever brought this odd term back in this odd sense back to any of his other published pages.

It is in the earlier quote where Bion explicitly handed the concept of "dream" over to his concept of contact-barrier, absorbing the former into the latter.

I will now closely examine Bion's often misleading and unclear words in the hope of reading in them some of his most promising meaning.

It may, however, assist the clarification of Bion's preceding piece if I first look into his next passage and then return to the core of his introductory lines.

In his next passage Bion claims that "the term 'contact-barrier' emphasizes the establishment of a contact between conscious and unconscious

DOI: 10.4324/9781003375159-5

and the selective passage of elements from one to the other" (1962, p. 17). Both Bion's terms *contact* and *selective passage* share the uncertain merit of being both visually and tactilely evocative, although they equally participate in the same demerit of luring the reader into believing that what these terms may evoke could ever provide him with any faithful insight into either the structure or the workings of the contact-barrier. The first reading of Bion's line may even warp away the crucial role that Bion himself is believed entrust contact-barrier with.

Bion's wording of his claim is doubly misleading. I will now carefully examine these two key terms – contact and selective passage – trying to gather what exact qualities of the contact-barrier each of these terms seems to refer to. I will now attempt to show that the qualities that they equivocally name are both believed to be quite crucial in both the structure and the workings of the contact-barrier and, therefore also, in the role that the contact-barrier is thought in this book to play in the structure and the workings of the human mind.

2 The Term "Selective Passage" – A First Note

What Bion seems to mean by *selective passage* is indeed *selective*, but it is not *a passage* in any sense the semantic field normally associated with this word would reasonably allow. On the other hand, Bion's term *selective* seems, indeed, to refer to a key psychical function of selection though in a nontrivial sense which, however, can hardly be read in Bion's words.

As I tentatively argued in the previous chapter, elements do not pass from one mental state to another in the current sense of some material object which would be moved from one point to another. This uninspiring and indeed misleading wording closely follows Freud's topographic view of the human mind and echoes Freud's language describing its parts and places forcing an unfortunately material overtone into his conception of the human mind.

The elements that are described to "pass" from conscious to unconscious were suggested, in my first tentative reading of Bion's theory in the previous chapter, to have to be continuously converted into new psychical elements or, more precisely, to have to be continuously dreamed into new psychical elements by the defeatingly complex cluster of dreaming functions called in this book contact-barrier.

The overwhelming complexity of this process entirely defeats the straightforwardness that Bion's luring term *passage* may carry into the uncareful reader.

The "passage" of these elements would once again seem to consist of a defeatingly complex conversion by which qualities and functions inherent in the conscious form of thought and the corresponding experience of reality into the qualities and functions inherent in the unconscious form of thought and the unconscious experience of reality. The "passage" of elements is therefore believed to require the continuous workings of a particular cluster of dreaming functions operating the contact-barrier or, once again, being the contact-barrier. This evidently argues against the passive undertone evoked by Bion's term *passage*.

Both Bion's terms – *selective* and *passage* – seem, therefore, to openly conflict with the exceeding complex dynamic of these continuous conversion processes.

I will soon examine Bion's *selective*.

3 The Term "Contact" – A Preliminary Note

The term *contact* seems to refer to a most crucial quality of the contact-barrier. The way Bion introduced this key part of his theory seems highly misleading. Once again, his unfortunate wording, heavy in its topographical and tactile overtone, may easily lure the reader in believing the straightforwardness of a process which drowns us all in its defeating complexity, its depth and its far-reaching consequences. Here, again, its innuendo of simplicity and readability that Bion's too uncarefully worded line lent this key term may again easily mislead the reader in following behind him and take the apparent triviality of the term, rather than wrestling to reach some insight into its recalcitrant meaning.

Once again, if my still preliminary and tentative reading of Bion's theory nears his elusive meaning at all, the term *contact* screens away the workings of the contact-barrier *continuously* converting elements newly presented to the mind into new psychical elements *as it dreams forms of thought into forms of thought* and, therefore also, *forms of experiencing reality into forms of experiencing reality*, thus *continuously creating both the conscious mind and the unconscious mind*. This would seem to be what pulsates with the marvel of psychical life within Bion's coarse term *contact* between conscious and unconscious. Again, in my tentative reading of

Bion's theory of contact-barrier, this way of seeing things may lend some concrete psychical substance and meaning to the term *contact*.

What Bion calls *contact* is continuously created by the *dreaming functions* as they convert qualities into new qualities as the contact-barrier continuously creates the conscious mind and the unconscious mind.

4 "Selective Passage" – New Remarks

I return to Bion's previous lines: "The term 'contact-barrier' emphasizes the establishment of a contact between conscious and unconscious and the selective passage of elements from one to the other" (cf. quote opening this chapter; 1962, p. 17). I will again focus on Bion's term *selective passage* though this time with an attempt at clarifying the role of the word *selective* in his theory of contact-barrier.

Evidently *selective* qualifies *passage*. How exactly does this qualification translate itself into either the structure or the concrete workings of contact-barrier?

The way Bion words it seems to leave yet another key function of the contact-barrier out of sight. Bion has indeed left this key function undescribed. For what exact psychical function is it that, in psychic reality, continuously *selects* the elements that Bion suggests uninterruptedly "pass" from the conscious to the unconscious and vice versa? What is the concrete psychical process which Bion once again does not describe but to which he gives the doubly slippery name *selective passage*? What psychical functions exactly *select* what and how? I now return to Bion's fundamental claim concerning the main aim of contact-barrier: "The 'dream' has many of the functions of censorship and resistance. These functions are not the product of the unconscious but instruments by which the 'dream' creates and differentiates consciousness from unconsciousness" (Bion 1962, p. 16). Bion's qualification of *passage* – his term *selective* – is now suggested to refer to the *selective function* of the cluster of *dreaming functions* crucial in continuously creating both the conscious mind and the unconscious mind. It may not be immediately evident, in light of Bion's words, what exact kind of elements this selective function directly operates on. I tentatively suggest that this highly specialized and sensitive psychical function is entrusted with two key tasks both instrumental in the structure and the workings of the contact-barrier. The first is expected to continuously decide, in each single instant of our psychical life, and relative to each single element newly presented to the mind, whether it should best be *dreamed* into a new element to be worked out by the conscious form of thought or the unconscious form of thought. What we immediately learn from Bion's lines is that the *dreaming functions* which operate the contact-barrier, or once again more precisely, *are* the contact-barrier, are particularly busy sharing this overwhelmingly complex work by "many of the functions of censorship and resistance." They therefore seem to directly operate on *every* element being newly presented to the mind *as it is dreamed into new psychical elements*. This *selective function* must continuously escort the *dreaming* of both forms of thought weaving their qualities together into the new psychical element. The same must be said about the experience of reality *concerning each single new element*. We may perhaps never be able to present with any rationally readable model for such degree of complexity.

It is a particularly remarkable quality of the contact-barrier to *continuously* create both the conscious form of thought and the unconscious form of thought *as it continuously converts new elements into new psychical elements*.

If this tentative reading invites any plausibility, the selective function would also seem to favour the view that the human mind may perhaps be seen as continuously *dreaming* itself into existence into both its awestruck structure, its ever-changing qualities and its defeatingly complex workings. This would, of course, meet the main aim of this book.

5 The Selective Function – New Remarks

A decision has to *continuously* be made, at each particular new step in this overwhelmingly complex process of determining what precise elements should best be *dreamed* into either the conscious mind or the unconscious mind. Although this quality – *best* – seems a general and natural expectation hanging on each such critical step in the workings of the mind, I am not prepared to deal with it in detail at such early point of the argument of this book. I will often return to it much later, however. But the general idea about the meaning of this quality – *best* – qualifying not only the fundamental workings of the contact-barrier but *all* psychical processes will always focus on the creative strength of the processes themselves immediately measured by the creative strength of the resulting elements and, therefore, on their inspiring and evocative power.

The depth and the evocative power of the way in which virtually every single element newly presented to the mind is *dreamed* into new psychical elements mirror the creative strength of the way in which both forms of thought were *dreamed* together in their way towards the creation of the experience of meaning. But in our way from elements newly presented to the mind and the creation of meaning, we are supposed to continuously create *the conscious mind* and *the unconscious mind* rather than Bion's *consciousness* and *unconsciousness* by constantly manging, with this precise and creative purpose, the key tools of censorship and repression. Only in the next chapter will I attempt to make clear both these concepts of *the conscious mind* and *the unconscious mind*. The creative strength of our continuously *dreaming* the human mind into existence translates itself into two very different ways: in the evocative and even inspiring power of our constantly making life and the world glittering with creative insight and meaning, sharing such foundational experience of the human mind with others, this being a task one should expect seeing even the foetus carrying long in his intimate relationships with the mother and the beauty of both the structure and the workings of the contact-barrier.

Chapter 4

The Conscious Mind and the Unconscious Mind

New Remarks on the Contact-Barrier

1 Introduction

Invited to briefly comment on the genesis of his book *North*, Seamus Heaney was driven to recount, in a long series of interviews he gave to O'Driscoll, how the sequence of six short poems he called *Bone Dreams* had shaped in his mind:

> The immediate stimulus was a dead-line: I was supposed to deliver a prose piece on the work of Barrie Cooke . . . and I was stuck. But Barrie at that time was doing a series of "bone boxes"; thinking about them brought up memories of bones I used to find in the fields around Mossbawn, so next thing a frolic of free association got started and ended up taking in the whole of Romano-Celtic Britain, from Maiden Castle to Hadrian's Wall. The chalkiness of bones, the chalk downs, the amorousness and adventure of that summer are behind those particular "dreams."
>
> (O'Driscoll 2008, p. 157)

This little prose piece is tentatively seen here as a large window opened over the works of how *dreaming* elements newly presented to the mind into the experience of meaning seems to imply *dreaming* both forms of thought together, as well as quite conflicting forms of experiencing reality into the continuous creation of both the conscious mind the unconscious mind, the former governed by the conscious form of thought, the latter by the unconscious form of thought.

An immediate result of this continuous *dreaming* of forms of thought and of conflicting experience of reality into the relatively unified experience of the creation of meaning came to be known as *the* conscious mind and *the* unconscious mind, both seen to be made of meaning, as it were,

DOI: 10.4324/9781003375159-6

together with the *dreaming functions* entrusted with continuously ripening both these "minds" into the continuous creation of meaning. Heaney's short prose piece is believed to already allow a glance at this tentative understanding.

If we now set ourselves to carefully follow Heaney's words and attempt to map out all that his words seem to both describe and evoke, his quite straightforward language may, however, soon drown us in the unreadable complexity of the web of emotions, unconscious phantasies, feelings, memories and thoughts that Heaney's short prose piece is alone teeming with, most of which are themselves well beyond straightforward readability. His words are sparing in details and yet overwhelming in their evocative strength.

As I tend to see it, Heaney's short prose piece sheds an inspiring light on the genesis, the structure and the qualities of both *the conscious mind* and *the unconscious mind* and on both the structure and the workings of contact-barrier in its key function of continuously creating *the conscious mind and the unconscious mind* as it creates the experience of meaning.

2 The Conscious Mind and the Unconscious Mind – A Note

If we now attempt to very closely follow Heaney's words, like a little child carefully follows behind his own little finger showing him the outline of some figure drawn on a piece of paper, they may perhaps lead us to some very moderate distance towards the enigmatic genesis of the experience of meaning.

I go briefly back to Heaney:

> Thinking about them ["bone boxes"] brought up memories of bones I used to find in the fields around Mossbawn, so next thing a frolic of free association got started and ended up taking in the whole of Romano-Celtic Britain, from Maiden Castle to Hadrian's Wall. The chalkiness of bones, the chalk downs, the amorousness and adventure of that summer are behind those particular "dreams."

Independently of the evocative strength of the sequence of six short poems the genesis of which he briefly recounts in his interview to O'Driscoll, Heaney's short piece of prose walks us swiftly beyond the edge of the unknown, the unknowable and the unthinkable, allowing us to take a brief though perhaps rather frightening glance at the sea of feelings and thoughts possibly pulsating with life beyond the frontiers of this mysterious realm. This brief glance invites us, alone through the evocative strength of Heaney's prose lines, to share with him some of his emotional experiences again possibly teeming with feelings and thoughts. We seem, more precisely, invited to *dream* what Heaney cannot possibly describe, or ever be fully aware of, and yet can ask his own words to evoke for us, that is, to ask us to *dream* his words into experiencing some of his own untellable experiences and dreams and thoughts.

In other words, as he walks us through the lines of his short prose piece, he imperceptibly drowns us beyond the edges of the unknown, the unknowable and the unthinkable, then bringing us swiftly back again into the world of sense impressions and of immediate readability of all that his words evidently point to. So we naturally follow him back and forth along his lines, his words inviting us to constantly cross over this mysterious edge in both directions, and indeed straddling both realms, almost word for word, even sound for sound and line for line, this sometimes happening even *within* the same word.

Here too Alice was right: "'It seems very pretty,' she said when she had finished it, 'but it's *rather* hard to understand! . . . Somehow it fills my head with ideas – only I don't exactly know what they are'" (Lewis Carroll, in: M. Gardner *The Annotated Alice*, p. 150; Jabberwocky'). Many words would therefore soon lose their jobs. They should rather kindly leave the page and allow those remaining to demand from the reader to urgently bring in all his capacity for *dreaming* what words can no longer tell. And yet quite puzzling though, we have the means to make all the words that have left us to nonetheless converge in the experience of meaning if only we keep *dreaming* those that stay in the page.

Most clinical hours somehow fill our heads with ideas – only we do not exactly know what they are. The same, however, may perhaps be said of virtually everything really interesting in life, even though we do not seem to have any precise idea of the psychical meaning of that we call *interesting*.

3 The Conscious Mind and the Unconscious Mind – New Remarks

I will now go briefly back to "so next thing a frolic of free association got started and ended up taking in the whole of Romano-Celtic Britain, from Maiden Castle to Hadrian's Wall." Immediately taken, the sentence is, again, quite intelligible. And yet neither Heaney nor anyone else would ever be equipped to form the remotest idea of the countless emotional experiences, unconscious phantasies, wishes, dreams, fears, nightmares and both *dreamed* and *undreamed* thoughts that pulsate within Heaney's one word: *memories*. Still less can he – or of course we – ever get a glimpse of the psychical processes continuously both underlying and linking all these psychical elements, many of which may well have been constantly into ever-new psychical elements and, eventually, into the experience of meaning. And yet the same happens endlessly. How crowded with uncountable feelings and thoughts is Heaney's little *taking in*? What, in both intellectual and psychical terms, does he exactly mean by *taking in*? How unreadably crowded are these two words brought together? How crowded are they by both recognized and unrecognized uncounted feelings, memories and thoughts, some pulsating with life within his six little poems he called *Bone Dreams*, some living in his mind though not in the poems? And indeed, for anyone who has read through the sequence of poems and even a brief analysis of them might soon be drowned in their depth and the sea of feelings and thoughts pulsating within them, making Heaney's "frolic of associations" failing to do even the remotest justice to. However, I have tried not to imply the poems themselves whatever their intrinsic qualities in the argument of this chapter.

The degree of complexity of the dynamic of psychical life ruling these unnumbered processes seems to lie entirely out of any possible rational assessment. It seems really puzzling that, although Heaney's statement opening his short prose piece is in itself quite intelligible – again: "Thinking about them [Cooke's 'bone boxes'] brought up memories of bones I used to find in the fields around Mossbawn" – the fundamental psychical events that this line speaks so clearly of run well beyond the edge of the unknown, the unknowable and the unthinkable – taking, once again, the term *unthinkable* in the weak sense of being impossible to directly observe, describe, predict, represent, organize, give them any rationally intelligible order, disclose its *modus operandi* within all these psychical processes, or indeed closely travel along the outcome of its dynamic by any conscious or rational means. Heaney's trivially readable lines lump all these unreadable processes together so as to make his description immediately – though only generally – intelligible. All this stands behind his sequence of six little poems, whatever their specifically literary qualities. The meaning, the music of his lines and all the other factors making for the literary qualities of this sequence are all entirely out of consideration in this chapter, however. Again, it is precisely all that lives within his words in his short prose piece, together with all that these words may evoke much of which we may have no conscious or rational access to or control upon, that may be *dreamed* into creating in us the emotional experience of meaning and make his prose piece surprisingly readable.

I do not think of any way leading us to the unique emotional experience of the creation of meaning that does not essentially unfold beyond the edges of the unknown, the unknowable and the unthinkable, no matter how crucially woven with what is known, knowable, thinkable, describable and in all ways reasoned. The core of the emotional experience of the creation of meaning is believed to crucially speak of the emotional experience of *dreaming* the human mind into existence. The former is seen in this book to be the core of the latter. Both experiences – of the creation of meaning and of *dreaming* the human mind into existence – are believed to mature into the experience of awestruck and of the mystery of things.

4 The Contact-Barrier and the Genesis of Meaning – A New Short Note

Incomprehensible as some Heaney's expressions and lines evidently are if we would force them under the powerful and yet strict lens of reason and consciousness, that is, strictly following the conscious form of thought alone, we can, of course, still closely follow them provided we keep *dreaming* both forms of thought together into the experience of meaning. However, what exactly are we supposed to do of Heaney's "so next thing a frolic of free association got started and ended up taking in the whole of Romano-Celtic Britain, from Maiden Castle to Hadrian's Wall"? As the cluster of *dreaming functions* entrusted with continuously ensuring the relative success of this quite current, and yet really prodigious achievement keeps operating properly, *it is also believed to continuously create both forms of thought* and, as I think we may see happening by closely examining Heaney's short prose piece, *both the conscious mind and the unconscious mind.*

Heaney's piece as well as my remarks on it may all look trivially clear. But again, it drowns us in unreadable complexities and yet marvels us as we may closely watch the genesis of meaning.

5 On Dreaming Functions – Further Remarks

So from an invitation to write a prose piece on his friend's "Bone boxes" to the fields around Mossbawn and the whole of Romano-Celtic Britain, from Maiden Castle to Hadrian's Wall, Heaney swiftly walks us through the impossibly long and impossibly winding way screened away by his trivially readable prose piece. This odd way has a clear beginning though not an end, unless pathology imposes one upon it, that is, unless pathology seriously disturbs and eventually stops this unending process of the creation of meaning.

Chapter 5

A Brief Historical Survey

1 Introduction

Freud once again stepped beyond the edge of history with his vision that "everything conscious has an unconscious preliminary stage" (1900b, S.E. 5, p. 612). Freud's view of the unconscious had fundamentally been associated with pathology. And yet Freud's early line suggests him already glancing beyond the horizon of pathology or perhaps even reshaping his own understanding of pathology. Even at such an early stage of his research, the unconscious is no longer entirely seen as the key agent in the aetiology of mental disturbance. Freud's line might well have set afloat a new discussion in the history of the research into the human mind, and certainly into the meaning of conscious. This discussion might have centred on the question of the role played by the unconscious in structuring all thought processes. However, it has not been for Freud to elaborate on this entirely new direction of research. Freud was far too focused on and absorbed by concrete problems of what he meant by pathology and the aim of curing them. As it had already happened with the key question of the dynamic of dream-thoughts discussed in Chapter 1, Freud turned an unpromising eye even on his own illuminating insight into the role of the unconscious in shaping the conscious, or rather, *the conscious mind*, as I tentatively called it in the previous chapters. He was driven, rather, to answers to the questions he was, by then, most eager to see dealt with. The role of unconscious processes in structuring the mind, deciding most of its qualities and guiding most of its workings still remains far too unsettled.

I will now examine Freud's early line and the new direction of research it raises, seeing it, however, in the light of the belief, central in this book, that the human mind continuously *dreams* itself into its deeply puzzling structure, its ever-changing qualities and its defeatingly complex workings.

DOI: 10.4324/9781003375159-7

ʔ A New Route

I will now go back to Freud's key early line: "Everything conscious has an unconscious preliminary stage" (1900b, S.E. 5, p. 612). Although this line has by itself alone walked Freud again beyond the horizon of current belief, his promising intuition has not immediately matured into a new area of research. His insight has been allowed to remain lost for decades among so many of his illuminating theoretical statements. Freud's early line, just as Riviere's insightfully put it about so many other of Freud's still unexamined insights and claims, which "have been left floating in the air" and "have not yet been explicitly woven into the texture of theory and technique" (1952, p. 17).

Forty years have indeed elapsed before Susan Isaacs, closely echoing Klein, ripened Freud's early insight into a new life: "The primary content of all mental processes are unconscious phantasies. Such phantasies are the basis of all unconscious and conscious thought processes" (Isaacs 1943a, p. 276). With Isaacs, psychoanalysis has just begun to glance at *unconscious and conscious thought processes*, rather than just (the) conscious and (the) unconscious. Even if we still struggle today to make substantial headways through the undelivered meaning of Isaacs' elusive "the basis of," her statement ventured far beyond the horizon drawn by Freud's early insight. Isaacs deeply reshaped Freud's early line. First, she ripened Freud's *unconscious preliminary stage* into a far clearer and far more promising *unconscious primary content*. Then, unlike Freud, she described the concrete nature of this content, no longer allowing it to remain an undetermined "preliminary stage" destined, Freud believed, to be soon left behind us at the pace of our mental growth. Moreover, Isaacs (1943a), cf. Isaacs (1952) both seem to side with the views that (1) this content is permanently active in *all* thought processes, conscious and unconscious; (2) it seems to play a key role in both the genesis and the workings of these processes and, therefore also, in their structure; and (3) the term *primary*, qualifying *content*, should, in Isaacs' line, be read in both its two main canonical senses – in its genetic sequence and as the top of a hierarchy of values (cf. OED adj. 1., 2.).

Again, unconscious phantasies – and no longer Freud's unqualified term *unconscious* – are therefore now seen to play a key role in *all* thought processes, conscious and unconscious. Isaacs' wording of her own key claim seems to suggest, again, that unconscious phantasies are believed to play a key role in both the genesis of these processes and their workings, thus leaving no one knows how promising new gate widely open for still untried research into the human mind. Although Isaacs' "the basis of," in her illuminating line, still remains a debatable expression today waiting for more illuminating clinical and metapsychological research, Freud's general *unconscious*, which he has always so deeply devalued, has crucially been ripened into the far more inspiring and promising *unconscious phantasies*.

3 Redirecting History

As I tend to see it, Isaacs' line made even more than ripen Freud's early statement into a new life, however. I believe it redirected the history of research into the human mind.

Freud viewed the unconscious processes "to be the older, primary processes, the residues of a phase of development in which they were the only kind of mental process" (Freud 1911, S.E. 12, p. 219). Freud's term *primary*, qualifying unconscious processes, bears only the first sense of the word (*OED* adj. 1.; cf. above). Freud, therefore, asserted here, as so often both directly and indirectly all along his very vast work, the unfavourable overtones that dominated his view of the unconscious and of its unfortunate role in the human mind. All the recalcitrant hopes that Freud allowed to man's future were heavily entrusted to the cares of reason. His last introductory lecture sombrely closed the development of his thoughts on such key question:

> Our best hope for the future is that intellect – the scientific spirit, reason – may in the process of time establish a dictatorship in the mental life of man. The nature of reason is a guarantee that afterwards it will not fail to give man's emotional impulses and what is determined by them the position they deserve. But the common compulsion exercised by such a dominance of reason will prove to be the strongest bond among men and lead the way to further unions.
>
> (1933a, S.E. 22, p. 171)

Exceptions to his unpromising assessment of what he saw as the unconscious realm of man's mind were rare and, in any case, inconsequential (cf. 1915a, S.E. 14, p. 190).

So Isaacs was already crucially reversing Freud's vision while opening a new wide way for other analysts, among whom Bion and Meltzer would soon stand out making the unconscious mind, and in particular emotions, the awestruck core of the human mind.

And yet this was the most visionary piece of insight with which Freud's genius has stormed into history:

> The unconscious is the true psychical reality; *in its innermost nature it is as much unknown to us as the reality of the external world, and it is as incompletely presented by the data of consciousness as is the external world by the communications of our sense organs.*
>
> (Freud 1900b, S.E. 5, p. 613)

This visionary line lies at the core of Isaacs' line: "Of all the fundamental debts we owe to Freud's genius, none more clearly marks the new epoch of understanding which he initiated than this discovery of *psychical reality*" (Isaacs 1943a, p. 269). We may still be only too far from seeing the reach of Isaacs' words: *a new epoch of understanding* such the depth of Freud's discovery.

Echoing Klein, Isaacs converted Freud's early line into an epiphany. Psychoanalysis still remains far too far from discerning, even indistinctly, how far Freud's vision would one day still take us.

4 The Psychical Translation of Instincts – A Note

Freud had already viewed the term *instinct* "as [the name of] a concept on the frontier between the mental and the somatic, the psychical representative of the stimuli originating from within the organism and reaching the mind" (1915a, S.E. 14, pp. 121–122). Although, in this key point, Isaacs seems closer to Freud, she nevertheless sheds a new light on Freud's understanding of instinct: "Phantasy is the . . . psychic representative of instinct. And there is no impulse, no instinctual urge, which is not experienced as (unconscious) phantasy" (Isaacs 1943a, p. 277). Isaacs' claim that every impulse, every instinctual urge is *experienced* as unconscious phantasies adds a more focused voice on both the richness and importance of the role of unconscious life in the human mind. This is yet another step, adding to Klein's illuminating shift of direction in working out the key question of the meaning of *being human*, even if her role in crucially deepening this key question still remains today unrecognized and unexamined.

5 A New Epoch of Understanding – New Remarks

Fifteen years after Isaacs' statement, Melanie Klein herself resumed much of the discussion on the role of the unconscious in structuring the human mind and in determining its workings by stating that Freud "made it clear that . . . the id is the foundation of all mental function" (Klein 1958, p. 236). The uncomfortable question of how exactly the id can possibly answer such crushing promise found in Isaacs' previously quoted line is an insightful and qualifying turn. Isaacs' claim implies, of course, that all impulses and instinctual urges are translated into psychical life. However, Isaacs' statement that unconscious phantasies are the primary content of *all* mental processes, conscious and unconscious, invites the question: what, then, is the primary content of unconscious phantasies? Two decades later a new turning point in this discussion ruffled the surface of current knowledge and, I believe, opened the way for yet another deep and lasting shift in understanding the human mind, as well as a whole new direction of research into the key question of the meaning of *being human*. I marginally recall Bion's view that "the emotions fulfil a similar function for the psyche to that of the senses in relation to objects in space and time" (Bion 1962a, p. 119). I will soon return to this key shift of understanding.

6 The "Mysterious Leap"

A crucial problem common to both philosophy and psychoanalysis is whether, and how exactly is it, sensorial excitations and even sense impressions are ultimately converted into psychical life. What is the interface between both? Scalzone and Zontini (2001, p. 263) call it the mysterious leap. They put it thus:

> One problem common to natural sciences and to those of the mind remains unsolved to this day: the form of the transition from the biological to the psychic. Despite all our efforts, the "mysterious leap" continues to confront us, but we must try to narrow the gap by seeking to extend our knowledge of "everything that lies between."

This key question seems to border on the neighbouring problem of drawing the frontier line between the external world and the internal world and the interface continuously articulating both. What exactly is it that continuously leads us *in both directions* across this much troubling line?

The "mysterious leap" will be taken in this book to cover the whole gap between sensorial excitations and psychical life. How exactly, then, do we continuously cross over this line in both directions? What exact psychical functions are entrusted with continuously leading us across this puzzling line?

This key question will tentatively be examined in this book in light of Bion's theory of dreams.

Isaacs' belief that instincts are experienced as unconscious phantasies seems to take us to the frontier of biology. Isaacs' understanding already seems to considerably shorten this "mysterious leap," to perhaps crucially narrow this unyielding gap.

If, however, Isaacs is right in seeing unconscious phantasies the primary content of *all* mental processes, conscious and unconscious, what is the primary content of unconscious phantasies? The question seems to gain a particular weight if we again closely follow Isaacs' claim that unconscious phantasies are the basis of all unconscious and conscious thought processes (cf. Isaacs 1943a, p. 276; cf. above). However, what psychical functions are those entrusted with continuously converting the primary content of unconscious phantasies, whatever it may exactly be, into unconscious phantasies? These psychical functions would seem to reach a further shortening of this odd gap and, therefore, the mysteriousness of this leap.

Emotions may perhaps take us a step closer to answer this key question. They would seem to further shorten the enigmatic gap, the mysterious leap. Unconscious phantasies would then be seen as theories about emotions – possibly the first theories the human mind is ever prepared to give form to. If this tentative understanding invites any plausibility, unconscious phantasies would perhaps no longer be the primary content of all psychical processes, conscious or unconscious, as Klein and Issacs. Emotions would then seem to be much closer to the privileged area of the continuous conversion of biology into psychic life. Therefore, we might be invited to see *emotions* rather than unconscious phantasies the basis of all unconscious and conscious thought processes.

But then the question would of course force its way in: what, then, are these psychical functions, which, by *directly operating on emotions*, are the first translators of biology into meaning? In this new condition, emotions would then seem to shorten Scalzone's and Zontini's "mysterious leap" even further, or perhaps would even shrink it down to nothing. In this tentative understanding, emotions, together with the psychical functions directly operating on them, or more precisely, *dreaming* them into new psychical elements, would be the key psychical elements filling up this as yet recalcitrant gap, actually being the interface between biology and psychical life. As it will soon be shown, however, the problem will continue to resist new, hopefully deeper steps into it. For it would then become clear, I think, that the psychical functions that continuously *create* the psychical link between both sides of this puzzling gap is not only emotions but, crucially, also the *dreaming functions* continuously operating not only on emotions but also on sensorial excitations. So it would then appear that there might be no "mysterious leap" at all, nor indeed any "leap," but rather a beautiful, indeed mysterious and defeatingly complex, cluster of *dreaming functions* both continuously creating and governing this interface.

Chapter 6

Alpha-Function as a Cluster of *Dreaming Functions*

1 The Awareness Clause

What is the exact nature of the elements on which the *dreaming functions being* the contact-barrier *directly* operate on?

Bion's definition of alpha-function carries a rather puzzling clause: "Alpha-function operates on the sense-impressions, whatever they are, and the emotions, whatever they are, of which the patient is aware" (1962, p. 6). Bion's *awareness clause* has often aroused either perplexity or a negligent reading. Analysts sometimes seem to have stored it away under the unmentioned heading of inconsequential oddities of Bion's language, thus ignoring it altogether. Few others have, however, tried to squeeze some meaning out of it, though as far as I am aware, with too modest yield (cf. Meltzer (1978b).

And yet Bion's odd clause seems to have somehow been inspired by Freud's view of the function of attention. Freud had given this function a key place in the workings of the mind. The following key line speaks for this view: "Its activity meets sense impressions half way, instead of awaiting their appearance" (Freud 1911, S.E. 12, p. 220). "Half-way," I gather, between sensorial excitations and their full emergence into consciousness. Attention is therefore believed by Freud not to *directly* operate on sensorial excitations themselves but rather on some already psychical elements, or some pre-psychical elements, the exact nature of which we, however, do not seem to know anything about.

As we learned from Freud himself, moreover, a preconscious attention escorts every dream in order to summon dream-work back into action every time the alarm of censorship preconsciously rings. This remarkable understanding adds a new weight to the crucial importance that Freud has always endowed *attention* with. The following key line speaks, again, of

DOI: 10.4324/9781003375159-8

the crucial role he gave *attention*: "a part of the attention which operates during the day continues to be directed towards dreams during the state of sleep, that it keeps a check on them and criticizes them, and reserves the power to interrupt them" (Freud 1900b, S.E. 5, p. 505). Attention, therefore, seems to be equipped to closely follow an unconscious narrative, even to intervene in the unconscious course of events and to sharply redirect it.

And yet the complexity of the internal work that Freud entrusts the preconscious attention with further increases our perplexity over the intricacies that would seem to live within Bion's awareness clause.

We may, of course, wonder what might have been Bion's purpose in postulating it. What exact role does this clause play within Bion's vision of the workings of the human mind? The defeating complexities of the mental processes implied in guiding Freud's pre-conscious attention encourage us to carefully investigate all that Bion's awareness clause seems to leave unsaid and screened away behind his uninviting language.

I am of course aware that, so far, I am still working on the unsubstantiated assumption that Bion's awareness clause had somehow been inspired by Freud's unfinished view of attention. I will soon return to this assumption hoping to lend it some plausibility.

4 Freud's Puzzling "Half-way"

Again the question what exactly in psychical life directs the pre-conscious attention and commands it into action every time the mechanism dreamwork should urgently be called back into action can only sharpen our interest in reading the workings of the still unnamed psychical functions and elements implied in Bion's awareness clause.

A step further into Freud's "half-way" seems enough for our tacit hopes for summary and simplification to be drowned in puzzlement: "excitations in order to reach consciousness must pass through a fixed series of hierarchy of agencies" (1900b, S.E. 5, p. 615). This hierarchy of agencies implied in continuously converting sensorial excitations into psychical life, and in particular into consciousness, together with the works of the psychical functions ensuring the defeatingly complex journey from stage to stage holds the reluctant key to the "mysterious leap" (cf. Scalzone & Zontini 2001, p. 263; cf. previous chapter).

Bion leaves all these psychical complexities altogether behind the puzzling backdrop of the awareness clause.

Strictly watched, in the light of Bion's own definition of alpha-function, the long winding way leading from sensorial excitations to awareness could then be walked from beginning to end before it makes any sense to call the concept of alpha-function on stage. Alpha-function would then be entirely left on one side all along this long and crucial psychical process.

So once again, what exact psychical functions are then entrusted with the key task of continuously leading us from sensorial excitations to consciousness? More essentially even: what psychical functions are entrusted with leading us along the long and winding way from sensorial excitations to psychical life?

5 The Awareness Clause: A New Note

What exact psychical functions are, then, those expected to *continuously* convert sensorial excitations into elements of the conscious mind? The key question seems to force the door open to the following question: what exact psychical elements are those on which alpha-function *directly* operates on which bear the complex name of *the sense impressions of which we are aware of?* Or more precisely: *what are the psychical elements resulting from dreaming sense impressions into awareness?*

It therefore seems obvious that under the light of Bion's definition of alpha-function, that before we reach the psychical complex state of awareness alpha-function can simply not operate.

6 Alpha-Function – New Notes

Although Bion's awareness clause clearly discredits the claim, alpha-function has nevertheless been often assumed to just bridge over the psychical route leading us from sensorial excitations to psychical life. Bion's unable claim would then leave behind it a host of key questions which I would believe still remain unaddressed today, together with an unknown number of key unexamined psychical processes.

Ogden is certainly not alone in incurring the same hasty step that alpha-function converts "raw sense impressions into elements of experience" (2003, p. 17). And yet though we rarely see Bion being clear about any of his concepts by sharing with the reader an immediately intelligible definition, this particular key concept is a welcome exception.

Furthermore, Bion, soon after having defined alpha-function, reaffirmed his clear view of the nature of the elements that alpha-function is conceived to directly operate on. He writes, "The more general statement of the theory [of alpha-function] is this: To learn from experience alpha-function must operate on the awareness of emotional experience" (Bion 1962, p. 8). Alpha-function, therefore, directly operates on *awareness*, or more precisely, on psychical elements which we are aware of, not on raw sense impressions or emotions. This, at least, seems clear in Bion. And yet, as just argued, the condition of being aware of anything seems a defeatingly complex psychical one.

We also sometimes meet the claim that beta-elements are untransformed raw sense impressions. And yet this fairly spread view about the exact nature of beta-elements seems again to directly conflict with Bion's own view in once again ignoring his awareness clause. For Bion seems to have again been quite clear in stating that "if alpha-function is disturbed, and therefore inoperative, the sense impressions of which the patient is aware and the emotions which he is experiencing remain unchanged. I shall call them beta-elements" (Bion 1962, p. 6). Beta-elements would, then, seem far more complex and sensitive elements than what common literature has made it.

10 New Remarks on Alpha-function

The closer we attempt to look into the question of Bion's awareness clause, the deeper the complexities clustering around it, and the greater the number of unknowns distancing us from the uninvited alternative of dodging the question as inconsequential.

At this still early point of the argument in this book, while struggling to lend plausibility to its main beliefs, we seem to have reached a rather odd stage of Bion's understanding of alpha-function. For we hardly know anything about the exact nature of the psychic elements alpha-function is postulated to directly operate on, or about the psychical functions operating it, or about its structure, or about its *modus operandi*, or indeed about its clinical merits. And yet the pages of psycho-analytical literature closer to Bion's thought teem with references to both alpha-function and alpha-elements. Puzzlingly, furthermore, clinical accounts speaking for its concrete clinical role and its concrete clinical merits still remain notoriously absent. It indeed seems odd that the concept of alpha-function is never clearly showed at work in detailed clinical reports. Should it be, it might perhaps then shed some new light on both its clinical and metapsychological merits. Analysts' puzzling reluctance to share extensive clinical data of what may live in the concrete course of the sessions that they purport to guide deepens our puzzlement. Even the so-called *vignettes*, which are too often brought to the pages of psychoanalytic literature with the doubtful purpose of speaking of both the depths and the complexities of the problems analysts are alleged to illuminate, are notoriously recalcitrant to provide the reader with de concrete evidence qualifying the concept to crucially assist the analyst in the clinic hour.

This puzzling void seems to favour the view that although the *idea* of alpha-function seemed potentially illuminating not only in the study of thought disorders but also as a key stepping stone in building up a more inspired and inspiring model of the mind, its *theory* may have promoted more verbiage than insight. The *idea* of alpha-function was first briefly sketched by Bion in his communication to the British Psycho-analytical Society in a still unpublished report. What appears to be the clinical core of that communication was brought into the public eye in Bion's paper 1962a, p. 115. This seems the relevant passage concerning the original purpose of the postulated concept and later of the theory:

> I have described previously (at a Scientific Meeting of the British Psycho-analytical Society) the use of the concept of alpha-function as a working tool in the analysis of disturbances of thought. It seemed convenient to suppose an alpha function to convert sense data into alpha-elements and thus provide the psyche with the material for dream-thoughts and hence the capacity to wake up or go to sleep, to be conscious or unconscious.
>
> (Bion 1962a, p. 115)

At this early point in Bion's work, however, he has not required the additional qualification of awareness of the sense impressions and emotions. The still unexplained clinical role of his awareness clause was still not yet in Bion's mind at this early time of his thought. And yet after more than half a century, his theory of alpha-function has still not filtered down to everyday clinical hour. Why exactly? The concept of alpha-function seems to have been allowed to spread through the literature in its abstract form under Bion's deliberate advice grounded on the conjecture that, in time, it would be "filled in" by concrete clinical data that would reveal all the strength of both its clinical and metapsychological import (1962). With some six decades already behind us, however, his postulate has not yet translated itself into substantial clinical change.

Chapter 7

Mother's Reverie

And the Mystery of Introjection

1 The Sensitivity of Projecting

The general idea of mother's reverie that we largely meet in the literature lays the focus too exclusively on the mother and her responsibility to *dream* back into them all that the foetus and the infant project into her. And yet in order for the mother to convert what she is urged by her baby – foetus or infant – to *dream* back into him, her babies are twice called to crucially engage in mother's potentially extraordinary achievement. The baby is first of all requested to be prepared to project into the mother his responses to whatever sense data reach him from external reality, his own body being, of course, part of the external reality. The available literature has it, with no exception known to me, that the baby eagerly expects the mother to just take his pain away from him, whatever the nature of his pain. Even the foetus' and the infant's earliest experiences of joy and excitement have to be lovingly *dreamed* by the mother back into them while they were not prepared to *dream* these experiences into an enrichment of their own psychical world is believed to be of crucial importance for the unending process of structuring the mind by continuously *dreaming* it into its awestruck structure and its ever-changing qualities, whether or not it may eventually grow galled by excess of excitation. Mother's reverie is crucial to assist the foetus and the infant to just begin to distinguish between joy and excitement, a distinction we so very often still struggle with today. The differentiation between the many sides of joy and excitement remains an important and often sensitive task throughout our lives. Mother's *dreaming* the difference between both in her foetus and her baby is believed to help us grounding this difference, protecting what is the experience of creation of meaning, the experience of beauty, of creativity in general, of gratitude, of generosity, from excitement.

DOI: 10.4324/9781003375159-9

I tentatively suggest, however, that projection into the mother may not always answer the urge to evade pain but also to earnestly answer the natural urge to share – to share with mother; soon to share with others, this being believed a key road towards the development of the mind.

Although projection into the mother – of sensorial excitations converted into emotions, unconscious phantasies, states of mind and thoughts that the foetus and the infant are not yet prepared all by themselves alone to *dream* into new psychical elements and even into qualities of their earliest personality – although such crucial process has generally been assumed to be both straightforward and successfully performed, projection is believed in this book to both be a vital and yet highly demanding task that may dramatically fail in several different ways and is indeed to actually very often miss its crucial psychical function. For the success of projections crucially depends on how the foetus or the infant experiences mother. Projections, particularly at early levels of the transference, are carefully tailored to the merits and the demerits of the analyst as the analysand perceives him. A rather unresponsive analyst can hardly expect a deep, early levels of transference coming naturally into the session. The analysand unconsciously cuts it to shape so as to spare himself from further pain not to once again be met by the dull, uncomprehending mother in addition to all those he may already have experienced at much earlier levels of his emotional experiences. Take, for instance, Bion's remark as he alluded to what he believes is "the extraordinary nature, the mystery of psychoanalysis": "Such a lot of analysts seem to be bored with their subject; they have lost the capacity for wonder" (Bion 1987, p. 15, Brasília, 3rd Seminar, 1975). How can the analyst who has lost his capacity for wonder, or even has never had it driving him lost in awe and perplexity, could ever expect to watch the transference anxiously travelling from the couch to the uncomprehending mother dully sitting on the chair? Inevitably, the lack of passion and the incapacity for the experience of awe would dominate the music of the analyst's voice, and the weight of this negative quality in the sessions may fatally hinder the evolution of the transference. The analyst-mother can hardly be prepared to *dream* the transference, particularly at early levels of the analysand's emotional experiences, back into his "foetus" and "infant" lying on the couch, anxiously expecting the relief of his pain coming from the unmerited mother, in the form of new creative psychical experiences, while the dull mother-analyst remains asking the time of the session to free "her" from "her" boring business.

A great number of other factors may well discourage projections. To invite the transference to gradually unfold along the many sessions in a way that *the truth* of the emotional experiences may eventually root and ripen into an ever richer experience of intimacy between the analysand and the analyst is believed to be an exceedingly complex and sensitive task, burdening the analyst with a frightening responsibility. The history of the transference can, of course, be carefully read in so many other ways. It surfaces analysis in the changes in the music of the analysand's voice, in pieces of evidence of creative thinking, dreams, the truth and the substance of what is communicated to the analyst, in the depth of the analysand's attachment to analysis, as well as, of course, in the history of the counter-transferential responses. But a key question always threateningly hovers over all our heads in every analysis: what key emotional experiences and thoughts have never travelled from the couch to the chair all along a whole analysis? But again, fundamental emotional experiences that have never shared with the analyst through projection evidently translate themselves negatively into the qualities of the analysis.

We of course all know that analysis is the analysis of the transference and of the counter-transference. Nothing that the analysand does not bring to the session can therefore join the matter of analysis. The weight of responsibility in inviting the transference and in particular in inhibiting projection particularly at early levels of emotional experiences and thoughts comes from the chair rather than from the couch. Failures in the evolution of the transference should primarily be addressed to the analyst.

2 The Key Role of Kindness in Promoting the Transference – A Note

Kindness is believed to play a key role in the crucial and sensitive process of fostering transference particularly at the earliest levels of emotional experience. Its central importance in the course of every analysis was first brought into the literature by Money-Kyrle through Donald Meltzer's belief that this is the first quality for anyone practising psychoanalysis to excel in (cf. Meltzer 1997a; Lima 2015, 2016). Its importance has, however, never filtered down into the clinic hour and indeed soon fell into neglect. And yet the analyst's kindness is seen in this book as a crucial piece of the setting hopefully brought by the analyst to every session. Kindness, however, is a particularly complex concept. It encompasses a sensitive cluster of qualities. By kindness I mean a passionate interest in the mental life of the patient, a deep, hopefully unendingly ripened respect for the meaning of *being human*, love for the truth, forbearance, tolerance, generosity and a sense of dignity. Absolutely central in this understanding of kindness, moreover, is the truth of the analyst's awareness of being helpless before the defeating complexity and sensitivity of the human mind. In the course of a supervision session with Donald Meltzer, I conveyed to Meltzer that

JM: I have recently noticed that I have often been worried with her, perhaps feeling her new steps so fragile, worried with the extreme complexity of this process and its *extreme* fragility. . .

DM: Well, yes . . . worrying about your patient is terribly important. . . In fact, the only way we have of keeping the patients safe is to be worried about them. Because when we're worried about them it's always because they have evacuated into us their own worry, and then to accept it, and not to try to analyse it away . . . to accept it along with our helplessness. . . . I mean, we are *very* helpless, really . . . and that's how we help our patients . . . it's by being helpless . . . *(smiling thoughtfully)* . . . it's extraordinary. . . (cf. Monteiro 2019, p. 148)

Being helpless – and being deeply true in our feeling *helpless*, being lost – deeply lost and yet not scare our *being* lost away into either the brutality of smugness or the many seductive side roads analysts are so prone to, one is believed to foster transference at early levels of the emotional experience.

In this understanding, soon kindness deeply retunes the music of the analyst's voice in ways that would seem difficult to come naturally to us.

Kindness should grow out of our awareness of the countless mysteries pulsating within the human mind and indeed weaving it. Furthermore, the lengthy road leading us to the discovery of kindness as a very central piece in every analysis also adds up to our understanding of the meaning of *being human*.

So kindness is believed to be a crucial factor in fostering the transference, particularly at deep levels of the emotional experiences and thoughts.

John Steiner raised a surprising link between kindness and truth. He was commenting on a line by Forster who, in his novel *A Passage to India*, aired the view that truth without kindness might easily swell into cruelty. This is Steiner's remark: "Forster's point is not just that truth without kindness can be cruel, but that truth without kindness is not fully true" (2016, p. 434). Although Steiner has not qualified *kindness*, and his line is not part of the argument in this chapter, the unexpected link he raised between *kindness* and *truth* invites reflection.

So nothing seems to support the widely spread assumption that projection is a straightforward psychical move naturally travelling from foetus and the infant to the mother – from the couch to the chair. Without projection, mother's reverie would hardly become as busy as it normally would be, and I believe the human mind might have been deprived of one of the most mysterious and most extraordinary process that it has been possible to identify and tentatively examine so far.

So projection may fail in many ways. Failures in projection, of whatever nature, are seen in this book as frightening threats to the potentially unending internal grow of both the analysand and the analyst, particularly at early levels of their emotional experiences, for they deprive mother's reverie from *dreaming* potentially key emotional experiences and thoughts that the analysand may refuse to deeply share with mother-analyst who may well be experienced as variously demerited and untrustful. Again: failures in projection should mostly be left at the analyst's door.

I will now focus in greater detail on another factor crucially implied in mother's reverie: the mystery of introjection.

3 The Mystery of Introjection – A First Note

The foetus and the infant are, however, crucially engaged in another task intimately associated with mother's reverie, even far more complex and indeed even far more crucial than the key task of projection. This is introjection – the mystery of introjection.

Introjection of the qualities of mother's reverie is believed to be of the utmost importance in making it possible for both the foetus and the infant to *dream* their own minds into existence in its structure, some of its fundamental qualities and some of its fundamental workings. As I would tend to see it, introjection largely determines the beginning of psychical life. Two among no matter how many qualities may occasionally live within mother's reverie and may travel back from her into her foetus' and her infants' minds, stand out far beyond all others in their role as foundational experiences of the human mind: mother's *dreaming* the foetus' and the infant's projections into her and the experience of the creation of meaning. The latter will be extensively discussed in this book. Not only these two qualities but indeed every other quality living in mother's reverie at each moment she is *dreaming* her babies projections back into them are both carried out back into them in the form of *dreamed* projections, but for the foetus and the infant to introject mother's own *dreams* into new qualities of their own personalities as well as new qualities of their thinking, they have themselves to *dream* the qualities of mother's reverie. Introjection is essentially a *dreaming* process. Introjection is seen in this book as a prodigious instance of *dreaming* our own mind into existence. And in this odd condition, it is also believed to be the epitome of the experience of the creation of meaning. Introjection of both these two key qualities of mother's reverie is a momentous emotional experience in the psychical life of us all. And yet unless interfered by pathology, this momentous step is unendingly *dreamed* into ever new, deeper and more creative strength of the personality. Exactly the same is believed to happen with every other quality carried into her foetus and the infant. Again, unless assaulted by pathology, they too are believed to be continuously *dreamed* into ever new, deeper and more creative qualities of their own – and our own – personality. This belief is both inferred from direct observation, particularly all along long analysis, but also supported by a postulate central in Bion's theory of dreams: that the creative strength of the unreadably complex dynamic of psychic reality is one of the two most awestruck qualities of the human mind, the other being its capacity to continuously *dream* itself into existence.

By *pathology* I mean in this book the psychical processes that irreparably damage both these two qualities – that capacity of the human mind to keep *dreaming* itself into an ever new, more creative life.

Introjection of the two most crucial qualities of mother's reverie – her capacity for *dreaming* her foetus' and her infant's projections back into them and, therefore, allowing them the unparalleled privilege of experiencing, by introjection, and therefore by *dreaming* it, her power to create of meaning – the vitality of the introjection of both these key qualities of mother's response vividly witnessed in one's urge to keep making life and the world glittering with insight and meaning, thus sharing with others, in gratitude and awe, the emotional experience of the creation of meaning.

4 The Mystery of Introjection – New Notes

By introjecting mother's reverie, that is, by *dreaming* the qualities of her reverie into qualities of the personality and of thought, the foetus and the infant are believed to keep crucially *dreaming* their own minds into their structure as well as into many of their fundamental qualities. But how exactly? What is the meaning of such mysterious process we use to call *introjection*? What exactly is it, furthermore, that determine the strength and the vitality of the foetus' and the infant's drive to introject the qualities of mother's reverie? Introjection of the two most crucial qualities of mother's reverie – the emotional experience of the creation of meaning and of mother's *dreaming* – seem paramount in creating the essentials of mental life in both the foetus and the infant and indeed in us all. Two factors seem to determine the strength of this urge, even transforming it into a fate: the depth of mother's passion for her foetus and her infant and the depth in which both the foetus and the infant are touched by the awe-inspiring, even unsettling experience of the creation of meaning. Both these experiences "wound" the foetus and the infant into mental life as well as into an awestruck link to the mother.

But how is it that the qualities of mother's reverie may so powerfully shape the qualities of the foetus' and the infant's minds and even grow in them into a fate?

5 The Mystery of Introjection – Further Notes

But the mysteries of introjective processes never cease to defeat research. "[Introjection] seems to me the most important and most mysterious concept in psycho-analysis. How does it operate and what does it mean?" (Meltzer 1978a, p. 459). In his very short treatise *On Memory* Aristotle famously wondered, "One might ask how it is possible that though the affection is present, and the fact absent, the latter – that which is not present – is remembered" (Aristotle, Mem., 450a25–26; tr. J. I. Beare; ed., rev. J. Barnes). It was surprising to see Aristotle, in the beginning of his little treatise, associating far greater mental activity to his view of *recollection* while a much more mechanical overtone to *remembering*. Recollection would then request a much greater assistance from the psychical than remembering, one might perhaps put it today. How psychical would recollection exactly be in Aristotle's way of thinking? How is it today? Where exactly should one draw the frontier separating biology and the psychical?

Perhaps unwittingly, Meltzer puts Aristotle's question on quite a different level of depth. Meltzer asks, "What is the difference between recalling an event or person and having introjected that person or event so that they exist 'in the mind', alive and independent of our self and will?" (Meltzer 1978a, p. 459). So what is now recalled has been endowed with a life of its own. How exactly independent of the self and of one's will, however? How exactly are we supposed to take Meltzer's *independent*? Meltzer's understanding seems to infuse a new weight to his own view – which he incidentally lent Bion as Meltzer was in the habit of doing – that the idea that the mind thinks is yet another empty myth of psychoanalysis (cf. Meltzer 1987, p. 558).

Consider Milton's lines:

If answerable style I can obtain   20
Of my celestial patroness, who deigns
Her nightly visitation unimplored,
And dictates to me slumbering, or inspires
Easy my unpremeditated verse: 24
          (Milton, *Paradise Lost* IX, 20–24)

Milton's lines were dictated by his internal characters – by his good, that is, loving, which crucially implies, inspiring internal characters. They alone gave him his lines for him to pen them down. They alone *dictate to him, slumbering, and inspire easy his unpremeditated verse.*

How alive and independent of his self and will is this inspired and inspiring figure, whom Milton does not know and does not ask anything from, knowing well that he has no power to command but is commanded by? I would wonder that Milton's *unpremeditated* verses are a particularly important piece of *recollection* – *of recollecting the dreaming mother by whom he discovered the unsettling experience of the creation of meaning, a recollection, though penned down in the immediately recognized form of particularly inspired verses, spoken in the language of awe before and gratitude for mother's love.* This is how I would tend to see all moments of *real* creativity.

Nevertheless, how dependent on introjective processes and particularly on the introjection of the qualities of mother's reverie are the internal characters? As said before, introjection of these qualities is believed to be carried out by *dreaming* them into new qualities of both the personality and of thought. Furthermore, introjection of these qualities is a potentially endless process for we are supposed to keep *dreaming* all these qualities into ever ripened others. What exact role do these *dreamed* qualities play in shaping the qualities of the internal characters – if indeed any? It would seem that the distinction between internal characters and introjected characters still remain in need of further investigation. Is there any substantial difference in the degree of reality between them? Any new points of light shed on this investigation might enable us to perhaps more rewardingly approach Aristotle's subtle question: "One might ask how it is possible that though the affection is present, and the fact absent, the latter – that which is not present – is remembered" (Aristotle, Mem., 450a25–26; tr. J. I. Beare; ed., rev. J. Barnes). How psychical may this "affection" exactly be? How *dreamed* into some new internal character? How alive and independent of our self and will may this "affection" be? The psychical processes continuously converting sense impressions into full psychical elements still seems in want of much further research.

6 Mother's Reverie and the Sense of Gratitude

Meltzer briefly describes a moving scene in the film *The Treasure of Sierra Madre* in which a couple of bankrupted men were lucky in finding a site plenty of gold. The gold was all laying within the bulky body of a mountain. After having removed an exhausting amount of earth from inside the mountain, they finally touched the gold. They then succeeded in extracting an immense amount of gold from inside the mountain. As they neared the end of the exploration, a conflict opposed them: a sensitive and grateful explorer insisted to return, in gratitude, to the now disembowelled mountain all the rubble they have removed from within it while taking the gold out of it, while the other man – a greedy and paranoid prospector – angrily opposed it (cf. Meltzer & Williams 1988, pp. 28–29).

Gratitude is believed to be profoundly implied in the endless work of introjecting the qualities of mother's reverie and in *dreaming* them into ever new qualities of the personality. The ways in which each explorer seeks reward from the gold they have both extracted from the inside of such bountiful mountain seem irreconcilably different.

The responsibility to carefully shield mother's inside from both internal and external assaults as well as to endlessly ripen her qualities in gratitude and awe closely stays with us as a guiding light throughout life. And yet, our awareness of the mysterious process of introjection and the sense of preciousness of the Mountain's inside seems always alarmingly fragile. The threat of ruining our being marvelled by mother's reverie and the awe-struck introjection of its qualities always frighteningly looms. This key factor lectures us all on the puzzling meaning of *being human*.

7 The Role of Passion in Creating New Dreaming Functions – A First Note

Introjection of the qualities of mother's reverie is believed to partly translate itself into a complex cluster of aesthetic experiences. These aesthetic experiences are believed to crucially participate in continuously *dreaming* our own mind into life, as well as in playing a mysterious role in endlessly enhancing the qualities of thought.

Just like the greedy and paranoid prospector of gold, however, it seems frightening for anyone of us to just recklessly turn our back on these sweeping aesthetic experiences, possibly collapsing the key role they are believed to play in both *dreaming* our own mind fully into life and keep endlessly ripening it in both its structure and qualities. This cluster of aesthetic experiences is a key power behind the trend to keep making life and the world glittering with insight and meaning. This trend speaks in the language of gratitude and for the qualities of mother's reverie and the joy inherent in generosity of sharing it with others.

Two factors, both mentioned before, are believed to crucially urge us all to keep introjecting the qualities of mother's reverie: the experience of *dreaming* the human mind into life and the awestruck experience of the creation of meaning. Both these factors lie in the heart of introjection of mother's qualities.

There is, however, yet another factor joining these two, and indeed crucially inhering them, in also making introjection of the qualities of mother's reverie an awestruck and in many ways ravishing experience. This other factor stands out in the rather surprising form in which Bion offered it: "When the mother loves her infant, what does she do it with? . . . my impression is that her love is expressed by reverie" (Bion 1962, pp. 35–36). As the lengthy, indeed hopefully unending discovery of the emotional meaning of mother's love, as well as the emotional experience of the discovery of the "wounding" beauty it inheres, stirred by it, seems to lead us into the paradoxical experience of an unending revelation – a revelation which may never cease to ripen itself as an ever enhanced revelation.

Nevertheless, love may be *expressed* by mother's reverie, but the *language* into which each of these – *love* and *mother's reverie* – are couched cannot ever be straightforwardly translated into one another. What, then, are the differences between both? What is it that lives in love though not in mother's reverie? I believe that the language of mother's love is essentially the language of mystery.

Our response to mother's reverie as an essential quality of her love may gradually be ripened in the form of a revelation: the awestruck revelation that the meaning of all emotional experiences may be matured into a matter of unending discovery.

The introjection of ever new qualities into the internal characters is a key way by which Meltzer believed the ripening of the personality may proceed unendingly (cf. 1973). Much of the roots of this awestruck quality of the human mind is believed to lie in the introjection of the qualities of mother's reverie.

8 The Foetus' Responsibility for Introjecting Mother's Reverie – A New Note

Although the mother may *teach* her foetus and her infant to think through the emotional experience of reverie, she cannot do the *learning* for them. *Learning*, here, means *introjection*. Both her foetus and her infant have to be able to endlessly *re-dream* it into new qualities of their personality, this being such a quite crucial step in *dreaming* their own mind into existence. They, therefore, should endlessly *re-create* the unique experience of *thinking*. This is a fundamental responsibility that we carry with us all lifelong. The depth with which we may experience this responsibility – foetus, infant and all – may speak for the depth of our sense of respect for the prodigy of mother's reverie, as well as of the depth of our gratitude to her. The complexity and endless richness inherent in the process of introjecting these qualities is believed to play a key role in enriching our understanding of the meaning of *being human*, and to perhaps bringing the importance of this meaning to each clinical hour.

9 On the Emotional Experience of Coherence and the Meaning of Hope

Bion reads the meaning of Poincaré's concept of *selected fact* as "the name of . . . the emotional experience of a sense of discovery of coherence" (1962, p. 73). I tentatively take the view that the epitome of the emotional experience of the discovery of coherence is the creation of new passionate links to the world. This is how *the sense of discovery of coherence* is believed to perhaps be best translated into our observable relationships with the world.

Every concrete instance of the sense of discovery of coherence is believed to play a key role in the genesis of the meaning of hope. This is believed to be an unending process. This tentative understanding may lend both psychical meaning and substance to the current concept of hope.

Passion may, therefore, live in the core of the experience of hope. Furthermore, passion also seems crucial in ensuring the vitality of thought such crucial emotional experience. This may perhaps allow us a glance at the defeating complexity that seems to live within what we use to call *hope*.

10 On the Meaning of Mother's Love – A New Note

The psychical complexity implied in the extraordinary process of creating a name for a feeling or a thing will tentatively be addressed in detail in another place. For now, I would just attempt to at least take a hint at the complexities burdening every foetus and every infant along the prodigy of introjecting mother's reverie.

> If the infant feels it is dying it can arouse fears that it is dying in the mother. A well-balanced mother can accept this and respond therapeutically: in a manner that it makes the infant feel he is receiving its frightened personality back again but in a form that it can tolerate – the fears are manageable by the infant's personality. If the mother cannot tolerate these projections the infant is reduced to continued projective identification carried out with increasing force and frequency. The increased force seems to denude the projection of its penumbra of meaning. . . . It behaves as if it felt that an internal object has been built up that has the characteristics of a greedy vagina-like "breast" that strips of its goodness all that the infant receives or gives leaving only degenerated objects. This internal object starves its host of all understanding that it is made available. . . . The consequences for the development of a capacity for thinking are serious.
>
> (Bion 1962a, pp. 114–115)

It would really seem an impossible task for the mother to still succeed, amidst such unimaginable emotional turmoil, accepting her foetus and her infant's projections, and accept them lovingly, that is, to keep *dreaming* all their projections creatively back into them. However, a quite critical point should, I believe, be emphasized. For perhaps the most precious quality of mother's love towards her foetus and her infant is the sense of the mystery of thought and of the creation of meaning. This quality is perhaps the deepest expression and the epitome of love. This deeply puzzling emotional experience – the sense of the mystery of thought and of the creation of meaning – should carefully be weighed as a central quality of the meaning of *being human.*

11 Mother's Plight and the Creative Strength of Passion – A Note

It seems imperative, however, to try to sharpen our impossible understanding of mother's emotional plight as she "meets" her foetus and later her newborn baby. Every attempt at it seems to hold a promise for us: the promise, that is, of failure. And yet without a serious effort to somehow take steps to at least hint at the sweeping storm of intensely conflicting emotions assailing the mother, we may remain entirely cut from seeing the prodigy of mother's reverie, on the one hand, and on the other hand, the unthinkably complex task that surely awaits the foetus and the baby to introject mother's reverie. In this light, not only thinking, but even *creative thinking* is believed to have its source, its substance and even its fundamental form in these two tightly combined prodigies: mother's reverie and the foetus' and the infant's capacity to introject it.

If we just altogether ignore the hardly reachable measure of both trying tasks and emotional experiences – of mother's, and of foetus' and of infant's – we may never be able to *hear* the echoes of these struggles in the course of the clinical hour.

We may, at any rate, try to perhaps hint at the over pressing demand of

> the baby's central preoccupations during his early experiences, in particular his lack of integration and fear of disintegration. The stressful task of taking care of a new *unknown* baby creates in a new mother a sense of loss of identity. The observations show how the impact of the baby's infantile terrors initially unsettles mother, preventing her from being able to understand his needs and feel emotionally close to him.
>
> (Miller et al. 1997, p. 100)

The over stressful mother may at times make it far too hard for the foetus, and soon the baby, to introject her reverie. These unintrojected experiences may live, in the adult's mental life, in many different forms. These many *undreamed*, and therefore, unintrojected emotional experiences are believed to surface in the sessions in many different forms. The many different voices in which these emotional experiences speak should confide in the analyst's gifted ear these particularly painful precocious experiences in the course of many sessions. They may have deprived the foetus and the baby from the capacity to give a name to feelings, thoughts and even to things, being perhaps inhibited to beginning to convert them into however precocious experiences of meaning. If well succeeded, such momentous experiences are also the beginning of making life and the world glittering with new creative insights and meaning.

In this light, a name given to either feelings, thoughts or things carry some loving, tender, kind, hateful, destructive or mad feelings into the thing we now name.

Only the creative strength of passion could perhaps breathe into the mother the strength to survive being so buffeted, sometimes from instant to instant, between extreme emotions even as she may at times experience her own sense of identity threatened when greeted by her now new baby.

But it would also seem an impossible task for the foetus and the infant to achieve the prodigy of introjecting mother's reverie amidst another unthinkable emotional turmoil, indeed a double emotional turmoil – the one trying his mother to the extremes of her best strengths, the other constantly threatening to throw to the whirlwind of yet another emotional upheaval all their efforts to somehow mould a sense of identity.

If, however, we do not seriously attempt to somehow hint at both these emotional turmoil even if no description would ever succeed to give a faithful voice to, we will never touch a remote feeling of their truth, and therefore, we may never be prepared to *hear* the echoes of their failures in the transference – of mother's reverie, as well as of the foetus' and the infant's failures in introjecting her qualities – both experiences speaking in the music of the adult's voices in the course of the clinic hour, as well as in the music of the voices of the analyst's own internal characters reacting to what we *hear*.

If, however, we would choose to ignore all serious attempts to somehow glance the truth of the emotional experience of both impossibly difficult processes – mother's occasional failures to *dream* her foetus' and her infant's projections back into them, as well as the foetus' and the infant's being forced to face their unreceived projections – we may perhaps miss out yet another extraordinary insight into the meaning of *being human*.

12 Introjection and the Foundation of Ethics – A Note

Now I briefly return to Bion:

> The increased force [of projections] seems to denude the projection of its penumbra of meaning. . . . It behaves as if it felt that an internal object has been built up that has the characteristics of a greedy vagina-like 'breast' that strips of its goodness all that the infant receives or gives leaving only degenerated objects. This internal object starves its host of all understanding that it is made available. . . . The consequences for the development of a capacity for thinking are serious.
>
> (Bion 1962a, pp. 114–115)

Bion's lines put the light on yet another extraordinary cluster of qualities of mother's reverie pulsating with life, promise and meaning. He again drowns us all in both perplexity and awe before the mysteries of introjection of the qualities of mother's reverie as well as on its overwhelmingly complex role in moulding both the structure and the qualities of the mind. The connection between the experience of the creation of meaning and the experience of goodness, even of the very genesis of the emotional experience of goodness, is yet another illuminating insight of Bion's. The links between *meaning* and *goodness* – or more precisely: *the emotional experience of the creation of meaning* and *the emotional experience of goodness* – allow us a privileged glance at the psychical meaning of goodness, as well as at the connection between a key psychical experience and the genesis of a key concept. Bion's lines draws our attention to the enigmatic journey we so often walk from emotional experiences to the creation of concepts. How many other emotional experiences converge and enormously enrich the concept of goodness? Is it possible, more generally, to carefully read back the unconscious emotional experiences that have played key roles in the genesis of most key concepts? What exactly is the role of emotional experiences and of unconscious phantasies in the genesis of concepts? How exactly does a cluster of emotional experiences ripen into a key concept? Is there *any* concept that does not translate, to some however undetermined extent, the work of *dreaming* sense impressions as well as psychical elements into the form of a concept? Together, the experience of the creation of meaning by introjecting mother's *dreaming* the foetus' and the infant's projections back into them, as well as the experience of mother's *dreaming* – together, both these experiences are believed to play a crucial role in lending the concept of goodness both psychical substance and meaning.

The experience of being stripped of such key goodness – feeling stripped, even, of *all* goodness – is certainly experienced as a terribly hostile, devastating assault made by a terribly hostile, devastating breast. The connections between being starved of understanding – that is, of mother's reverie, of mother's *dreaming* the foetus' and the infant's projections back into them – crucially assisting the foetus and the infant *dreaming* their own minds into their budding structure and qualities – the connections between *being starved of understanding* and the concept of *badness* seems, again, crucial: we seem to *dream* the unsettling emotional experience of being *starved of mother's understanding* into the extremely creative form of a key concept – that of badness, of evil.

Here again, the long winding way leading from a key psychical experience to a key concept heavy with psychical meaning seems yet another awestruck quality of the human mind and another road of research.

But Bion's lines lead us to an elaborated face of badness: the one translating the experience of being starved of all goodness into the *concrete* experience of an internal world crowded by degenerated objects.

Furthermore, the extraordinary experience of sharing with mother, through introjection, her *dreaming* their own projections into the creation of meaning should soon begin to ripen into a foundational quality of the meaning of *being human*. The experience of the good mother is inseparable from the experience of hope. Being stripped of all goodness implies the experience of being stripped of all hope. Again, this terrible deprivation of goodness and therefore also of hope takes a more concrete form: an internal world full of degenerated figures.

Bion's lines are believed to open a number of promising ways leading us somewhere near the psychical foundation of Ethics.

13 The Meaning of Goodness – A Note

But Bion's previous quote may force a new question into our perplexity: *what exactly is the psychical meaning of goodness? What is the psychical meaning of badness?* For their genesis, now read in the light of Bion's lines, may speak of their psychical meaning as perhaps nothing else with paralleled depth. Bion's the foetus' and the infant's "increased force [of projections] seems to denude the projection of its penumbra of meaning" should perhaps be view, rather, as a deep change in the *psychical substance* of projections: what is projected into the mother may no longer be his fear of dying but his desperation for mother's unresponsiveness, adding up to, and be confused with his previous fear, possibly transforming it into terror not only without name but deprived the access to the experience of meaning.

Bion's "The increased force [of projections] seems to denude the projection of its penumbra of meaning" seems to refer, rather, to a swift change in the *nature* of the emotional experience that the foetus or the infant tried – in vain – to project into the uncomprehending or refusing mother. The foetus' and the infant's responses to the uncomprehending mother put a frightening weight of responsibility on the analyst. For he seems called to read these emotional experiences in the form of an unreadable disturbance of the transference at deep levels of the emotional experience and of the counter-transference, both these disturbances being themselves what the analyst is urgently requested to read. At that far more sensitive level of transference, acute attention to the slight nuances of changes of the music of both the analysand's and the analyst's own voices seem of paramount importance.

14 An Enigmatic Projection

I will now briefly return to Bion's claim that "the infant personality by itself is unable to make use of the sense data, but has to evacuate these elements into the mother."

Sense data in themselves do not seem objects of projection, however. Being a psychical function, *projection* does not seem equipped to *directly* operate on sensorial excitations. For sense data to be operated on by projection as well as by mother's *dreaming* them back into her foetus or her baby, a previous conversion of sense data into some sort of psychical elements seem needed. I am unprepared to step into the lengthy philosophical discussions of what sense data exactly consist of and whether sense data are to be taken as equivalent to sense impressions. I am equally unprepared to argue whether *sense impressions* should be taken as an equivalent term as *perceptions*.[1] What seems immediately relevant to the argument in this book is what, of these three categories of phenomena – sensorial excitations, sense impressions and perceptions – require psychical life. The view that I will uniformly take throughout this book is that sense data, as well as sensorial excitations, do not imply any psychical work. I will, therefore, take *sense data* and *sensorial excitations* interchangeably. I closely follow Bion throughout in this choice of terminology. I also closely side with Bion's claim that "there are no sense data directly related to psychic quality, as there are sense data directly related to concrete objects" (Bion 1962, p. 53, cf. **Chapter 13**). So what, then, does it exactly mean for the foetus or the infant to evacuate *sense data* into the mother? By now, and mainly because of Bion's awareness clause (cf. previous chapter), it would seem quite clear that alpha-function falls short of the task of continuously converting sense data into psychical life. We, therefore, would seem bound to postulate a function which somehow continuously bridges over the gap between neurology and the psychical – a function, that is, continuously crossing us over the key line drawn between non-psychical and psychical.

However, some of the foetus' immediate, no-psychical responses to sensorial excitations stir by themselves alone mother's psychical responses. Physiological responses in the foetus might perhaps induce psychical responses in the mother, not, however, because they have been *projected* into her but because the mother has *perceived* his purely physiological responses to whatever stimuli untranslated into the foetus' and the infant's psychical life. In these circumstances, it is the mother who converts the infant's sensorial excitations by *dreaming* them into new psychical elements in her baby. The mother would, then, forestall her baby's *dreaming* sensorial excitations by *dreaming* them for him. These purely physiological responses of the foetus' or the infant's may stir her into reverie projected into them. It would then be the mother, not the foetus or the infant, to convert their sensorial excitations into some psychical life, thus infusing the result of her *dreaming* them into her baby. She would then offer her foetus the experience of her *dreaming* sensorial excitations into psychical life. This seems a priceless stepping stone for us all in our unending way to meaning. The mother's conversions would continuously create a unique link between her foetus and her infant and herself, being the most privileged author of the unparalleled experience of critically assisting creating their own mind. This, I believe, is the foundation of intimacy. This also seems why Meltzer viewed the emotional experience of intimacy to be the source of thought, stirring thought into life (cf. 1986, p. 27). This seems another reason why Meltzer believes that the most important factor of the setting is to offer the analysand *the concrete experience of a thinking mind in the room*.[2]

But mother's reverie crucially assists stirring her foetus' and her infant's psychical life into existence in still another deeply subtle and perhaps even more powerful way: by making her reverie carry into them the strength of her own passion for them, and with it, the awe-inspiring mystery of bringing a human mind into life.

The mother herself seems to project her own thoughts into her foetus, her infant and her child mostly through the music of her voice, the uncountably many different emotions shining in her eyes and her face, her smile and the countless many ways of shaping, and misshaping, her smiles, the sweetness or harshness of her bodily movements as well as the many dreaming functions ways in which she holds her baby, being herself the privileged reader of her little oracles of their own undeciphered enigmas. She must constantly read into the enigmatic signs she must be the privileged interpret of and continuously converting them into mental life. Before converting her foetus' and her infant's purely physiological "words" into emotions and thoughts, they perhaps may keep responding purely physiologically to the stirs and ruffles of existence. She is thus believed to be the uncomprehending witness of perhaps the deepest of all human mysteries, that is, of the creation of mental life.

15 On the Enigma of Joy – A Note

How many of mother's emotions and thoughts and wishes may still live today in the adult's mind? How all these pieces of mother's mental world may still be heard in the many voices of the adult's personality and thoughts in the transference? It may take us all a whole life endeavouring to string all these countless pieces of mother's together into a relatively unified internal figure which we use to call *internal mother*. Nevertheless, this tentatively unified internal figure is hopefully *dreamed* into ever new, more inspiring others. One of the many ways in which the best of our internal mother may live inside us is in our more inspiring ways of thinking. Not, however, because of the *form* of thinking but because of its creative strength, as well as of its *dolcesa*, both invisibly drawn out of both gratitude and awe for the prodigy of mother's capacity for reverie. Another extraordinary way in which this elusive and enigmatic figure can best prove its vitality is what in us guides the *dreaming functions*. This also seems what in us best celebrates the experience of joy.

Notes

1 For a relatively recent discussion of important aspects of the philosophy of perception and of the philosophy of representation particularly focusing on Kant, v. Gomes 2014.
2 Personal communication.

Chapter 8

What Is a Dream?

1 Introduction

If my tentative reading of Bion's drafted theory of contact-barrier is at all faithful to his undelivered meaning, Bion invites us, even perhaps urges us to cautiously re-examine the question, *what is a dream?*

> The sleeping man has an emotional experience, converts it into alpha-elements and so becomes capable of dream-thoughts. Thus he is free to become conscious (that is wake up) and describe the emotional experience usually known as a dream.
>
> (Bion 1962, p. 15)

So what we are all used to call a dream is, to begin with, not a dream. A dream, in Freud's sense, is, in Bion's, an emotional experience. In light of Chapters 2, 3 and 4, therefore, a dream, in Freud's sense, is, in Bion's, an *undreamed* emotional experience, that is, an interrupted dream. So in still other words, in Bion's eyes, dreams are emotional experiences which have not yet been woven into the texture of our personality and the qualities of our thinking. So in the eyes of Bion's contact-barrier, dreams, in Freud's sense, are of a failed *dream*.

Furthermore, "As far as dreams give us direct access to its [the contact-barrier] study they retain the central position in psycho-analysis that Freud assigned to them" (1962, p. 17). Bion's "As far as" invites *and only as far as*.

So at their best, dreams, in Freud's sense, are now entrusted with the puzzling task of lecturing us on either qualities or the workings of contact-barrier. It would, therefore, seem that, if the dream fails to shed some new light on the contact-barrier which it is assumed to be closely

DOI: 10.4324/9781003375159-10

associated with, the dream, in Freud's sense, may confidently be edged into irrelevance.

In other words, the dreams that prove unsuccessful in their new, unexpected responsibility should be dropped from the central role that Freud and indeed generations of able analysts closely queuing up behind him have entrusted them with, being now seen as not much more than just a failed emotional experience in need of further psychical work so as to make it some interesting psychical piece.

2 What, Then, Does It Exactly Mean to Interpret a Dream?

If further research would eventually lend deeper credit to Bion's unexpected claims, analysts may have a trying challenge awaiting for them. For where exactly, in Bion's view of dreams, can we find the latent content of a dream? Where are we to both find and follow the many labours of Freud's *dream-work*? Where are we to meet the fulfilment of wishes that, in Freud's eyes, is dreams' only psychical function (cf. Freud 1900b, S.E. 5, p. 579)?[1] How should we, then, listen to dreams in the course of any clinical hour? Should we, from now on, focus on trying to closely read, in each dream, what it teaches us about the structure, the qualities and the workings of the contact-barrier it should be associated with rather than struggling to read the forbidden wishes spurring the dreamer to compose it? Should we rather tend to see, in such surprising view of dreams, a far more inspiring and clinically useful view of the meaning of dreams? What, after all, should we, from now on, understand by *the meaning of a* dream? What, then, in this new puzzling light is an interpretation of a dream? How exactly should we then interpret a dream if we no longer seem to know what a dream exactly is? Is a dream no longer a psychical entity with a definite structure and end but rather a cluster of psychical phenomena which we have, so far, lumped together under the misleading name of *dream*, stuffing these many indistinct things into a far too narrow and uninspiring concept? Would these many elements be too many for an interpretation to be ever attempted and awkwardly offered to the analysand? Is the analyst ever prepared to carefully go through these new trying ways? Would he ever be? What exactly have we all been doing for decades when we believed we were interpreting a dream, usually equating it with its narrative? Is it that, in the end, we may perhaps be more able to read the history of the transference and the counter-transference in the workings of the contact-barrier? How far away may we now suddenly find ourselves from everything Freud and, indeed, generations of experienced analysts who have closely followed him, have so firmly claimed about dreams, trusting their own views with the frightening responsibility of guiding their clinical thoughts in everyday consulting rooms?

3 What, Then, Is a Dream?

Bion's next step in deepening his understanding of the psychical significance of contact-barrier took him even farther away from Freud, leading us into even greater perplexity. For Bion now states that

> the ability to "dream" preserves the personality from what is virtually a psychotic state. It therefore helps to explain the tenacity with which the dream, as represented in classical theory, defends itself against the attempt to make the unconscious conscious. Such an attempt must appear indistinguishable from destruction of the capacity to dream.
>
> (Bion 1962, p. 16)

Bion identifies in dreams a key function that he himself had just given to the contact-barrier: the function, that is, to continuously preventing the unconscious to become conscious or, in the language I suggested before, to continuously prevent *the unconscious form of thought* to disrupt *the conscious form of thought*, possibly leading to psychotic states. Although, however, Freud has indeed identified what he described as the *general* tendency of the unconscious to infiltrate itself the conscious, thus threatening the conscious form of thought to collapse into psychotic episodes, I am not aware that he has ever singled out this specific function about the mechanisms of dreams. Since the only function of dreams, in Freud's eyes, has always been to slyly meet the dreamer's forbidden wishes, the tenacity with which the dream defends itself against the attempt to make the unconscious conscious should perhaps be read, rather, as the dreamer's tenacity not to interrupt himself in his guilty task.

To the purpose of preventing this infiltrating move from the unconscious into the conscious mind possibly collapsing it, I have added the equally crucial function of the contact-barrier preventing the *conscious form of thought* to hostilely infiltrate *the unconscious mind* collapsing it into mindlessness.

We soon find yet another line of Bion's further adding to all that has already been discussed before about this particular function. He wrote, "The contact-barrier is . . . also responsible for the preservation of the distinction between conscious and unconscious and for its inception. The unconscious is thus preserved" (1962, p. 27). Not only what I called before *the unconscious mind* is supposed to be preserved as the fundamental source of mental life by the continuous work of the contact-barrier, but exactly the same holds for *the conscious mind*.

The continuous creation of both *the conscious mind* and *the unconscious mind* is expected to prevent the unconscious mind to collapse the conscious mind into psychosis, as well as the conscious mind to collapse the unconscious mind into mindlessness.

I would recall that, in my tentative reading of Bion's theory of contact-barrier, I introduced both these concepts – *the conscious mind* and *the unconscious mind* – in the belief that they might usefully replace the questionable concepts of *the conscious* and *the unconscious* (cf. chapter 2).

Note

1 Is this the only function that can be assigned to dreams? I know of no other (Freud 1900b, S.E. 5, p. 579).

Chapter 9

Bion's Theory of Dream-Work-Alpha

Part I

1 Introduction

The fundamentals of Bion's sketchy theory of *dream-work-alpha* was shared with us in the form of Bion's fragment dated August 1960s:

> The methods of dream-work-alpha are not the same as those of dream-work which is related to interpretation of dreams, but are the *reciprocal* of dream-work and are related to the capacity to dream, i.e., to transform into dream, events that are grasped only on a rational, conscious level. In this way alpha is the reciprocal of dream-work. Furthermore, it suggests that the element of "resistance" in dream-work, as elucidated by Freud, is a compound of two elements: resistance, as described by Freud; and a felt need to convert the conscious rational experience into dream, rather than a felt need to convert the dream into conscious rational experience. The "felt need" is *very* important; if it is not given due significance and weight, the true dis-ease of the patient is being neglected; it is obscured by the analyst's insistence on interpretation of the dream.
>
> (Bion 1992, p. 184)

It is immediately clear that Bion's sense of the term *dream* has nothing in common with Freud's sense of the same term.

2 Bion's Theory of Dream-Work-Alpha – First Notes

Bion equates the capacity to dream with the capacity to transform into dreams events that are grasped only on a rational, conscious level. For the sake of the clarity of the argument, I will henceforth use the italic form

DOI: 10.4324/9781003375159-11

of the word "dream" and "dreaming" every time it seems clear that they refer to Bion's sense of both these terms. So in this clearer form, Bion's previous fragment begins by stating that dream-work-alpha converts the conscious and rational experiences into *dreams*. I tentatively take Bion's view to invite the claim that a key function of dream-work-alpha is to *continuously* convert conscious and rational experiences into *dreams*, and therefore, to state that conscious and rational events are supposed to be continuously *dreamed* into new *dreams*.

Two key questions will travel along this whole book: (1) what exactly is the new condition of the conscious and rational experiences after they have been converted into *dreams*, and (2) what exactly does this conversion consist of?

Question (2) may perhaps be better reworded into this one: what psychical functions are entrusted with continuously converting conscious and rational experiences into *dreams*, and how do they operate such momentous conversion?

3 Bion's Theory of Dream-Work-Alpha –
A New Introduction

Bion introduces his sketchy theory of dream-work-alpha in the form of an apparently trivial chain of events:

> This chain of events, as far as I am able to tell, is something like this: suppose I am talking to a friend who asks me where I propose to spend my holiday; as he does so, I visualize the church of a small town not far from the village I propose to stay. The small town is important because it possesses the railway station nearest to my village. Before he has finished speaking, a new image has formed, and so on.
>
> The image of the church has been established on a previous occasion – I cannot now tell when. Its evocation in the situation I am describing would surprise no one, but what I now mean to add may be more controversial. I suggest that the experience of this particular conversation with my friend and this particular moment of the conversation – not simply his words but the totality of that moment of experience – is being sensorially perceived by me and converted into an image of that particular village church.
>
> I do not know what else may be going on, though I am sure that much more takes place than I am aware of. But the transformation

of my sense-impressions into this visual image is part of a process of mental assimilation. The impressions of the event are being re-shaped as a visual image of that particular church, as so are being made into a form suitable for storage in my mind.

By contrast the patient might have the same experience, the same sense impressions, and yet be unable to transform the experience so that he can store it mentally. But instead, the experience (and his sense impressions of it) remains a foreign body; it is felt as a "thing" lacking any of the quality we normally attribute to thought or its verbal expression.

To the first of these products, that of dream-work-alpha, I propose to give the name, "alpha-element"; to the second, the unassimilated sense impression, beta-element.

(Bion 1992, pp. 180–181)

This, then, is Bion's only attempt I am aware of to describe the fundamentals of his theory of dream-work-alpha. He gave his description the form of an unbroken narrative. A number of other fragments, many in the form of quick notes scribbled on occasional pieces of paper, others left in a recording machine spanning no one seems to exactly know how many months or years, dealing with the same concept and playing an uncertain part in his concept of dream-work-alpha, survived in the printed page in the form of many posthumous fragments gathered by Francesca Bion in *Cogitations* 1992.

In this and in some of the next chapters, these scattered fragments will be argued to form a relatively unified new theory. This will be called in this book Bion's *theory of dream-work-alpha*. This theory will be shown to be central in both Bion's theory of dreams and in his visionary model of the mind. It is also believed to eventually play a key role in the future of psychoanalysis.

4 On What Bion Is Unable to Tell

I will now attempt to closely follow Bion's narrative almost line by line, trying to see in it Bion's attempt to answer his own preliminary question: "Is it possible to get nearer to describing what [dream-work-]alpha does?" (Bion 1992, p. 64). We will soon find out what seems to have advised Bion to word this apparently trivial question in his wisely groping words.

Bion begins his narrative by gently cautioning the reader about what he has just cautioned himself against: to tacitly assume the plain readability of such an apparently pedestrian narrative.

Indeed, Bion gently begins his narrative by warning the reader – as well as himself – of all that, in this apparently uninspired and uninspiring narrative, he is surprisingly unequipped to tell.

Bion writes, "This chain of events, *as far as I am able to tell*, is *something like this*" (my emphasis). And indeed, we very soon discover with surprise that what Bion is able to tell about such apparently trivial chain of events is, after all, not much more than a few notes scribbled on the margins of all that he is able to tell. The latter – what he cannot tell – gradually emerges to be precisely what Bion most focuses on, even though this is exactly what, in his trivial narrative, most tries him being precisely where the core of his theory of dream-work-alpha best lives.

5 Bion's Second Chain of Events

So paradoxically, again, it is precisely the second chain of events – the one increasingly evading the strength of his privileged grasp – that will soon be shown to defeat him – and us – the core of his theory. What stops him in his efforts to share with us what he intuits and yet cannot see, it soon emerges, is exactly what, of his narrative, lives beyond the edge of the unknown, the unknowable and the unthinkable.

In different words, the very core of his new theory, being, of course, what the keenest focus that his privileged researching eyes falls the deepest on, and where the illuminating promise of this new theory is believed to most clearly live, is exactly what he can least tell.

From this point of his narrative on, we will see Bion trying his most to walk his uncertain way along what he sees less, treading on an uncharted land and inviting us to closely follow him. By clearly proceeding along these lines, Bion once again shows himself unwaveringly faithful to his vision that what seems to matter most in the human mind is believed to pulsate beyond the edges of the unknown, the unknowable and the unthinkable. This is taken throughout this book to be one of the most awestruck qualities of the human mind. Gradually, I would hope, this vision may filter down into the clinic hour as well as into our slow grasp of the meaning of *being human* deeply illuminating it.

6 A Detailed View of the Two Chains of Events – A First Step

I will next attempt to closely follow Bion's two narratives, the one that he knows what he can tell, the other what he knows he cannot. I will attempt to very carefully follow both as Bion walks along the former while sharing with the reader the findings about his *dreaming* the latter.

As his friend asks him where he was going to spend his holiday, Bion realizes that, at this moment, he visualizes the church. He further realizes that the image of the church has been established on a previous occasion though he cannot tell when.

We may wonder – though in vain – what psychical role might this image have already played, or still been playing in his mind, as well as what exactly was it that Bion may have asked that image to do for him. Still less does he – or indeed we – know what it exactly means for an image to "become loaded with psychical events."

What, indeed, can it possibly mean to *load an image with psychical events*? By "loading it with events," and also entrusting it with psychical functions, we surprisingly convert a quite pedestrian image of a pedestrian church into an important psychical element pulsating with life and playing key roles in psychical life.

7 An Enigmatic Image – First Note

Bion has also no idea how he has transformed an image of a common object – in the case, a common village church – into such an unreadably complex psychical phenomenon – a phenomenon which, currently taken, would easily evade our inattentive eye, seeing in it nothing more than a common image of a common church.

This is already part of the narrative that Bion is not able to tell: "I do not know what else may be going on, though I am sure that much more takes place than I am aware of." How exactly much more is his "much more"? How essential is it? How many other easily nameable elements have always been playing key psychical functions in his mind, and indeed in everyone else's, without his – and ours – slightest consciousness of? How uncountably many other elements *continuously* play countless many different roles in each one's mind without our being not vaguely aware of? How many unnameable psychical elements and functions are continuously playing quite crucial psychical roles unnoticed by our unaware eye?

What psychical elements and what psychical functions continuously guiding all sides and all movements of our mental life are those which we have *any* awareness of?

8 The Core of Bion's Theory Being the Core of What He Cannot Tell – New Notes

We will soon begin to hint that what Bion believes he does not know about the role of this apparently pedestrian image goes indeed far farther than what he is sure goes on in his mind about it: "I do not know what else may be going on, though I am sure that much more takes place than I am aware of." Nor are we, puzzled readers, prepared to discern that his research into this now surprisingly conspicuous image is going to lead him – and us – right to the heart of a new theory about the ever enigmatic workings of psychical life, and that this sketchy theory, being once again about what seems to pulsate beyond the edges of the unknown, the unknowable and the unthinkable, is believed to play an unsuspected central role in both his theory of dreams and in his visionary model of the mind.

9 The Two Chains of Events – Introduction to the Second One

I will now briefly recall the beginning of Bion's narrative.

As his friend was asking him about where he was going to spend his holidays, Bion realized that he "visualize[d] the church of a small town not far from the village I propose to stay." He also noticed, however, that "the image of the church has been established on a previous occasion – I cannot now tell when."

An image of this church has, therefore, been previously worked out by Bion himself into some psychical element which he might then have previously endowed with some kind of internal life, as well as with an internal function, without, however, having realized it.

But Bion candidly believed that "its evocation" – the evocation of an image of this church – "in the situation I am describing would surprise no one." Colloquially, Bion's remark may invite an easy agreement.

If, however, we carefully reread the line, we may perhaps begin to puzzle over the psychical mechanisms operating behind the unpremeditated evocation of this image.

Bion was evidently aware that he ignores virtually everything about both the psychical functions this image has been surprisingly entrusted with. And yet, he alone has, of course, endowed it with a mysterious life of its own and therefore has created its qualities and its workings. Bion may, furthermore, have even continued to deepen the unknown internal life of this image.

This sudden image now swells to puzzling importance. Its still unknown psychical role will very soon confound us all. So if we examine Bion's words a little closer, the unpremeditated evocation of this image ought, indeed, to puzzle everyone – even if "in the situation I am describing [it] would surprise no one."

We may not even notice that if we just convert Bion's apparently trivial statement into a question we may immediately feel somehow lost about it: *to what exact psychical purpose has this pedestrian image been evoked?* Surprisingly, we may be entirely unable even to draft a groping tentative answer to this apparently trivial question, perhaps hinting that we may never be equipped to risk trying it.

For now things really change.

10 The Second Chain of Events – A New Step

"The impressions of the event are being re-shaped as a visual image of that particular church and so are being made into a form suitable for storage in my mind." Bion's colloquial "so" is a gross *non sequitur*. The false innuendo that this little "so" wriggles into the line is that the second statement of this line – "are being made into a form suitable for storage in my mind" – trivially follows from the first. Bion's misleading "so," so unobtrusively dropped into the line, may perhaps comfort the reader by luring him into not realizing that we are already fully operating beyond the edge of the unknown, the unknowable and the unthinkable, this being perhaps the main reason why this is a central piece in the second chain of events – precisely the events Bion cannot tell, his little "so" being an immediate witness to.

In other words: Bion's little "so" may play the luring service to the hasty reader: it may screen away from him the rather troubling fact that this odd area of mental life – again: beyond the edge of the unknown, the unknowable and the unthinkable – seems where alone we may ever meet the meaning, and hopefully follow the workings of, the core of Bion's theory of dream-work-alpha.

Bion's unfortunate "so" may even lure us into the belief that we may perhaps be spared the trouble of striving to read the exact meaning of each of the two statements that this same "so" pretends – falsely – to connect: "The impressions of the event are being re-shaped as a visual image of that particular church" – this being the first of these two statements – and "are being made into a form suitable for storage in my mind." Therefore, the innuendo that this "so" offers the inattentive reader doubly misleads him. For as it will soon become clear, the *psychical* link between these two statements seem to condense the still unrevealed core of Bion's theory of dream-work-alpha, which, once again, lives altogether in what Bion cannot tell.

So it gradually emerges that what Bion cannot tell is, again, exactly what matters most in his illuminating new theory.

Furthermore, this little "so" may invite the reader's hasty eye not to realize that he has no access to the psychical meaning of any of these two statements, let alone the connection between both. And yet Bion kept groping through his uncertain way towards the meaning, which, however, he knows he can never grasp.

The key question seems, nevertheless, this: although he can really never grasp it by the means that the canon of psychoanalysis puts at his service, by *dreaming* his own vision, he cannot really *grasp* it at the level of this canon but he can *create it* – and keep creating it unendingly, this being how we may reach the meaning of things – unendingly created meaning of things.

The way Bion proceeds along his narrative, bringing his new theory to life, offers us another impressive piece of evidence of how Bion entrusted the task of guiding him through this uncharted field with *dreaming*. The same about knowledge as well as about understanding. This has most crucial consequences.

11 Alpha-function – An Odd Point in Bion's Discussion of Dream-Work-Alpha

At this point of the discussion of Bion's theory of dream-work-alpha, we may perhaps be invited to carefully reread Bion's classical theory of alpha-function. For now Bion seems to have drafted two theories of alpha-function: one sketched in *Learning*, the other in the very pages in which he drafted his theory of theory of dream-work-alpha that are now under scrutiny. Each of these drafted theories of alpha-function branches out from a different concept of alpha-function. These are very different concepts giving birth to two very different theories. The immediate difference between both concepts lies in the awareness clause, central in the former, absent in the latter.[1] In the former – the *Learning* version – alpha-function is postulated to *directly* operate on emotions and sense impressions, which we are aware of, continuously converting them into alpha-elements (cf. 1962, p. 6; cf Chapter 6).

However, this requirement is absent in Bion's concept of alpha-function as he describes it in his theory of dream-work-alpha.

Although the *conceptual* difference between both versions of alpha-function lies in whether or not the awareness clause is entrusted with a key role in the workings of alpha-function, the difference between both these theories that each concept branches out into is of the utmost consequence for Bion's theory of dreams.

As I tend to see it, the difference between both theories is this: while in the *Learning* version the psychical functions operating on the sense impressions and the emotions which we are aware of are altogether indistinctly wrapped up in the abstract term *alpha-function*, they are brought to the centre stage in the dream-work-alpha version of the theory. In the *Learning* version, Bion did not allow us the slightest hint at the nature of the psychical functions operating the so-called *alpha-function*. In his theory of dream-work-alpha, however, the psychical functions operating it seem to entrusted with *directly* operate on sense impressions. The "alpha," closing the name *dream-work-alpha*, qualifies *dream* inviting the idea of a transformative psychical factor operating *directly* on sense data. This distinction is absent from the *Learning* version of the theory of alpha-function. And yet, again, this difference proves of far-reaching consequence. This tentative view will soon be discussed in detail.

12 The Prodigy of Introjection – New Notes

> The infant personality by itself is unable to make use of the sense data, but has to evacuate these elements into the mother, relying on her to do whatever has to be done to convert them into a form suitable for employment as alpha-elements by the infant.
>
> (Bion 1962a, p. 116)

The name that Bion himself has already given to this "whatever has to be done" is *reverie – mother's reverie*. The awareness clause has no role to play in the notion of mother's reverie. Exactly the same happens in his theory of dream-work-alpha. This "whatever has to be done in order to convert sense data into alpha-elements" seems to imply that mother's reverie is entrusted with providing the foetus, the infant and the child with what is required for equipping them to begin bringing their own mind into life. It is important to make the concept of alpha-element clearer. By alpha-elements I tentatively mean, in this book, the first, and in that way, the most primal psychical elements that can be operated on by the most primal psychical functions of the foetus and the infant.

I would believe that it is the strength of mother's passion for her foetus and her infant, and for the mystery and the brimming joy of bringing them to life, that is, the key factor in her reverie, being what would sweep them into mental life, "forcing" them to create, in turmoil and awe, their own experience of *dreaming*. The prodigy of introjection is the prodigy of the discovery of *dreaming* and of the unsettling experience of the creation of meaning.

13 Dream-Work-Alpha, Mother's Reverie and the Prodigy of Introjection – A New Note

I would once again address the reader to Bion's previous quote. Since sense data do not seem, in themselves alone, to be objects of projection, they do not seem to leave behind them their primary condition of neurological phenomena before they had somehow been *dreamed-work-alpha* into some kind of psychical condition that at least would equip them to be projected into the mother.

The cluster of *dreaming functions* specifically entrusted with converting sense data and primary emotions into alpha-elements is now called, by Bion's himself, *mother's reverie*. And yet, this seems to exactly be what Bion's dream-work-alpha is altogether about: how is it that we continuously convert sense data, as well as a host of unspecified "impressions," into alpha-elements. The epitome of this mysterious conversion is, in Bion's theory, a pedestrian image of a pedestrian church.

Soon the complexity of this image defeats us. To this exact extent, Bion's dream-work-alpha should largely be seen as a drafted theory, not, however, of the workings of mother's reverie, but more precisely, I would think, of the workings of the foetus' and the infant's as they strive to introject the fruits of mother's reverie. In perhaps more precise words, Bion's theory of dream-work-alpha seems about how the foetus, the infant and indeed we all may continuously convert sense data into alpha-elements by *dreaming* them. This amounts to state that Bion's theory of dream-work-alpha is essentially about the workings of some fundamental *dreaming functions*.

14 Mother's Reverie and Dream-Work-Alpha – A New Note

Nevertheless, I will now re-examine Bion's same lines once again though this time I will just tentatively remove alpha-elements as the end purpose of his view of mother's reverie. Instead, I will focus, rather, on what I would believe is the fundamental aim of mother's reverie. I will, therefore, reword Bion's statement into this alternative version: the infant personality by itself is unable to make use of the sense data but has to evacuate these elements into the mother, relying on her to do whatever has to be done to convert them into the sweeping discovery of the prodigy of the experience of meaning and, therefore, also of the unique discovery of the emotional experience of thinking. These are, of course, momentous experiences and foundational of the human mind. Furthermore, they are both believed to be *the* inspiring source of two other emotional experiences both also seen, in this book, to again be foundational of the human mind: the emotional experience of passion and of the experience of awe.

None of these experiences seem in any way dependent on alpha-elements. On the contrary: *these experiences are believed to create the alpha-elements,* to "force" them into life – if *alpha-elements* could ever speak of psychic reality.

Another crucial discovery forced into mental life by mother's reverie is sweeping aesthetic experiences. These two emotional experiences – the emotional experience of revelation, and the aesthetic experiences that revelation are believed to spark off – are both seen as key sides of the epitome of thinking.

Mother's *dreaming* the foetus' and her infant's projections, as well as the prodigy of introjection, are both believed to be governed by specific clusters of *dreaming functions*.

15 Theory of Alpha-function Versus the Theory of Dream-Work-Alpha – A Note

I have described previously (at a [undated] Scientific Meeting of the British Psycho-analytical Society) as a working tool in the analysis of disturbances of thought. It seemed convenient to suppose an alpha function to convert sense data into alpha-elements and thus provide the psyche with the material for dream-thoughts and hence the capacity to wake up or go to sleep, to be conscious or unconscious.

(Bion 1962a, p. 115)

Once again, Bion's *thus* is a huge *non sequitur*. This time, however, not only is it a *non sequitur*, but the way the statement is composed invites reading this *thus* as yet another source of unwelcome confusion. For Bion's *thus*, so naturally dropped into the line, screens away the fundamental problem of postulating a cluster of psychical functions entrusted with continuously *providing the psyche with the material for dream-thoughts*.

Bion's *hence* is yet another *non-sequitur*. For again it begs the question of how exactly dream-thoughts are equipped to lead us into one or the other states, or indeed to both simultaneously provided the cluster of dreaming functions that has been called, in this book, *contact-barrier* continuously governs this process.

In the words of his communication to the British Psycho-analytical Society, we seem to meet exactly the same operations converging on exactly the same functional purpose that has been entrusted before with mother's reverie, now suddenly confided to the cares of a version of *alpha-function* to which the requirement of the awareness clause has been dropped.

Note

1 Since I am not aware of when the theory of dream-work-alpha has first been published, the terms "former" and "latter" refer to the order they are mentioned in this chapter.

Chapter 10

Bion's Theory of Dream-Work-Alpha

Part II

1 The Dynamic of Psychical Life – A Note

> We are now confronted with the task of investigating the development
> of the relation . . . of mankind in general to reality, and in this way of
> bringing the psychological significance of the real external world into
> the structure of our theories.
>
> ("Formulations"; cf. Freud 1911, S.E. 12, p. 218)

As far as I am aware of, it was in these lines of Freud's "Formulations" that
the problem of the relations of mankind to external reality first formally
walked its surprisingly new way into psychoanalysis. As I would see it,
this is what Freud's historic paper is crucially about. This setting up of the
reality principle proved to be a "momentous step" (Freud 1911, S.E. 12,
p. 219).

Bion's theory of dream-work-alpha is believed to add a new dimension
to Freud's settling the problem by rooting the core of such crucial question
beyond the edge of the unknown, the unknowable and the unthinkable.

Freud's illuminating insight may again be given a wider dimension if we
examine it against the backdrop of Guthrie's view:

> The Presocratics may fairly be said to have been preoccupied with the
> nature of reality and its relation to sensible phenomena. This question
> of the relations between reality and appearance remains at the root of
> things, and in one form or another constitutes the fundamental differ-
> ence between rival philosophies.
>
> (Guthrie 1971, p. 4)

We indeed meet echoes of this quite central question everywhere in life
and in countless different forms. Just like the curtains of the B Bartok's

DOI: 10.4324/9781003375159-12

The Bluebeard's Castle, we are told that the curtains of our own eyelids were just raised and put before a puzzling question: "where now is the stage: within or without" (Prologue, Libretto by Bélla Balázs 1884–1949).

Where, indeed, is the stage? Where, indeed, is it, the stage, at each moment of life, is it outside, inside or both?

Bion's theory of *dream-work-alpha* is a visionary approach to the mysterious process of continuously converting external reality into internal reality, thus continuously creating the external reality.

Continuously converting external reality into internal reality constantly creating the former should essentially be entrusted with *dreaming functions*, the fundamental part of which is believed to develop beyond the edge of the unknown, the unknowable and the unthinkable is a visionary and indeed priceless gift that Bion offered to history.

2 "Reshaped as a Visual Image"

> The impressions of the event [Bion's meeting with his friend and their conversation] are being re-shaped as a visual image of that particular church and so are being made into a form suitable for storage in my mind.
>
> (Bion 1992, pp. 180–181)

In the previous chapter I have argued that Bion's little "so" is a major *non sequitur*. This little unprotruding "so," carelessly dropped into the line, screens away from the reader's eyes what exact psychical functions are entrusted with *re-shaping* Bion's "impressions of the event" into the image of this church, transforming it in such a crucial and yet defeatingly complex psychical element. This short "so" also hides from the reader's awareness exactly how these psychical functions have succeeded in carrying out this mysterious conversion. And yet what this unsuspected "so" screens away from the reader's eyes is believed to be no less than the core of Bion's theory of dream-work-alpha.

As these unnamed psychical functions convert Bion's "impressions of the event" into an image of a common church, they profoundly transform Bion's perception of that church into a whole new, defeatingly complex psychical element, endowed with fundamental internal functions.

This group of psychical functions operating this conversion would soon be called *dream-work-alpha*. This new puzzling psychical element will soon be claimed by Bion himself not only to be central in his theory of dream-work-alpha, but central in the workings of the human mind. Bion would, of course, call it *alpha-element*. The name soothes us. It may perhaps even lure us into no longer attempt to gain a glimpse of the psychical processes that it gives a general name to, never mind to extensively investigate into it. Otherwise, it would soon defeat us. For we do not seem to have the means to form the remotest idea of all that we do not know, can never come to, and may not even succeed to think about, in any predominantly rational terms, about what this term is now asked to name. What exactly is the genesis of this now defeatingly complex psychical element? What is its extraordinary internal life? Why exactly is this now transformed perception of a pedestrian church such an important model of much of the process of continuously bringing the human mind into existence – indeed of continuously *dreaming* the human mind into its awestruck structure, its ever-changing qualities and defeatingly complex workings? This is not only part of all that Bion cannot tell: it also is, I would believe, the core of his theory of dream-work-alpha.

Where indeed, then, is the stage? Where is the stage of the interface between what is out and what is in? How many stages there are in this stage?

3   Moving From Unknowns to Unknowns, and From Unknowables to Unknowables

But I will now go back to Bion's own words, trying to very closely follow them:

> I do not know what else may be going on, though I am sure that much more takes place than I am aware of. But the transformation of my sense-impressions into this visual image is part of a process of mental assimilation. The impressions of the event are being re-shaped as a visual image of that particular church, as so are being made into a form suitable for storage in my mind.

At this exact point of his narrative, Bion cautiously moved from "my sense impressions" to "the impressions of the event," by which he carefully avoids being unduly specific about what exact sense impressions have been brought into this image – have been *dreamed-work-alpha* into this image, or as I would, once again, put it, have been *dreamed* into it. This deliberately unqualified sense of "impressions of the event" leaves no door open for the easy innuendo that Bion knows what exact sense impressions he was referring to. He himself had no idea exactly what they were. Bion, therefore, makes it clear that he himself does not know, and can never come to know, not only what "impressions of the event" are exactly these that now seem to crowd this mysterious image, but he does not even know anything about their nature, this being one reason why Bion, again cautiously, lumps together much of what he is not aware of about his meeting with his friend. He carefully calls the unspecific term *event* to assist him in telling us the little he still can. Are some of these "impressions" emotions? Are they unconscious phantasies? Are they also some of his own thoughts that he is not remotely aware of? Are they also new ideas? Are they perceptions of which he may not be aware of? What exactly are they? And yet these sense impressions live in the core of what he cannot tell. "The impressions of the event are being re-shaped as a visual image of that particular church."

As said before, Bion has no precise idea, and can never come to have, of all that lives within what he cautiously call *event*. As he goes on composing his narrative, Bion's restraint shows him relentlessly moving from unknowns to new unknowns and from unknowables to new unknowables. How much is the much more that he is now aware he does not know is taking place? And yet nothing seems to demur him from groping along his most uncertain way beyond the edge of the unknown, the unknowable and the unthinkable, where all these processes seem to unfold, so far from the grip of his incapable language, telling what he is capable of telling, though using that incapable language to draw our concern and acute interest to all that he cannot.

4 "Reshaped as a Visual Image" – A New Note

Not only the psychical functions entrusted with *reshaping* Bion's "impressions of the event" into an image of this church are, of course, an essential part of what Bion cannot tell but *a fortiori*, their concrete workings too are another crucial part of it. Is this what we meet in the workings of the contact-barrier, that is, in the workings of the cluster of functions that the contact-barrier has been suggested to essentially consist of? Is it that both processes – *contact-barrier* and *dream-work-alpha* – share exactly the same cluster of dreaming functions? I do not think this is the case but cannot discuss this point at this early point of the argument in this chapter. As said earlier, Bion's theory of dream-work-alpha is about how external reality is converted into psychic reality. Exactly the same, however, can – and I think must – be said of contact-barrier. As also said before, all these psychical functions are viewed as *dreaming functions* in the sense I have always given to this term in this book.

One of the most extraordinary and yet also disconcerting steps in Bion's theory of dream-work-alpha is that this already enigmatic reshaping of his sense impressions of that event some pieces of which Bion was aware of, though most he was not, ends up in an incomprehensible image full of incomprehensible life. Puzzlingly, this conversion is described by Bion as *mental assimilation*.

If we closely reread the following lines of Bion's narrative, we find it is so full of unknowns that it might have invited some measure of inattention to some of them by many readers. For he wrote, "The transformation of my sense-impressions into this visual image is part of a process of mental assimilation."

We of course must come carefully around yet another disconcerting, though again quite crucial question: what psychical functions entrusted with *continuously* carry out this incomprehensible task? And yet this task seems to lie at the core of *mental assimilation*, or perhaps more precisely, essentially *be* what Bion calls *mental assimilation*.

In this tentative understanding, *mental assimilation* is seen to be too large and loose a name of a process implying no one seems prepared ever to glimpse how many unknowns and how many unknowables pulsate under it.

5 Again the "Mysterious Leap"

The question of the "mysterious leap" raised by Scalzone and Zontini was first discussed in Chapter 5. This is the question they put:

> One problem common to natural sciences and to those of the mind remains unsolved to this day: the form of the transition from the biological to the psychic. Despite all our efforts, the "mysterious leap" continues to confront us, but we must try to narrow the gap by seeking to extend our knowledge of "everything that lies between."
>
> (Scalzone & Zontini 2001, p. 263)

Bion's theory of dream-work-alpha is believed to be a visionary step into this key question for it seems to convincingly approach the key problem of *what exactly are the objects the dreaming functions that dream-work-alpha essentially is believed to* directly *operate on*.

This question seems to border the neighbouring problem of drawing the frontier line between external reality and internal reality. How do we *continuously* convert the external world into psychical life? What psychical functions have we entrusted with *continuously* lead us across this much troubling line in both directions? Bion left us with a precious piece of a tentative answer: "Contact with reality is *not* dependent on dream-work[-alpha]; accessibility to the personality of this contact *is* dependent on dream-work[-alpha]" (Bion 1992, p. 45). In other words, the external world *has to be continuously dreamed-work-alpha* into psychical elements. But again this key problem stands out in our sometimes hasty way: *what are the first objects to be dreamed-work-alpha into some psychical elements? What exactly are the first objects that the cluster of dreaming functions which dream-work-alpha essentially directly operate on?* This might perhaps answer Scalzone's and Zontini's key question, and a fundamental step in Freud's key question of men's relations with external reality which he first approached in his "Formulations." In more general terms, the "mysterious leap" will be taken in this book, in more general terms, for the frontier between sensorial excitations and psychical life. How exactly, then, can we continuously cross this line *in both directions*? In Chapters 12 and 13 I will again return to this problem to hopefully re-examine it in still new depth. While I am not aware that anything in Bion's 1962 version of alpha-function allows any fundamental light on this same problem. Bion's 1992 version of this concept, however, promises a surprising new light on the same key problem which I am not aware having seen before or after in psychoanalysis. Putting it in a language that I believe is both clearer and more precise, these clusters of *dreaming functions* are entrusted with govern *mental assimilation*. I will soon attempt to show how Bion's language of alpha-element – of its genesis, its structure and its workings – may be more intelligibly translated in the language of *mental assimilation*.

So again, as he proceeds with his narrative, Bion journeys us along the edge of the unknown, the unknowable and even the unthinkable, being careful in pointing to us all that he cannot tell, pulsating with life beyond that mysterious edge. And at the same time, Bion invites us to trust *dreaming-work-alpha* as the privilege language of understanding what he – and we – can less see. Bion's odd narrative shows us a promising way for us to grope through that which could never be told, by trusting *dreaming* our way along, teaching us how to trust the truth of our inspiration and our insight.

6 What Is an Alpha-Element?

Why, then, is it that the core object of Bion's own research suddenly evades his own grip and compels him to start *postulating* rather than *describing*? The closer he observes, the less he can describe. And the closer he nears the heart of his insight, the more the words evade his grip and farther away he – and we – are from immediately understand what he really means as we closely follow him well into what he cannot tell. And yet, puzzlingly, the deeper we intuit the meaning of his view, the more our fascination as the true witness to our understanding.

Why exactly is it that he can no longer have access to the key piece of his own narrative though it again is the very heart of his deepest insight? What is it that seems to live within this disconcerting image? Why exactly, once again, are the psychical functions converting the unknown and unknowable "impressions of the event" into an image of a church suddenly transforming a pedestrian picture of a pedestrian church into such a defeatingly complex psychical element? What exactly, furthermore, is this very odd element important for? What exact dreams are these dreams so crucially at work in *dreaming-work-alpha* the unknowable "impressions of the event" into such a mysterious picture of such a common church? They are certainly not dreams in Freud's sense. What exactly are they, then? It seems remarkable that alpha-elements are certainly not a *sine qua non* condition for the possibility of *dreams* and *dreaming* and, therefore, of continuously *dreaming-work-alpha*. On the contrary, in light of both Bion's theory of alpha-function and of dream-work-alpha, it is precisely the *dreaming* – the *dreaming-work-alpha* – that *creates* the alpha-elements. What, however, is its genesis? What is its internal structure? How many *dreams* and memories and thoughts and unconscious phantasies are intensely living within every alpha-element? Are alpha-elements concrete instances of *mental assimilation*? What, then, is an *alpha-element*? What exactly do we need the concept of alpha-element for?

I will next discuss Bion's quote.

7 What Is an Alpha-Element – Further Notes

Although I have not put the term into the argument, my tentative reading of Bion's theory of contact-barrier (cf. Chapters 2, 3, 4, 6, 7 and 8) also submits a detailed rereading of his theory of alpha-function. Both this rereading and Bion's theory of dream-work-alpha show that the mechanism Bion called *alpha-function* is not only convenient to tentatively approach disturbances of thought but is seen as a foundational process of the human mind. Both the theory of contact-barrier and that of dream-work-alpha are believed to be fundamental steps into the problem first formally raised by Freud in "Formulations" of the relations between mankind and external reality, an evidently crucial part of which being the psychical processes determining the continuous conversion of external reality into internal reality.

In this fundamental quote, Bion just jumps over the key problem of the exact nature of the objects that alpha-function *directly* operates on. He just called them *sense data*. And yet Bion's awareness clause immediately collapses this undiscussed assumption (cf. Bion 1962, p. 6; cf. my discussion of Bion's theory of contact-barrier, particularly Chapter 6). The drafted theory of dream-work-alpha would seem to remain unclear on this key problem, but further discussion of it, in Chapters 12 and 13, is believed to settle the problem.

The question of what exactly endows us with the prodigious capacity for being both conscious and unconscious seems to have been left untouched by Bion in this theory. I have, however, approached it in detail in my tentative reading of Bion's contact-barrier (cf., again, Chapters 2, 3 and 4).

I am not prepared even to conjecture whether the discovery of Kant's two categories of sensibility – space and time – should as well be rooted beyond the edge of the unknown, the unknowable and the unthinkable through what cluster of dreaming functions operating any of these theories.

8 "The Totality of that Moment of Experience"

> The experience of this particular conversation with my friend and this particular moment of the conversation – not simply his words but the totality of that moment of experience – is being sensorially perceived by me and converted into an image of that particular village church.

What does it exactly mean *to convert the totality of that moment of experience into an image*? Neither Bion nor, indeed, anyone else seems equipped even to roughly guess what psychical elements live within this odd object bearing the disconcertingly long name *the totality of that moment of experience*. What sensorial excitations, perceptions, emotions, unconscious phantasies, ideas, memories, doubts, wishes, thoughts, psychical functions themselves, most of which are unconscious, have trod their ways into this odd unknowable psychical object? What, furthermore, does it exactly mean to *perceive* sensorially *the totality of that moment of experience*? What does this exactly mean? What cluster of psychical functions is believed to operate the prodigy of this enigmatic conversion? In Bion's language, this is the cluster of psychical functions operating dream-work-alpha. These functions, however, are believed to fundamentally operate beyond the edge of the unknown, the unknowable and the unthinkable.

But Bion's vision does not stop there: he goes further, ventures further and risks further. For, again, he held, "The impressions of the event are being re-shaped as a visual image of that particular church, as so are being made into a form suitable for storage in my mind." What exactly does Bion's elusive word *re-shape* stand for in psychic reality? What transformations of psychic reality are given the name *re-shape*? What exactly are we talking about? No one seems equipped to tell or ever become prepared to do so. And yet we may *dream* it and, as discussed in the previous chapter, observe, describe, discuss and understand many of their effects.

9 On Mental Assimilation

As we closely follow Bion's narrative, we watch his own words beginning to evade his command. He, however, goes on venturing to add that "the transformation of my sense-impressions into this visual image is part of a process of mental assimilation." What part is this? We want to believe that we know that the object Bion ventures to call "the totality of that moment of experience" is *trivially* perceived by him and *trivially* converted into an image of that particular village church. We may perhaps want to believe we know it, and yet we know only too well that we do not and will never come to. By playing with names that we give to unknown and unknowable objects and processes, we may easily fool ourselves into the belief that we now know what we have named. As said before, furthermore, we also do not know, and do not seem equipped ever to come to know what exact psychical functions work out this prodigy, never mind *how* exactly do these functions really operate so as to achieve such mysterious end. And yet, once again, this would seem to lie at the core of the workings of the human mind.

Like a little drop of clean water, as soon as it is put under the lens of an electronic microscope, it reveals the disconcertingly complex world of the Brownian motion, a simple image of a simple church, having been converted into a defeatingly complex new psychical element called *alpha-element* by our having achieved the prodigy – so common and yet so mysterious, so ordinary and usual and yet so awestruck – of *dreaming-work-alpha* "the totality of that moment of experience" into a new psychical element no one, once again, seems prepared to know what it is, may overwhelm us with its unreadably complex and beautiful internal structure, as well as its unreadably complex and beautiful internal life.

What, then, is an image? What may it become? What may it be *dreamed* into? Bion's theory of dream-work-alpha also shows us – as most lines of his – that there are questions, that there is an unending host of questions that may always remain unanswered, that we may never be equipped to offer them any convincing answer, that, once again, they look far too complex for us to reasonably venture into any tentative answer. His theory of dream-work-alpha adds up to my tentative view that so many lines of his are endowed with a promise: they end in the light of new perplexity. This would seem one of Bion's most precious insights: illuminating perplexity is the fate of most questions concerning the human mind.

The role Bion gives alpha-elements in his theory of dream-work-alpha may perhaps shut us within a paradox: Bion tells us time and time again that he has no idea what he is talking about. His repeated claim could hardly be more firmly substantiated. And yet he shows us the way beyond the edge of the unknown, the unknowable and the unthinkable guided by the discovery of the priceless merits of uncertainty and the invitation to rely on inspiration, insight and intuition. These are all believed to be different voices of *dreaming*.

10 On Mental Assimilation – New Notes

Bion's theory of dream-work-alpha might perhaps be seen as a tentative investigation into both the workings of mother's reverie and of the foetus' and the infant's introjection of the outcome of her reverie. As such, it is believed to provide us with a useful clinical tool allowing us to tentatively observe where the cluster of *dreaming functions* governing both key processes – mother's reverie and the foetus' and the infant's unending work of introjection – might perhaps have failed, or even may be failing at any moment of any session in either the analysand, the analyst or in both.

It seems unclear, furthermore, what the limits of thought his far better version of Bion's theory of alpha-function are. Does it end with the genesis of alpha-elements? Does it go farther than that, in which case the concept of alpha-elements would have to be seen as an artificial and, to my tentative understanding, unfortunate limit inadequately imposed upon an awestruck though unreadably complex psychical piece playing a crucial role in *mental assimilation*?

Mental assimilation, therefore, is best translated by continuous creative psychical processes. It does not primarily refer to the qualities of our knowing or understanding something but again to the enhancement of the complexity of the structure and of the qualities of our internal world. How exactly is it, furthermore, that "mental assimilation" is concretely carried out by dreaming-work-alpha the *totality of that moment of experience* into a pedestrian image of a pedestrian church? This is yet another prodigy to *dream* an uninspiring image into a whole new psychical entity now endowed with an internal structure and an intense internal life of its own.

The same may be shown to happen with concepts and even words without which human language would not seem possible as I hope to show in another book. This, again, is why I take Bion's theory of dream-work-alpha an insightful piece on the workings of *dreaming functions*.

11 On the Enigma of Perceptions – A Note

I will briefly return to Bion's lines:

> The experience of this particular conversation with my friend and this particular moment of the conversation – not simply his words but the totality of that moment of experience – is being sensorially perceived by me and converted into an image of that particular village church.

There is a word in Bion's lines which I will now particularly focus on: the word *perceived – sensorially perceived*.

Bion's theory of dream-work-alpha may also be seen an illuminating investigation into both the genesis and the extraordinary internal structure of perceptions. Bion hints at how he transformed the sense impression of a church into the unending complexity of a perception as a complex psychical element.

The image of a common church has been dreamed-work-alpha into an extraordinary psychical element. We used to call this psychical element a *perception* – a new perception. We, however, now know that what lives within this particular perception is an unknowable psychical element called *the totality of that moment of experience*. Perceptions are seen in this book as sense impressions *dreamed* into new complex, hopefully creative psychical pieces. In this tentative understanding, a perception should then be seen as a psychical element endowed with a genesis and an internal life of its own whether or not closely associated with an image. In this odd condition, perceptions should be continuously operated on under the creative strength of the unreadably complex dynamic of psychic reality continuously *dreaming* virtually *all* perceptions into ever new psychical elements. As just said before, the creative strength of the unreadably complex dynamic of psychic reality is one of the most extraordinary and indeed awestruck qualities of the human mind, and one that most profoundly speaks of the meaning of *being human*.

Dependent on the qualities of these *dreaming functions*, perceptions may either ripen into new awestruck psychical pieces being themselves now even endowed with an inspiring capacity, or may wither into dull, unliving elements, further fostering neglect and indifference. The qualities of the *dreaming functions* which convert sense data and sense impressions into perceptions are crucially important in making life and the world glittering with meaning. This view finds an echo in Keats' brief line: "The great beauty of Poetry is that it makes everything every place interesting" (Keats 1970, *Letters of John Keats*, p. 315).

> – that the qualities of the *dreaming functions* may make virtually everything fascinating.

12 Kant on Imagination – A Note

I will now briefly look at two passages of Kant's first edition of his *Critique of Pure Reason* (1781), calling them both to join the argument of this chapter. Quite unexpectedly, both these passages are believed to be heard in Bion's theory of dream-work-alpha. This is Kant's first passage:

> That the imagination is a necessary ingredient of perception itself, has, I suppose, never occurred to any psychologist. This is so partly because its power has been limited by psychologists to reproduction only, and partly because they believed that the senses not only supply us with impressions, but indeed also assemble these impressions and thus something more than our receptivity for impressions, viz., a function for their synthesis.
>
> A120 (Kant 1996, p. 168)

Kant's *function for their synthesis* seems to be entrusted with a task which, in Bion's theory, would seem to correspond to the workings of the cluster of psychical functions continuously converting sense impressions into perceptions. Kant's elusive *something more* seems to be given the name, in Bion's thought, of *dreaming*. Both these new views of perceptions – Kant's and Bion's – are now believed to be extraordinary creative achievements.

Bion, however, moves Kant's *something more* altogether beyond the edge of the unknown, the unknowable and the unthinkable by which he allows history a glimpse of its defeating complexity and awestruck beauty. Although along wisely different ways, both Kant's *imagination* and Bion's *dreaming functions* are believed to assist us in *dreaming* the human mind into further and hopefully more creative existence. This tentative understanding seems to be a whole new vision of perceptions, of both their nature, genesis and awestruck structure. Depending on the creative strength of the *dreaming functions* that have converted sense impressions into new perceptions, each new perception is endowed not only with a life of its own but also with new psychical functions. In each response to the external reality, a perception should be seen to *dream* what it perceives into a whole new object, now believed to be immensely enriched by new emotions, unconscious phantasies, memories, thoughts and feelings and perhaps even new ideas. In view, however, of the creative strength of the unreadably complex dynamic of psychic reality believed to be continuously at work in the human mind, perceptions are supposed to be unendingly *redreamed* into ever new psychical elements. This potentially endless richness both creates the internal life of each new perception and ensures its vitality. This extraordinary quality of perceptions is heard in Keats' line, and it is of critical assistance for each one of us to keep making life and the world glittering with creative insight and meaning.

This perhaps continuous and powerful reworking of perceptions is believed to manifest itself in the form of raising new emotions, unconscious phantasies, both conscious and unconscious thoughts, ideas, perhaps enhancing the qualities of insights and values. All these psychical elements are, again, believed to speak in the voice of the intense internal life of perceptions.

Depending on the qualities of the *dreaming functions* governing the creative strength of the unreadably complex dynamic of psychic reality, the qualities of perceptions may be endlessly ripened. This seems crucial in making virtually every instant of our lives so much more inspiring. The same holds of virtually every new clinic hour.

This would seem to be the critical difference between imagination when seen in the eyes of psychologists, as Kant puts it, and when examined under Kant's and Bion's illuminating insight. The former reproduces the senses and assembles them into images, the second gives them life – endless life, endlessly different lives.

14 Kant on Imagination – A New Note

In the beginning of the previous section I proposed to briefly look at two of Kant's short pieces on imagination, both in the first, 1781 edition of his *Critique of Pure Reason*. As just said previously, they are both believed to speak in the language of Bion's theory of dream-work-alpha.

This is Kant's second piece:

> This power we call imagination; and the act that it performs directly on perceptions I call apprehension. For the imagination is to bring the manifold of intuition to an *image*; hence it must beforehand take the impressions up into its activity, that is, apprehend them.
>
> A120 (Kant 1996, p. 168)

If, again, I am at all allowed to see the transformative strength of Kant's *imagination* distinctly echoed in the conceptual language of Bion's theory of dream-work-alpha, Kant's view of the imagination *performing directly on sense impressions* would perhaps now be far more precise and fascinating if we would now see it in the light of Bion's theory dream-work-alpha, by having the emotionally lifeless sense impressions of a perception being continuously *dreamed-work-alpha* into a new, potentially inspiring perception, endowed with an internal life of its own as well as a new psychical function.

Another line in this second piece of Kant's also speaks of how Bion's theory seem to endow sense impressions with the mystery of meaning as we *dream* them into a new perception. This is the line: "The imagination is to bring the manifold of intuition to an *image*." I would again tentatively reread the line as if saying that the *dreaming functions* entrust an image – just like the image of a church – with meaning, with the unique experience of meaning, thus "forcing" perceptions into full psychical life, transforming a host of "impressions" into the unity of alpha-elements – in Bion's language, or again, in my tentatively preferred language, into the unity of the experience of meaning, to which I will extensively go back in Part III.

In his puzzling and yet deeply inspired theory of dream-work-alpha, Bion seems clear about two points: (1) what he cannot be clear about and (2) that which he cannot be clear about is exactly what is most important in his theory and, in the light of his theory, in the human mind.

Here again, Freud might have tended to ignore the unknown, the unknowable and the unthinkable; here again, Bion tended to ignore the known, the knowable and the thinkable. Here again, this is what Bion seems to put all his passion and all his genius. Here again this is what he believes the core of the human mind most pulsates with life. And here again this is where we may best meet, in awe, the meaning of *being human*.

15 A Transformation of What No One Seems to Know What It Is Into Something Else Which No One Seems to Know It Is

Dream-work-alpha is, therefore, claimed to have converted an object which no one seems to exactly know what it is into another object which no one seems to exactly know what it is. The former is what Bion calls "the totality of that moment of experience"; the latter is a pedestrian image of a pedestrian church suddenly converted into an defeatingly complex and enigmatic psychical entity endowed with an internal life of its own and crucial psychical functions. The upshot of this odd conversion is two-fold: it is, on the one hand, the awestruck creation of the experience of meaning, and it is, on the other hand, yet another piece in the unending task of *dreaming* the human mind into its defeatingly complex structure, its ever-changing qualities and its overwhelmingly complex workings.

16 On the Deft Ears of Psychoanalysis – A Note

In Bion's hands, most conclusions, and therefore also most theories, no matter how hastily scribbled down on paper, eventually prove to be new doors ajar into new, more inspiring perplexity and awe. As it unfolds, Bion's visionary model of the mind moves us closer to a few famous lines heard along millennia of the most insightful philosophical thought, two of which are believed to be Heraclitus' fragment 45 and Aristotle's from *De Anima*: "One would never discover the limits of soul, should one traverse every road – so deep a measure does it possess" (Heraclitus, frg. 45.; ed., tr. Robinson). And then Aristotle's: "To attain any knowledge about the soul is one of the most difficult things in the world" (Aristotle, *De Anima*, 402a10–11; tr. J. I. Beare; ed., rev. J. Barnes). Both these lines largely preside over this whole book. None of them could ever be heard by psychoanalysis, so deafened by its faith in the virtue of knowledge and reason, so deafened by the misfortune of smugness. But then Bion is extensively argued to have matured both lines – Heraclitus' and Aristotle's – into a whole new dimension, seeing it seeing the human mind to essentially pulsate in an unreadably complex and awe-inspiring life beyond the edge of the unknown, the unknowable and the unthinkable, and to see the light of uncertainty to guide us along both research as well as virtually every clinical hour.

Chapter 11

The Enigmatic Fabric of Mental Life

1 Introduction

This chapter examines another key fragment of Bion's. It is dated 29 July 1959:

> [1] Into the realm of the dream flow the sense impressions associated with the coming into being of the reality principle [2] and the pre-verbal impressions associated with the pleasure principle. [3] None of this can be associated with consciousness, memory, recall, unconscious, repression or suppression unless transformed by dream-work[-alpha]. [4] The domain of the dream is the storehouse in which the transformed impressions are stored after having been transformed. [5] Dream-work[-alpha] is responsible for rendering pre-communicable material 'storable' and communicable; the same for stimuli and impressions derived from the contact of the personality with external world. [6] Contact with reality is *not* dependent on dream-work[-alpha]; accessibility to the personality of this contact *is* dependent on dream-work. [7] The failure of dream-work[-alpha] and the consequent lack of availability of external or internal psychic reality [to the personality] gives rise to the peculiar state of the psychotic who seems to have a contact with reality but is able to make singularly little use of it either for learning by experience or for immediate consumption.
>
> (Bion 1992, p. 45)

For the sake of clarity of the discussion, I numbered all the relevant lines of this fragment. The discussion of this fragment is the discussion of each numbered lines. The numbers are shown in bold and within square brackets.

DOI: 10.4324/9781003375159-13

In the following discussion, all the occurrences of the terms *dream* and *dream-work* are taken to be shortened forms of *dream-work-alpha*, of Bion's coinage.

As an introduction to my tentative discussion of lines **[1]** and **[2]**, I will recall a key passage of Freud's "Formulations" (1911)

Freud put as follows:

> It was only the non-occurrence of the expected satisfaction, the disappointment experienced, that led to the abandonment of the attempt at satisfaction by means of hallucination. Instead of it the psychical apparatus had to decide to form a conception of the real circumstances in the external world and to endeavour to make a real alteration in them. A new principle of mental functioning was thus introduced; what was presented in the mind was no longer what was agreeable but what was real, even if it happened to be disagreeable. This setting-up of the *reality principle* proved to be a momentous step.
>
> (Freud 1911, S.E. 12, p. 219)

Then Freud added, "The new demands made necessary a succession of adaptations in the psychical apparatus."

> (Freud 1911, S.E. 12, pp. 219–220)

Freud both intuits into this momentous shift and describes it in its rough lines. I believe that Bion insights into the depth of its underlying mechanisms. This fragment argues that dream-work-alpha is the core of this change.

2 Discussion of Bion's Fragment

[1]

I tentatively read line **[1]** as claiming that dream-work-alpha plays a fundamental role in working out "the coming into being of the reality principle." What exact role is, then, this? Bion's line seems to suggest that the sense impressions directly implied in showing us – infants and adults alike – the deceiving nature of the manoeuvre of evading frustrations by hallucinating are exactly those that have been *dreamed-work-alpha* into new psychical elements. What makes these psychical elements *new*,

I suggest, is exactly that they are now suddenly seen as *experiences* of frustrations. This now seems to be the main quality of *the same sense impressions* now revealed by our having *dreamed* it into a new psychical element. Once *dreamed-work-alpha*, this modification of our experience of these sense impressions – that is, the sudden discovery of the deceiving nature of the manoeuvre of evading frustrations by hallucinating – seems to meet Freud's idea that "it was only the non-occurrence of the expected satisfaction, the disappointment experienced, that led to the abandonment of the attempt at satisfaction by means of hallucination." Again, the *discovery of the disappointment as a new quality of these sense impressions* is believed to be revealed to us by having *dreamed* it into a new psychical element. This much would seem to be in Bion's line. This would already seem a huge demand Bion burdens dream-work-alpha with.

In other words, Bion seems to claim that *dreaming-work-alpha* some sense impressions may deeply modify our experience of them and, therefore, also what we think about them. But does this modification go as far as to introduce a new principle of mental functioning, as Freud puts it? And does this new principle of mental functioning, postulated to be created by dreaming-work-alpha sense impressions into modifying our experience of them, fully answer what Freud expects it to perform, that is, to make us realize that "what was presented in the mind was no longer what was agreeable but what was real, even if it happened to be disagreeable"? Does this particular cluster of *dreaming functions* achieve such momentous change in both the structure and qualities of psychical life so as to lead us to the *discovery of reality*? How much work must we ask from dream-work-alpha or, in my preferred language, from some specific cluster of *dreaming functions*? How long would it take us to *discover reality*? Does it take us the time of a *dream*? Of an analysis? Of a life? Do we ever discover reality? Do we not, rather, modify it, *dream* it into reality – into realities? How many realities may we *dream* reality into? No one knows what is the time of *dreams* – of *dreaming. Dreams* and *dreaming* are out of time. How deeper, how more creative – how more endlessly creative may we *dream* reality under the creative strength of the unreadably complex dynamic of psychic reality? How telling is the strength of this *dreaming* trend in re-shaping the meaning of *being human*.

However, "the new demands made necessary a succession of adaptations in the psychical apparatus." What exactly is it that governs this succession of adaptations so crucial to seal and indeed continue the discovery of reality? We are, of course, once again back to Freud's key question of his "Formulations" of the relations of the human mind with reality.

Bion's [1] raises the question of the role of *dreaming functions* in guiding these relations.

If this tentative reading of [1] would invite any plausibility, we would be confronted by the unkind question of how exactly, as we continuously *dream* the human mind into its awestruck structure, its ever-changing qualities and its defeating complex workings, do we continuously reshape reality, impoverishing it, defacing it, making it an endless source of wonder, keep making life and the world glittering with creative insight and meaning.

Be as it may be, line [1] seems to invite the ever-taxing question: what is reality?

[2]

If my tentative reading of line [2] nears Bion's meaning at all, the line seems to claim that pre-verbal impressions associated with the pleasure principle must also be dreamed-work-alpha into some form of psychical life so as to succeed, as in line [1], to modify the way we experience them, and therefore also, the way we respond to them. Here again, the *dreaming* of these impressions ought to modify both the structure and qualities of the psychic world so as to create an alternative response to continue to be governed by purely physiological response to reality. Here again, by *dreaming* the objects of the external reality into new objects of the internal reality, alter the way we experience the objects of external reality.

Just as with line [1], line [2] too seems to raise a central problem in both Bion's theory of dreams and his visionary model of the mind: what exactly is the nature of the elements that the cluster of *dreaming functions* primarily entrusted with sparking the human mind into life *directly* operate on? Is it possible that *dreaming functions directly* operate on sense data?

I will now briefly return to the closing lines of the key piece of Bion's that opened my discussion of his theory of dream-work-alpha (cf. Chapter 9):

> *Freud* meant by dream-work that unconscious material, which would otherwise be perfectly comprehensible, was transformed into a dream, and that the dream-work needed to be undone to make the now incomprehensible dream comprehensible. *I* mean that the conscious material

has to be subjected to dream-work[-alpha] to render it fit for storing, selection, and suitable for transformation from paranoid-schizoid position to depressive position, and that *unconscious pre-verbal material has to be subjected to [the same] reciprocal dream-work[-alpha] for the same purpose.*

(Bion 1992, p. 43; my emphasis)

All the other numbered lines of this fragment further elaborate on the question, is it possible that *dreaming functions directly* operate on sense data?

[3]

This line seems pivotal in both Bion's theory of dreams and in his visionary model of the mind.

As it is worded, **[3]** seems to stand as a draft of the view that dream-work-alpha is just central in continuously *dreaming* the human mind into existence, this being, once again, a shortened form of one of the two fundamental aims of this book, the other being that Bion's so many lines on dreams and dreaming left behind him most often as scattered and unworked pieces may nevertheless be brought together in the relatively unified form of a theory, called in this book Bion's theory of dreams.

If I am reading **[3]** any faithfully, this line seems to claim that nothing psychical can ever be brought to life without having been *dreamed* into this unique condition.

Once again, the key problem that Freud sets himself to approach in "Formulations" is a dauntingly ambitious one: "We are now confronted with the task of investigating the development of the relation . . . of mankind in general to reality" (Freud 1911, S.E. 12, p. 218). Bion's whole fragment, and line **[3]** in particular, seem both to crucially address Freud's key question and to shed an unprecedented light on it.

De Masi seems to add his voice to this tentative understanding: "The preverbal unconscious material must be constantly subjected to dream-work, which operates outside of consciousness. Bion is concerned with the birth of the emotions, of affective symbolization and the foundation of psychic life" (De Masi 2000, p. 5). The opening words of **[3]** seem crucial: "Nothing of this." How crowded with life his "this" is. How much of the human mind pulsates within his notoriously brief "this"? How many emotions and unconscious phantasies and unmanageable conflicts and sweeping joys and wishes and thoughts constantly stir within this little "this"? De Masi's word brings things into a much deeper focus: "Bion is concerned with the birth of the emotions . . . and the foundation of psychic life." Although the words may not be explicitly there, this is what this extraordinary fragment seems mostly to be about. The end line of Bion's previous quoted piece lends further substance to this view: *unconscious pre-verbal material has to be subjected to [the same] reciprocal dream-work[-alpha] for the same purpose.*

The role played by *dreams* and *dreaming* and *dreaming functions* in approaching the foundation of psychical life is what Bion's theory of dreams and his visionary model of the mind that this theory is believed to branch out into is about.

[4]

In order to carefully follow [4] it seems useful to begin by examining Bion's unfortunate term *store*, which he so often resorted to. We are all familiar with the use Bion has often made of the idea of "storing" alpha-elements, the building blocks of thoughts and dreams in his theory of alpha-function. However, from all the angles we may examine the verb *store*, it always returns the same unevocative meaning. The term (and cor-relates) does not seem to lead us anywhere but the pedestrian idea of tak-ing some concrete objects aside from a particular collection of material things and put them on wait for as long as they would remain unneeded. Whenever required, these stored objects would then be called back into the appropriate stream of actions. The storage of things is therefore psychical elements into ever new, hopefully more creative ones – into new emotions, unconscious phantasies, ideas, insights, values, thoughts and qualities of the personality, thus continuously maturing our psychical world. The crea-tive strength of this extraordinary process is seen in this book, the key measure of mental health. These new psychical elements are hopefully endowed with a richer meaning and, therefore also, are potentially both more deeply evocative and inspiring. Severe disturbances of this other-wise unending process are described in this book by the term *pathology*. The focus of this concept falls on what impairs these qualities and their concrete translation into the many sides of life rather than on symptoms, an auxiliary gesture, not a crucially creative step. When called back, fur-thermore, the stored objects are expected to be found in essentially the same state in which they had been stored. This uninspiring sense of the word seems all that the term "store" may be prepared to yield.

It seems, therefore, rather puzzling how Bion insisted in calling back to his pages a term that could hardly betray more dramatically the unreadably complex dynamic of psychical life, and doing such injustice to the defeating complexity of his own concept of alpha-elements. Once again, Bion's language seems to exhibit the doubtful merit of being visually suggestive though massively misleading.

Unless we are referring to psychotic or mindless states, "the transformed elements," as Bion himself puts it, are expected to mature unendingly by being converted by *dreaming functions* into ever new emotions, new sources of insights and of new ways of thinking.

If we now take [3] and [4] together, Bion seems to very persuasively hold that the psychical world is edged by the workings of *dreaming functions*. All that is psychical has been *dreamed* into this new odd condition, or dreamed-work-alpha into it. Bion, therefore, would seem to again claim that all that is conscious has to be *dreamed* into *being conscious*, and all that is unconscious has as well to be *dreamed* into *being unconscious*.

As said in previous chapters, a fundamental quality of the dynamic of psychical life is that the clusters of *dreaming functions* are believed to *continuously re-dream all psychical elements into ever new ones* – into new emotions, unconscious phantasies, ideas, insights, values, thoughts and qualities of the personality, thus continuously maturing our psychical world. Unless hindered by pathology, to be continuously transformed into ever new, hopefully more creative psychical elements by this awe-struck dynamic is the fate of all the "stored impressions" the moment they have been *dreamed* into their new condition. So [4] seems to lend an even clearer voice to the view that psychical life turns around the creative strength of the unreadably complex dynamic of psychic reality continuously *dreaming* the human mind into itself, this being the epitome of the mystery of creativity.

[5]

This is believed to be yet another crucial line in both Bion's theory of dreams and his visionary model of the mind.

The first part of the line – "Dream-work[-alpha] is responsible for rendering pre-communicable material 'storable' and communicable" – seems to add two new claims to all those that the previous lines of this extraordinary fragment, as well as all the other fragments studied up to this point in the argument of this book, have already revealed.

I will next attempt to examine both these claims [5] is composed of as well as what seems to link them.

The more conspicuous of these two claims is that Bion entrusts some still unspecified cluster of *dreaming functions* with rewriting precommunicable material into a new language capable of being apprehended by others, crucially, of course, by the mother. Bion seems clear in again establishing dream-work-alpha as *the* psychical factor entrusted with this extraordinary task. Such shift in both the *structure* and the qualities of the human mind is so overwhelming that we may perhaps not always be prepared to assess either the complexity and the beauty implied in this shift or the depth of its consequences. I am tentatively assuming that an emotional experience or even a stimulus resulting from some contact with external reality is in a pre-communicable state if we are not prepared to project it into the mother.

Both parts of [5] seem to lend new strength and substance to [4] though in different ways. *Dreaming-work-alpha* pre-communicable material into new psychical elements profoundly changes its qualities. One of these extraordinary new qualities, [5] states, is to render it communicable. What perhaps is more remarkable in this new quality is that we can easily read in it the concrete truth of the fundamental belief on this book: that the human mind is continuously *dreamed* into its awestruck structure, its ever-changing qualities and its defeatingly complex workings. This new quality, emerging from a primitive state of being pre-communicable by *dreaming-work-alpha* psychical elements fully freed to be continuously *re-dreamed* under the creative strength of the unreadably complex dynamic of psychic reality.

Again, to dream-work-alpha pre-communicable material into communicable material seems to imply yet another momentous change in both the structure and qualities of the mind. This change seems to translate itself into the exceedingly complex psychical mechanism capable of creating a new language and a new emotional experience of *the other*, endowing this new figure with a reality of an entirely different nature, that is, *the other as object of projection*. The depth of this change in both the structure and qualities of the mind may drown us in both perplexity and awe because of the immense complexity of the shift. This shift seems to imply some sense of hope, of expectation, of a clear sense of purpose, of direction.

Furthermore, the moment a pre-communicable element is *dreamed-work-alpha* into a new psychical element, it falls into the privileged new condition of being freely exposed to the creative strength of the unreadably complex dynamic of psychic reality, being continuously and indeed endlessly *re-dreamed* into ever new, hopefully more creative psychical elements. This extraordinary phenomenon leads us once again back to the fundamental belief of Bion's theory of dreams: that the human mind *dreams* itself into itself.

The second claim of line **[5]** reads, "Dream-work[-alpha] is responsible for rendering pre-communicable stimuli and impressions derived from the contact of the personality with external world 'storable' and communicable." This new line adds yet another crucial voice to **[1]**–**[4]**, making it even clearer that *dream-work-alpha* is the name Bion gives to the psychical factor entrusted with continuously *dreaming* the human mind into existence. This second claim has a crucial role in guiding the interface between external reality and internal reality. It entrusts dream-work-alpha with *continuously* assisting bringing the personality into existence.

Furthermore, the second part of line **[5]** seems take a new key step in clarifying a fundamental problem often raised before: what is the nature of the objects that dream-work-alpha *directly* operated on. This is, of course, crucially related with the problem of the "mysterious leap" between biology and psychical life discussed in Chapter 5 and again in this chapter, as well as between external and internal reality. The whole of this fragment is a very central voice in the key question of the meaning of *being human*.

[6]

This line is yet another crucial piece in both Bion's theory of dreams and his visionary model of the mind. It seems to have a unique role in strengthening the rather disconcerting view that dream-work-alpha is entrusted with continuously converting sense data, or sensorial excitations, into psychical elements. Dream-work-alpha – or indeed the *dreaming functions* – seem entrusted with taking the first step in *dreaming* psychical life into existence and, therefore also, in crucially ruling the interface between non-psychical and psychical.

This line both inherits from the voice of the second part of **[5]** and lends it even further strength and substance. This new line speaks once again sharply for the key role of the *dreaming functions* in *continuously* shaping the human mind into life, form and workings.

So once again, the cluster of *dreaming functions* operating the dream-work-alpha is entrusted with the unparalleled role of being the first psychical mechanism translating external reality into psychical life.

Line [6] is, of course, yet another key step in approaching Freud's fundamental problem of "Formulations" of the relations between what has often been described before.

This problem, so far so recalcitrant to the endless efforts of both philosophy and psychoanalysis, may perhaps have now been brought under a whole new light. We may come to know the external reality by *continuously creating it* – by continuously *dreaming* it into *the concrete reality* of psychical life, thus continuously creating both the external reality and the mind itself. So as the human mind continuously *dreams* itself into existence, it unendingly *dreams* it *also* into an unendingly new psychical entity. Another awestruck quality of the human mind that Bion's extraordinary fragment invites us to glimpse at is that *dreaming* the human mind into existence as well as reality continuously transforming it into an ever new psychical entity are both unending processes. Furthermore, as they are both *dreamed* into existence, they are both potentially endlessly ripened.

But lines [1]–[7], as indeed Bion's therefore of dreams and visionary model of the mind are believed in this book to offer history the gift of a new, surprisingly insightful light into the question Guthrie masterly formulated:

> The Presocratics may fairly be said to have been preoccupied with the nature of reality and its relation to sensible phenomena. This question of the relations between reality and appearance remains at the root of things, and in one form or another constitutes the fundamental difference between rival philosophies.
>
> (Guthrie 1971, p. 4; cf previous chapter)

The "mysterious leap" (Scalzone's & Zontini; cf, Chapters 5 and 11) may still remain mysterious, as indeed virtually everything in psychical life. However, now seen in the light of Bion's first six lines of this fragment, the "mysterious leap" is more mysterious, though we may now know much more deeply about its mysteriousness, which moves us much closer to the experiences of awe and wonder about the beauty of psychical life and, again, the meaning of *being human*.

Lines [3], [4], [5] and [6] of this fragment now seem to lend greater substance to my tentative reading of both [1] and [2].

[7]

This line seems, again, to establish that *dreaming* is *the* key factor in working out the human mind into existence. Unlike all the previous ones, however, the line focus on a peculiar form of psychical life, qualifying it as *psychosis*.

Although it is not in Bion's line, the question would nevertheless seem invited by it: how far mental disorders of whatever form may, or perhaps should primarily be seen as failures of the workings of *dreaming functions*.

Line [7] both encircles and crowns Bion's crucial fragment and, in a way, also crowns the core of his theory of dreams: it crucially depends on which of the *dreaming functions* the very existence of the human mind and, in particular, the emotional experiences of the external reality and the internal reality. This seems to put a final word in all that lines [1]–[6] have been struggling to work out and hopefully make clear.

Line [7] seems to lend a particularly compelling voice to the central belief of this book: that the human mind continuously and endlessly *dreams* itself into existence.

This fragment, dated 28 July 1959, seems to particularly strengthen the belief, expressed by the end of Chapter 1, that only those steps which edge us unendingly to the disturbing experience of perplexity before the host of the unknowns, the unknowables and the unthinkables peopling the human mind may have any chance of allowing us a glimpse of the truth of psychic reality and of the experience of wonder before it. Most of Bion's pages show him pursuing this illuminating insight, no matter how many unsettling ends he seems to have clashed against all along his long way. This is one main reason why perplexity stirs up in most of his lines.

Every step walking us towards the truth of psychic reality also seems to walk us along a fundamentally uncertain, winding way bordering on what we are most unprepared to see. *Dreaming* and *dreaming functions* are both believed to be our privileged guiding light all through that unending way. This fragment speaks as perhaps no other of Bion's of both the defeating complexity and the awestruck beauty of the meaning of *being human*.

Chapter 12

The Dreaming Ego

1 Introduction

> The dream is the mechanism by which (1) the ego links the sense data of external experience with the associated conscious awareness of the sense impression[s]; (2) the stream of unconnected impressions and events are made suitable for storing in memory; (3) these stored events are reviewed and one is chosen which enables facts already "known," i.e. stored, to be harmonized so that the relationship between them is established and the place of each element seen in its relationship to the whole; (4) the interplay between paranoid-schizoid position and depressive positions is made possible by a selected fact which is known as the "harmonizing or unifying fact" spatially and the "cause" temporarily, or when time is an essential element in the relations between elements.
>
> (Bion 1992, p. 44)

These four lines might at first be read as an outline of a whole new theory of dreams. A closer reading of each of these lines seems, however, to show that these four lines partly add to the previous fragment and partly confirm not only the preceding one but a few others already discussed. In this chapter, however, I will focus on line [1] alone.

Bion's new fragment begins with the statement: "The dream is the mechanism by which (1)–(4)." This opening statement promises a view of dream in the form of a sequence of qualities characterizing what Bion, at this exact point of his developing thought, understands by dream. In other words, lines (1)–(4) defines Bion's new conception of dream. Here again, however, that which Bion calls *dream* seems to emerge more as the psychical factor entrusted with continuously bringing the human mind into existence. Together, lines (1)–(4) renews our hopes of seeing the key question *what is a dream?* be offered a less questionable and conflicting

DOI: 10.4324/9781003375159-14

understanding. And yet this was certainly not the question moving Bion into research. To my best awareness, this particular question has never, *per se*, moved him into it. As often said before, what this book believes that has really swept Bion into a life-long research was his extraordinary intuition that all that seems interesting in the human mind pulsates beyond the edge of the unknown, the unknowable and the unthinkable. His theory of dreams is certainly not about dreams, in Freud's sense, and certainly not about dreams, in any sense I am aware of this word.

But as just said, this chapter focuses on line (1) of the aforementioned fragment alone. It therefore examines Bion's quite surprising claim that one of the key qualities of dreams is the mechanism by which the ego links the sense data of external experience with the associated conscious awareness of the sense impression[s]. This, then, is the line that this chapter will now attempt to examine.

2 An Odd Link

One word in Bion's line seems to hold the key to much of our puzzlement about Bion's view of what exactly the ego is: the word *links*. Much of this puzzling and yet deeply inspiring line falls back on the meaning of this little word. So what exact psychical elements and functions are believed to lend both substance and meaning to this little crucial word?

Bion's introductory line to this fragment gives us a first key clue: "The dream is the mechanism by which the ego *links* the sense data of external experience with . . ." (my emphasis).

The ego is then believed to "link" two groups of elements. The first – say A – is composed of elements that do not seem to have any connection with psychical life: the sense data of external experience. The second – say B – is formed by elements deeply involved with psychical life: the conscious awareness of the sense impression[s] associated with the sense data of that external experience. Having in mind lines **[3]**, **[4]**, **[5]**, **[6]** and **[7]** of the previous fragment, we seem bound to believe that Bion's concept of *ego* is *in itself* a cluster of *dreaming functions*, operating within dream-work-alpha, entrusted with *continuously* converting A into B – converting the elements in A into elements in B. In other words, the elements in A are expected to be continuously *dreamed* into the elements in B. Again, while the former does not seem to have anything in common with psychical life, the latter are all key psychical elements being, of course, new psychical elements. I may perhaps be allowed to just recall lie [6] of the previous fragment: "Contact with reality is *not* dependent on dream-work[-alpha]; accessibility to the personality of this contact *is* dependent on dream-work." The key factor continuously converting the unspecialized elements in A into the highly specialized elements in B is now what Bion calls the *ego*.

These new psychical elements seem, therefore, to result from an extraordinary sequence of transformations that the ego, in its new condition of a highly specialized cluster of *dreaming functions*, is now entrusted with.

Surprisingly, the ego is now believed to operate *directly* on sense data of external experience. This comes as yet another persuasive piece of argument favouring the view that at least some clusters of *dreaming functions* seem to operate *directly* on sense data. Once again, this suggests that Bion's theory of dreams may bring a whole new light on the key question of the "mysterious leap" over the gap between biology and psychical life, or even more generally, between external reality and internal reality first discussed in Chapter 5 and again in Chapter 11 as well as the previous. Listening again to both Scalzone's and Zontini's voices, "Despite all our efforts, the 'mysterious leap' continues to confront us, but we must try to narrow the gap by seeking to extend our knowledge of 'everything that lies between'" (2001, p. 263). If my tentative reading of the first line of Bion's new fragment invites any plausibility, this line and indeed a large part at least of his theory of dreams would seem to offer this key problem an unprecedent new light.

3 The Dreaming Ego and the Extreme Sensitivity of Sense Impressions

This highly specialized cluster of psychical functions operating the extraordinary sequence of steps that Bion expects the ego to *continuously* perform seems to have huge consequences in continuously changing our conception of both the structure and the qualities of the human mind. We may once again realize how much we should entrust *dreaming functions* with continuously *dreaming* the human mind into existence, into its overwhelmingly complex structure and its ever-changing qualities.

The first step that Bion asks the ego to bring about consists in *dreaming sense data* into *sense impressions*. This extraordinary understanding is already present in the previous fragment, in each one of the lines discussed in the previous chapter, though not specifically charging the ego with such very crucial undertaking. The complexity of this converting process is awestruck. By *dreaming* sense data into sense impressions, the ego seems, of course, to continuously *create* sense impressions as new psychical elements. This conversion, however, seems of the utmost consequences. For the ego hands sense impressions over to the dynamic of psychic reality, though it imposes severe restrictions upon its awestruck strength. For as Bion puts it, dream-work-alpha is believed to answer

> a felt need to convert the conscious rational experience into dream, rather than a felt need to convert the dream into conscious rational experience. The 'felt need' is *very* important; if it is not given due significance and weight, the true dis-ease of the patient is being neglected; it is obscured by the analyst's insistence on interpretation of the dream.
>
> (Bion 1992, p. 184)

Each new step in the workings of the *dreaming ego* – continuously *dreaming* sense data of external experience into sense impressions of which we are made, by the same *dreaming ego*, both aware and conscious of our awareness, into a new *dream*. This prodigious achievement is what seems to live in this extraordinary *link*. This link results in further modifications of both the structure and the qualities of the mind, thus adding yet another voice to the fundamental belief of Bion's theory of dreams and his visionary model of the mind that the human mind continuously dreams itself into itself.

By lines **[3]** of the fragment discussed in the previous chapter – "None of this can be associated with consciousness, memory, recall, unconscious, repression or suppression unless transformed by dream-work[-alpha]," the second part of **[5]** – "Dream-work[-alpha] is responsible for rendering pre-communicable material 'storable' and communicable; the same for stimuli and impressions derived from the contact of the personality with external world", **[6]** – "Contact with reality is *not* dependent on dream-work[-alpha]; accessibility to the personality of this contact *is* dependent on dream-work," and **[7]** – "The failure of dream-work[-alpha] and the consequent lack of availability of external or internal psychic reality gives rise to the peculiar state of the psychotic who seems to have a contact with reality but is able to make singularly little use of it either for learning by experience or for immediate consumption" – by these absolutely central lines in Bion's theory of dreams and his visionary model of the mind, we seem strongly invited to see the *dreaming ego* offering the human mind the immense privilege of ensuring that the sense data associated with sense impressions may also be converted into psychical life and, therefore, *dreamed* into the experience of meaning and, therefore, not to allow forgotten in the realm of mindlessness. The *dreaming ego* is believed to make systematic use of the mechanisms of resistance and censure not, however, in Freud's sense but in Bion's as he brought both concepts into his sketched theory of contact-barrier (cf. 1962, p. 16; cf. Chapter 2).

If my tentative reading of Bion's line of the fragment that this short chapter proposes to discuss invites any plausibility, this seems another way how, in Bion's visionary understanding of the ego, we are opened the way to keep making life and the world glittering with creative insight and meaning, as well as to move closer to Keats: "The great beauty of Poetry is that it makes everything every place interesting" (in: Gittings 1990, *Letters of John Keats*, p. 315). If, again, my tentative reading of Bion's line is at all faithful to his meaning, the role he now addresses to the ego may invite us to watch the way we live our lives. For the moment we convert the consciousness of being aware of sense impressions itself into a new *dream*, and the sense impressions are *dreamed* into a new psychical element, the sense data associated with both with this new psychical elements resulting from having also *dreamed* sense impressions into them as well as this consciousness itself into a new *dream*, the sense data themselves are believed to become new psychical elements and, therefore, endowed with psychical life, having a place in the dynamic of our psychic reality, and in particular in our memory as a precious source of ever new *dreams*. It is in this sense that we may perhaps be invited to offer a more caring look at the sense data and of sense impressions, this being the new responsibility that Bion's line entrusted with the ego. This is what seems to live in Bion's awestruck *link*.

4 On Uncertainty – A Brief Note

As so often before, we once again watch Bion inviting us to cross the edge of the known, the knowable and the thinkable, though drowning us in both perplexity and awe. This seems the trying frontier along which we are continuously led to walk uncertainly. Every time we resist recoiling from the trying experience of uncertainty, we may feel invited to trade *knowledge* for *dreaming*, the brutality of certainties for the creative light of uncertainty, the safeness offered by the strength of reason for the inspiring fragility of hope and the experience of awe and passion. How sad is the analyst to crown his insightful uncertainties with certainties in virtually every session so woven by perplexity and unknowns?

We are always free to avoid the unsettling experience of the creation of meaning as an unending fascination. The history of psychoanalysis seems to largely hinge on this frighteningly fragile line. It is always at everyone's hand the frightening freedom to cower before the sweeping experience of awe and of the loyalty to passion. This seems the very same fragile line along which we silently walk along in virtually every hour of our lives having always to decide on which side of that line we feel more inclined to live.

Bion equates the capacity to dream with the capacity to transform into dreams events that are grasped only on a rational, conscious level (cf. section 2 CH 8).

Chapter 13

How Conscious Is Conscious and Unconscious Unconscious?

1 On How Conscious Is Being Conscious – A First Note

Chapter 11 discussed a fragment of Bion's. As I again tend to see it, this is perhaps the single most important fragment on dreams and dreaming in Bion's theory of dreams. I am now back to it.

Lines [3], [6] and [7] seem to make clear that *dreaming* draws a clear line between *neurologically conscious or unconscious* and *psychically conscious or unconscious*. We may alone be *neurologically* conscious of something, but not just *psychically conscious* of anything. Bion's previous fragment argues we may hardly conceive a mental state in which we are conscious of anything without also being not only just unconscious of the same thing but perhaps even *essentially* unconscious of the same thing. For to be conscious of something – to be *psychically conscious of something* – seems to imply having *dreamed* the thing we are now (psychically) conscious of into a new psychical element. In the eyes of my tentative view of Bion's theory of dreams, the crucial operator of this extraordinary conversion is *dreaming functions*. As it was said before, the *dreaming functions* are postulated to enjoy two key qualities: to be responsible for continuously converting the human mind into itself, a quality that has usually been described as *dreaming* the human mind into existence, and to continuously take us beyond the edge of the unknown, the unknowable and the unthinkable, where most interesting psychical phenomena are believed to both root and grow. The conversion of any elements newly presented to the mind and, in particular, the conversion of sense data of experience into new psychical elements is, therefore, believed to essentially run beyond the edge of the unknown, the unknowable and the unthinkable. This implies that every psychically conscious object is an extremely

DOI: 10.4324/9781003375159-15

complex object and an awestruck psychical achievement. A psychically conscious object and a neurologically conscious form of the same object are two objects of essentially different nature.

Exactly the same can be said of states of being unconscious of something: again, we may be *neurologically unconscious* of something, though not *psychically unconscious* of the same thing. But to be psychically unconscious of something implies to *dream* that object into this psychical condition which, again, is an awestruck psychical achievement.

2 The Unreadably Complex Dynamic of Psychic Reality and the Problem of How Conscious Is Conscious and Unconscious, Unconscious – Further Remarks

To this already unreadably complex and indeed awe-inspiring part of the structure and the workings of the human mind centred around contact-barrier, we still have to closely consider another equally crucial factor in continuously shaping the human mind into both its structure and its ever-changing qualities: the *creative strength of the unreadably complex dynamic of psychic reality*. As said before, this dynamic is believed to be guided by *dreaming functions*. This dynamic is seen in this book as one of the most extraordinary qualities of the human mind. If unhindered by pathology, this pivotal factor is believed to operate by *continuously* reworking virtually *all* psychical elements of whatever kind into ever new, hopefully more creative psychical elements. Therefore, every psychical element – conscious or unconscious emotions, unconscious phantasies, ideas, thoughts, *dreams*, psychical functions themselves entrusted with whatever task, even qualities of the personality – are, then, believed to be continuously *re-dreamed* into ever new, and again, hopefully more creative elements, being perhaps endowed with new qualities, and even endowed with new psychical functions. Such fundamental modifications, however, seem to imply that the very qualities of *being conscious of something* and of *being unconscious of something* seem themselves to be *continuously* modified – if these expressions may ever be convincingly argued to have substantial meaning in psychic reality. Although we will very soon see how deeply – and indeed how often – both these qualities are believed to be reworked into *qualitatively* different ways, this for now is just one way in which both are argued to constantly vary.

Perhaps the most awe-inspiring conversion is carried out by the foetus' and the infant's *dreaming* mother's reverie into the prodigy of introjection.

3 The Unreadably Complex Dynamic of Psychic Reality and the Problem of How Conscious Is Conscious and Unconscious, Unconscious – New Remarks

The dynamic of being (psychically) conscious or unconscious of something seems so unreadably complex that I would not believe that we may ever be equipped to grasp, by any current rational means, either its intrinsic complexity or the depth of its beauty. And yet we may keep struggling to very closely follow the virtually countless effects of this dynamic and perhaps even intuit its awestruck beauty. This is one reason why I disagreed with Bion's insistence in calling into his pages the term *storing* alpha-elements.

As it will again be argued in the next sections of this chapter although following a slightly different line of approach, virtually every conscious piece is believed to be *continuously* operated on by *dreaming functions* that convert its quality of *being conscious* into different qualities of *being conscious*. Exactly the same is believed to hold for every piece of unconscious material, pre-verbal or not.

So again, every time we are said to be conscious of something, we are also believed to be unconscious of that same thing. Putting it into more precise words, every piece of *the conscious mind* is also believed not just to be a piece of *the unconscious mind* but even to *essentially* be a piece of *the unconscious mind* (for the concept of *the conscious mind* and *the unconscious mind*, cf. Chapter 4). The idea of drawing a clear line between both conscious and unconscious as if it would be possible to put clear names to essentially unclear objects, or again in a more precise language, to always clearly distinguish between *the conscious mind* and *the unconscious mind* – between what exactly is conscious in *any* element of *the conscious mind* and what is unconscious in that same element – may perhaps never be possible such the complexity of the workings of the *dreaming functions* weaving both forms of thought together so as to *continuously create* both these "minds." And yet, we may often attempt to clearly follow the characteristic stamp of each *form of thought* at work and try to read the dynamic of both at work together (cf. Chapter 4). This should of course often be carefully observed at work in the course of the clinic hour in both the analysand and the analyst.

4 On Being Conscious of Something and Unconscious of Something – A New Note

Yet another factor that adds up to both the already overwhelming complexity of the dynamic of psychic reality as well as to its awestruck beauty is that by *dreaming* elements in both the conscious mind and the unconscious mind we are believed to potentially enhance their qualities. This is a potentially unending process. This extraordinary quality of the human mind may even lead us to give substance and form to new ways of thinking and new forms of knowledge. "Poetry . . . awakens and enlarges the mind itself by rendering it the receptacle of a thousand unapprehended combinations of thought" (Shelley 1821a, Harvard p. 10; and Shelley 1821b, Oxford p. 680). What exactly is conscious and what unconscious in Shelley's line? What are the conscious processes and the unconscious at work in making possible Shelley's line? How far have we to go beyond the edge of the unknown, the unknowable and the unthinkable if only we want to follow him? What exactly is conscious in the workings of the analyst's internal characters in the concrete course of the clinic hour as they speak to the analysand in their many voices through the analyst's throat?

Bion's theory of dreams is the more inspired way I am aware of in psychoanalysis to allow us a glimpse of the unending enigmas living the experience of *being conscious of something* and *being unconscious* of *something*.

5 Neurologically Conscious and Psychically Conscious – A New Note

I will now ask another crucial fragment of Bion's to assist the argument in this book. This new fragment reads as follows:

> The conscious material has to be subjected to dream-work[-alpha] to render it fit for storing, selection, and suitable for transformation from paranoid-schizoid position to depressive position, and that unconscious pre-verbal material has to be subjected to reciprocal dream-work[-alpha] for the same purpose.
>
> (Bion 1992, p. 43)

With the exception of the crucial reference to the role of the *dreaming functions* in ensuring it's possible for the dynamic of PS↔D to gradually develop into inner maturity, this fragment has often been in the argument of this book in the more general form that both all that is conscious and all that is unconscious have to continuously be *dreamed* into ever new, hopefully more creative psychical elements. It seems interesting, however, that in this particular piece, Bion focuses on the unconscious pre-verbal material rather than the pre-verbal impressions associated with the pleasure principle, as he does in line **[2]** of the fragment studied in Chapter 13. I am unprepared to see whether any of these two groups of phenomena somehow enriches the other.

This view has also been in the argument of this book in the more elaborated form that it is alone by *dreaming* elements of whatever nature into new psychical elements that the human mind is believed to continuously *dream* itself into existence.

The role of *dreaming functions* in ensuring PS↔D to develop creatively and unending is, of course, crucial to escort the continuous conversion of elements newly presented to the mind into new emotions, unconscious phantasies, ideas, thoughts, and even new qualities of the personality without which would be just impossible, making it possible that all these new qualities would keep *dreaming* the human mind into ever richer existence.

6 How Conscious Is Conscious? – A New Note

So in this new fragment Bion emphasizes the key role of *dreaming* in continuously converting the former conscious elements into the latter conscious elements, this being postulated the only way left for us to raise the former into their new condition of psychical conscious elements.

The most fundamental consequence of this continuous process seems to be that each such conversion is believed to assist *dreaming the human mind into new existence* and, therefore, to somehow add to its defeatingly complex structure and to its ever-changing qualities.

The way in which this new fragment seems to strengthen even further the already overwhelming impact of the previous one (that is, lines **[1]–[7]** of the fragment discussed in Chapter 13) is by making it even clearer that it is by *dreaming* conscious elements into new conscious elements alone that it becomes meaningful to talk about being conscious of anything. So the new fragment lends further weight to the view that without *dreaming* conscious material into new conscious material, conscious material would never be meaningfully conscious. Without, therefore, this continuous conversion, consciousness would never be fully consciousness. But how insufficiently conscious exactly? How exactly *fully* is this "fully"? What is the exact depth of this often reckless "fully"? How many different levels of "being fully conscious" of anything? How unconscious is the unconscious qualities of this "fully conscious" something? How many different qualities may the phenomenon described as *being psychically conscious of something* really have in any one of us as we mature psychically? How many different levels of *being unconscious of the same thing* can the phenomenon described as *being unconscious of something* have? How different may the role of being unconscious be in psychical life dependent on the depth of our being unconscious of something? How inspiring may an unconscious element be in each single moment of its unconscious life?

Since the unreadably complex dynamic of psychic reality is endless, I am unable to see any limit for the depth of the emotional experiences of *being conscious* and of *being unconscious of something* except an assault on this prodigious dynamic by *pathology*. I therefore take *pathology* as the name for the processes which hinder the workings of this dynamic.

Another immediate implication of these tentative differentiations is that we may be conscious of something even if we remain *mindlessly conscious of it*. By being *mindlessly conscious of something*, I understand the mental state in which we are unequipped to create the emotional experience of *meaning*. This other surprising phenomenon – that one may be mindless and yet conscious of an object – leads us right to the key question of the genesis of meaning and of its importance in deciding whether new steps in continuously *dreaming* the human mind into existence have successfully been achieved.

Whether the emotional experience of *meaning* is recognized is tentatively seen in this book as a crucial separating line between non-psychical conscious and psychical conscious.

7 How Conscious Is Conscious – Further Remarks

If every time we are psychically conscious of something we are also – and indeed we are *essentially* – unconscious of that thing, how exactly conscious are we of that which we are conscious of? Again, how many different meanings of being conscious *of the same thing*, as well as of *being unconscious of something* we all come to experience external reality, even from moment to moment, as we continuously keep *dreaming* virtually all psychical elements into ever new ones? And how many different levels of being conscious of something, as well as of being unconscious of something, may be experienced by different parts of the personality? This seems so unreadably complex, so awestruck that it may compel us to closely rethink the meaning of *being conscious of something* as well as of *being unconscious of something*. Furthermore, I do not think that we are equipped to very closely follow the intricacies generated by the creative strength of the unreadably complex dynamic of psychic reality, still less, perhaps, the awestruck beauty of these extraordinary psychical phenomena. However, neglect and indifference are always lurking, this being one reason why I would believe that we should watch the way we live our lives.

8 How Unconscious What Is Conscious Needs to be Dreamed Into So That What Is Conscious May Mature Into the Condition of Being Psychically Conscious?

To be conscious of something and unconscious of something are both claimed in this book to be unreadably dynamic and complex processes. Again, we are believed to be *simultaneously* conscious and unconscious of uncountably many different things and at so many different levels of depth and of complexity at the same time. Once again, attempts at summary and simplification seem to carry with them a promise of failure and may leave widely open the easy door for smugness.

So again, conscious elements have already been *dreamed* into their new condition – that of *being conscious* – being now, therefore, *simultaneously both conscious and unconscious psychical elements*.

Bion's key line on the importance of converting all conscious and rational elements into *dreams* – indeed to continuously *dream* them into new *dreams* – plays a key role within his theory of dreams as well as in his visionary model of the mind. I therefore return to my belief that *only* then can we properly see conscious as conscious, and rational as rational – as *psychically conscious* rather than *neurologically* conscious and *psychically* rational rather than merely operatively rational. So we do not and, I believe, could never really come to know how conscious is what is conscious. What is conscious may be conscious in countless many different levels of *being conscious*.

So how unconscious does conscious need to be *dreamed* into so that conscious may best mature into being conscious? And how unconscious should all that is rational need to be *dreamed* into best being rational, that is, more inspiring and better capable of assisting us to keep making life and the world glittering with creative insight and meaning? Although this does not seem possible to exactly determine, we seem invited to see the *dreaming functions* continuously maturing what is conscious and what is rational into potentially unending levels of depth, that is, of inspirational and evocative strength and, therefore, of creativity.

The trouble of being conscious is when it is not enough unconscious.

Chapter 14

Freud's Wrestling With "The Fact of Consciousness"

1 "How Does a Thing Become Conscious?"

Since his earliest working days, Freud wrestled with a question which had swelled in his hands into a haunting riddle. He called it "the fact of consciousness." Soon this question led him to struggle with a neighbour other. He described this other question as "the genesis of the fact of consciousness."

There is enough documented evidence to show that this recalcitrant riddle – the fact of consciousness – has travelled him all along his many working years. The question, however, always stood proudly defiant and indeed unbending even before the strength of his genius.

Freud's disappointment with the hardships that this question posed him soon wrang in his early voice: "No attempt, of course, can be made to explain how it is that excitatory processes in the ω-neurones bring consciousness along with them" (Freud 1895, *Project*, S.E. 1, p. 311).[1] No less than 43 years later we still surprise him worrying the question though now in an unhopeful key:

> We know two kinds of things about what we call our psyche (mental life): firstly, its bodily organ and scene of action, the brain (or nervous system), and, on the other hand, our acts of consciousness, which are immediate data and cannot be further explained by any description. Everything that lies between is unknown to us, and the data do not include any direct relation between these two terminal points of our knowledge.

> (Freud 1940 [1938], S.E. 23, pp. 144–145)

DOI: 10.4324/9781003375159-16

A dismal undertone of conceding defeat evidently rings in this later piece. A key line in his last passage on the same question raises perplexity, however. This is Freud's claim that everything that lies between these two terminal points of our knowledge is unknown to us. It does not seem clear within what conceptual frame Freud was exactly rooting his claim. Was Freud focusing on the domain of neurology? Was he thinking of the field of psychical life? Was he straddling both? For unless he expected us to value perhaps too much his word *direct* ("and the data do not include any direct relation between these two terminal points of our knowledge"), which might diminish the key importance of the question, this seems a rather surprising statement for Freud himself to have made so much to shorten the gap between both extreme points: the brain and the acts of consciousness. Even so, never "the fact object of consciousness" lessened its grip on him. The last word that I am aware that Freud has given this question speaks, once again, for his long-lasting perplexity about it: "The starting-point for this investigation is provided by a fact without parallel, which defies all explanation or description: the fact of consciousness" (Freud 1940 [1938] S.E. 23, p. 157). Very few problems have demanded so much from Freud's genius throughout all his many working days without receiving the privilege of his insight, even if the question seems to have always remained close to his heart. Indeed, "The division of the psychical in what is conscious and what is unconscious is the fundamental premise of psychoanalysis; and it alone makes it possible for psychoanalysis to understand the pathological processes in mental life" (Freud 1923, S.E. 19, p. 13). In his wrestling with "the fact of consciousness" we suddenly find Freud trying his way out of such recalcitrant riddle through what might at first appear a narrow side door. This apparently narrow passage was given the form of a question: *How does a thing become conscious?*

To my best recollection, this question has first been both asked and answered by Freud himself. He indeed pondered over it and groped along a new, promising way into the genesis of "the fact of consciousness." For indeed, Freud carefully pondered: "How does a thing become conscious? The question . . . would thus be more advantageously stated: 'How does a thing become preconscious?' And the answer would be: 'Through becoming connected with the word-presentations corresponding to it'" (1923, S.E. 19, p. 20). What, however, does it exactly mean, at the level of psychic reality, for an object to become "connected with a word"? How is it that such "connection" *creates* a new psychical element, or a new key quality of an already existent psychical element? Why exactly is each of these countless new *psychical* elements now called *"conscious things"*? Should each of these "connections" be said to bring changes on either the structure or the qualities of the mind? How is it that by "connecting an object to a word" we come to perceive the new object resulting from this connection as a new object in perhaps both the external and the internal world? Exactly how different is the connected object from the unconnected object at the level of psychic reality? Is it that each time we connect a new object with a word we are justified in believing that we have somehow modified either the structure or the qualities of the human mind? In other words, how exactly does the connection between a thing and a word modify either the structure or the qualities of the human mind? Are we prepared to describe this difference and devise how exactly this difference translates a change in either the structure or the qualities of the psychical world?

Freud believed that his concept of *word-presentation* might have afforded him the means to getting him closer to a satisfactory answer to his key question: *How does a thing become conscious?* (cf. 1915a, S.E. 14, pp. 201–204, and Annex C pp. 210ff.). Unfortunately, I have been unable to closely follow him in argument that his concept of *word-presentation* and his discussion of it could allow us any new step in clarifying his fundamental question.

Elsewhere I will tentatively examine the key question of the role of words in structuring psychical life and, in particular, in the genesis of the quality of *being conscious*.

I am not aware that Bion has offered a single page to Freud's "the fact of conscious." Nor am I aware that he had ever examined Freud's key question: *how does a thing become conscious?* And yet Bion's theory of dreams is believed to have shed a brighter light on Freud's lifelong unyielding questions than ever before or after in the short history of psychoanalysis. Bion's theory of contact-barrier and of dream-work-alpha are believed to be key steps in this direction. Both these theories seem to show that the fact of conscious is not exactly the fact of conscious: it is a countless number of facts of conscious for each single object we become conscious of. What exactly is the psychical genesis of the fact of conscious? How unconscious has each single psychical step been in leading us to the fact of conscious? How often has unconscious steps been called to assist in the genesis of the fact of conscious? How unconscious is the fact of conscious?

Note

1 This was the name Freud gave, in his *Project*, to the group of neurons which he entrusted with the task of forming perceptions. cf. also Strachey's "Key to Abbreviations in the *Project*" (S.E. 1, p. 294).

Chapter 15

What, Then, Is a Dream?

1 Introduction

It is usually assumed that the narrative of a dream faithfully renders the dream we claim that we have had. Bion opposes this popular belief. The following couple of lines is how he opens the three odd pages into which he crammed virtually all he left us with on his theory of contact-barrier:

> The sleeping man has an emotional experience, converts it into alpha-elements and so becomes capable of dream-thoughts. Thus he is free to become conscious (that is wake up) and describe the emotional experience usually known as a dream.
>
> (Bion 1962, p. 15)

Both Bion's little *so* and *thus* are huge *non sequiturs*. Much of the defeating complexity of both the structure and the workings of contact-barrier that both these little words screen away have been discussed before in Chapters 2, 3, 4, 6, 7, 8 and 12. This chapter resumes the discussion in Chapter 8: "What Is a Dream?" Bion's new lines claim that what we believe that is a dream is, to begin with, not a dream. What exactly is it, then? Now Bion claims that the text which we use to read as a narrative of a dream and commonly refer to as a dream is a narrative of an emotional experience.

Bion has always been notoriously recalcitrant in pursuing and providing answers. I do not recall him leaving many with us to soothe the pain of our uncertainty. Many of his pages converge in the belief that no answer may ever lead us anywhere nearing the truth of psychic reality as the fundamental object of psychoanalytic research and practice. I am also not aware that he has ever taken up the concept of *the truth of psychic reality*.

DOI: 10.4324/9781003375159-17

Rather, Bion seems to experience answers to dangerously neighbour the misfortune of certainties about the human mind. The closer we are to experiencing the soothing effect of answers, the farther away we seem from trusting *dreaming* as the privileged way leading us beyond the edge of the unknown, the unknowable and the unthinkable as the realm where all that grips us with fascination and perplexity in psychical life is believed in this book to pulsate with life.

This chapter goes back again to the question, *what is a dream?*

Bion's previous quote seems to leave floating in the air a promise of something far more complex than just an answer to a question.

2 "What We All Ordinarily Understand by a Dream" – First Remarks

> When a patient reports a dream to us and we are satisfied that he means by this what we all ordinarily understand by a dream [this is an indication] that there is a failure of dream-work-alpha.
>
> (Bion 1992, p. 68)

In some of his hastily drafted fragments, Bion sometimes abbreviated his own term *dream-work-alpha* down to *dream-work*, sometimes even just *dream*, or even only "α," even if this last too contracted choice surfaces in his so many pages once or twice only. All these forms of the same still not entirely defined concept are usually rendered, all along this book, by *dreams*, *dreaming* or *dreaming functions*.

In the light of Bion's theory of dreams, therefore, a dream, in Freud's sense, is, in Bion's, a failure of the workings of some *dreaming functions*. In other, hopefully clearer terms, a dream, in Freud's sense, is an interruption of the workings of the *dreaming functions* in converting some elements, whatever their nature, into new, hopefully more creative psychical elements. What exactly is the nature of this failure? Is this failure coming from the couch, the chair, or from both? If the failure comes primarily from the chair, it may stir, and even deepen, the one primarily coming from the couch. I will next attempt to describe how.

3 "What We All Ordinarily Understand by a Dream" – New Remarks

When we again attempt to examine what exactly it is that we usually mean by a dream, though now looking at it in the light of Bion's theory of dreams, a dream seems to be, in the first place, a lump of no one exactly knows what emotional conflicts that the analysand shares with the analyst in the form of a narrative, associations and, crucially, the changes of the music of his voice as he goes along both recounting this narrative and imparting his associations to him. As just said previously, however, the dream that is shared with the analyst is now seen as a disturbance of the workings of some *dreaming functions*. What the analysand tells the analyst is, therefore, the report of a failure.

The narrative of a dream, in Freud's sense, seems to carry into the analyst an expectation, often even an unuttered hope: the hope, that is, of listening from the analyst a word which might help him out of an unresolved lump of emotional conflicts possibly rooted in the depths of his mental experiences. What, however, the classical analyst is inclined to *hear* is not the sensitive nuances of the music of the analysand's voice conveying to him whatever emotions, conflicts and thoughts he may have lumped together into that piece of narrative but rather an easy door left ajar by the analysand to once again share with him what the analyst believes he knows about dreams and, in particular, about the analysand. The classical analyst is certainly not inclined to offer the analysand *the concrete experience of a thinking mind in the room*, nor the inspiring experience of uncertainty, nor the truth of his own feeling the need to convert his experiences into new *dreams*, nor his being uncertain about the meaning of *being human* strongly advising him to hold up conclusions, but the unhearing mother always being sure about the sea of enigmas and unknowns defeating her foetus' and her infant's minds.

If Bion's tentative understanding invites scrutiny, we may perhaps find ourselves in a rather odd crossroad, never knowing what direction to take. For if the analyst approaches the analysand's dream within the classical conceptual frame, the end result of his labour on any particular dream may speak of how poorly he may have *heard* the analysand's report so as to lead him, sometimes even urge him to further miscarry a creative piece of psychical work which has already been disturbed and interrupted. As he trusts the analyst a dream, the analysand may be asking the analyst to assist him give a better, perhaps more creative form to the intricate lump of emotional conflicts, unconscious phantasies and confused thoughts emerging in the form of a rather disruptive interference of his *dreaming* work, this disruptive interference taking the form of what we call, in classical language, a dream.

Dreaming psychical elements into ever new, hopefully more creative ones is potentially endless. This seems one of the most awestruck qualities of the human mind and yet another inspiring guide to a deeper insight into the meaning of *being human*. In stark contrast with dreams in Freud's sense, *dreaming* is the name I have been giving to the workings of the cluster of psychical processes believed to continuously bring the human mind into the unending marvel of its structure, of its ever-changing qualities, and of defeatingly complex workings.

Not only, furthermore, the creative strength of the unreadably complex dynamic of psychic reality has a beginning but hopefully not an end, but its creative vitality is supposed to mature unendingly, the fundamental measure of its vitality being the strength and depth of *passion* – of our passionate experience of the revelation of mother's reverie. Severe disturbances of this process, or unrecovered disturbances of this creative strength are what it is called in this book *pathology*. The strength of this passion is the response to the depth of the awestruck experience of mother's reverie and the prodigy of introjecting the qualities of mother's reverie. The strength of this drive may be deepened under the guidance and the stir of ever-maturing gratitude.

In the opposite end of this line of thought we meet Freud's idea of dreams as a psychotic movement involved with frustrated wishes, not with values. A dream, again seen in the light of Bion's theory of dreams, is an emotional experience

> that is developmentally unsuccessful in that it is an attempt to fulfil the functions which are incompatible; it is in the domain of the reality principle and the pleasure principle, and represents an attempt to satisfy both. That is to say, it is an attempt to achieve frustration evasion and frustration modification and fails in both.
>
> (Bion's 1992, p. 95)

4 On Dreams as Evidence of Nightmaring Processes – A Note

The fragment that opens this chapter claims that a dream is a disturbance of the workings of the *dreaming functions* and, therefore, of *dreaming*. This view seems to imply that some of the functions operating within this cluster of *dreaming functions* have possibly been momentarily nightmared or have been degraded into nightmaring functions. It would, therefore, seem important to investigate, in the session, what parts of the analysand's personality seem to be nightmaring his felt need to convert *every* psychical element into new *dreams*, or his passionate links to the world into hate, or neglect and indifference, or have been perverted into an eager devotion to the ugly and the false. I would believe that the analyst might perhaps "see it" live in the music of the analysand's voice, hearing it in his counter-transference, that is, in his own *dreaming* all that the analysand projects into him, but perhaps particularly, in his *dreaming* the music of the analysand's voice, assisting him to resume *dreaming* what his dream, now in Freud's sense, seems to have been nightmared. In other perhaps clear words. In the light of Bion's remarks, the analysand's dreams may be usefully seen as evidence that the analysand has nightmared some of his own *dreaming processes*. A dream, in Freud's sense, should in this tentative understanding be seen as evidence of a nightmare. It would then be expected that the analyst would *dream* the analysand's dreams into resuming his damaged *dreaming processes* rather than read in them the crooked answer to forbidden wishes. The analysand's *dreaming functions* may have been assaulted into dreams, thus thwarting the analysand drive to continue *dreaming* his emotional conflicts into new creative pieces of his own psychical world.

In this light, dreams may be privileged calls for the analyst to try to see what, in the analysand, in himself or in both, seem to be persistently night-maring the analysand's efforts to hopefully branch out his own *dreaming* processes into new qualities of his own personality. It is, again, in this sense, I would believe, that the analyst is now expected to try to work out the analysand's nightmaring processes back into resuming his disturbed *dreaming functions*. This would hopefully restore the key function of continuously converting psychical elements into ever new experiences of meaning and, in particular, to keep *dreaming* paranoid-schizoid elements into new passionate links to the world.

5 Elaborations 1, 2, 3 . . . n of the Same Dream

In light of Bion's theory of dreams, interpretations are, then, believed to be *dreams* that should assist the analysand restoring the disturbed workings of *dreaming functions*.

This, I would believe, is why Bion's next fragment is so important:

> It is advisable to revert to the patient's dream over and over again – elaborations 1, 2, 3 . . . *n*; but not simply as dreams to be interpreted and related to a stimulus. They must be related to the dream-work[-alpha] that the stimulus has stimulated.
>
> (Bion 1992, p. 184)

"They must be related to the dream-work[-alpha] that the stimulus has stimulated" – the stimulus being, I would believe, the active nightmaring processes that have been thwarting and threatening the workings of dream-work-alpha, that is, of the *dreaming functions*, this being exactly why the dream has emerged – why the creative thinker unfortunately turned into a dreamer, not a *dreamer*. This is also why I would believe that the dream projects into the analyst a plea, speaking from a remote source, worded, I would think, in a very early language, certainly not for the analyst to interpret as forbidden wishes, but mostly, in the more or less desperate hope to be *heard*, that is, to be offered *the concrete experience of a thinking mind in the room* (cf. next chapter).

Again, dreams are therefore believed to bring with them the evidence that *dreaming processes* have somehow been disturbed. In this tentative light, interpretations should not focus on the hidden text of forbidden wishes but rather on trying to read, in the narrative of the dream, what might have broken the workings of the *dreaming functions*, thus disturbing the dreamer away from the experience of creativity and, therefore also, of intimacy. The disturbance of the experience of intimacy with mother, in the transference, may move the dreamer to recall the dream and report it to the analyst. This would then be the remotest – though perhaps the truest – content of every dream.

By reading the same dream 1, 2, 3 . . . *n* times also seems important to assist the analyst himself to restore his own capacity to *hear* the remote, early language of the analysand's, as well as to closely follow the changing nuances of the music of the analysand's many voices in the session, as well as of the voices of the analyst's many internal characters, the analyst's internal characters being the acutest "audience" of the analysand's remotest language. By carefully trying to read, in the narrative of the dream, where exactly the creative process of *dreaming* may have been disturbed, the analyst may perhaps assist him resuming these more creative psychical processes and perhaps restoring in his own emotional experience the marvel of creating meaning.

6 "We Are Deeply Helpless"

So Bion views dreams as emotional experiences that the dreamer may have not been able to convert into new creative psychical elements. However, how many emotional experiences and conflicts may *simultaneously* live within the same dream? How complex is the attempts and failures that each single dream speaks for?

This seems one reason why Bion believes it is so important to return to the dream over and over again though always focusing on exactly what has disturbed the workings of the *dreaming functions* rather than, again, the revelation of the forbidden wishes.

In Bion's fragment the "*n*" seems important. For it once again invites us to focus on the unending wonder of the defeatingly complex dynamic of psychical life in which the work of the *dreaming functions*, entrusted with governing this dynamic and, again, continuously *dream* the human mind into full life.

I would believe, furthermore, that an important quality of dreams is the emergence, in the analysand's dreams, all along the history of every analysis, of aesthetic experiences, maturing in both the analysand and the analyst. The history of these experiences emerging along the clinic hours is a key guiding light to the analyst of the depth of the experience of intimacy between the analysand and the analysand at deep levels of the dynamic transference and counter-transference.

Chapter 16

The Soul and the Stone

> Within the soul the faculties of knowledge and sensation are *potentially*
> these objects ["all existing things"], the one what is knowable, the other
> what is sensible. They must be either the things themselves or their
> forms. The former alternative is of course impossible: it is not the stone
> which is present in the soul but its form.
>
> (Aristotle *De Anima*, III, 8, 431b26–29; ed. Barnes 1984)

Fifteen centuries later, Aquinas, quoting the last line of Aristotle's passage, added an illuminating remark to it. Aquinas wrote: "'It is not the stone which is present in the soul but the representation of the stone' And yet, the object of thought is the stone, not the representation of the stone" (Aquinas, *Somme Théologique*, I, Q.76, Art.2, Sols. 4; ed. 1990).[1] Aquinas' remark creates a fracture and yet reveals a treasure. For how exactly is it that the object of thought being the stone, not its representation, we nevertheless are still believed to work on the object of thought by working on its representation? How is it that the representation of the stone emerges into our mind? What is the exact psychical nature of this representation? What is its genesis? Through what *psychical* means does the representation of the stone come into psychical life? What is the role of *psychical life* in bringing this new representation into our mind? How – if at all – is this new representation converted into a new psychical element? What exactly, in other words, does the dynamic of psychical life rework this new representation into?

I would believe that Kant, and two centuries later Bion added something crucially new to these questions.

DOI: 10.4324/9781003375159-18

I would first recall Kant's insight into the complexity of perceptions:

> That the imagination is a necessary ingredient of perception itself, has, I suppose, never occurred to any psychologist. . . . This undoubtedly requires something more than our receptivity for impressions, viz., a function for their synthesis. (A120) –
>
> (Kant 1996, p. 168)

I do not know whether Bion was aware of Kant's illuminating insight into the genesis of perceptions. What exactly is Kant's "something more" that the genesis of perceptions requires? What exactly is this "function of synthesis" that psychologists have never been aware of and yet without which perceptions would be nothing but mere "impressions"? Kant asks what he called *imagination* to provide for this "something more," this mysterious "function of synthesis."

Two centuries later Bion came up with an answer to a question he had not asked. Kant's "something more," his enigmatic "function of synthesis" is tentatively seen in this book to be worked out by dream-work-alpha, or once again, in my preferred language, *dreaming functions*.

For Bion argued that sense impressions have to be *dreamed* into perceptions, thus continuously converting sense impressions into psychical elements (cf. Chapters 10, 13 and 14, particularly Chapter 13). Even more importantly, in view of the dynamic of psychical life, perceptions – as indeed all psychical elements of whatever nature – are believed to be continuously matured by the workings of *dreaming functions* operating on them, closely following the guiding principle of the *creative strength of the unreadably complex dynamic of psychic reality* into ever new psychical elements. Therefore, in Bion's view, perceptions become new psychical elements, endowed with new qualities and new psychical functions while still operating as perceptions. As the *psychical* qualities of perceptions are enhanced, the depth and richness of perceptions too are believed to be enhanced. This is what allows us to keep making life and the world glittering with insight and meaning. The psychical life crucially coming in the process of building up perceptions seems what Kant insighted under the name of *imagination*.

For as long as sense impressions, or sensorial excitations, are not *dreamed* into psychical life, they may be responded to in either mindless or psychotic ways.

At this point we may meet Aquinas' extraordinary remark: "And yet, the object of thought is the stone, not the representation of the stone." The object of the perception is the thing we sense, not its representation.

The stone, therefore, must be *dreamed* into the soul – it must be *in* the soul, to put it in Aristotle's language, *in* the intellect, in Aquinas' – in the very odd condition of being *essentially* a new psychical element. Hence the importance of the question: what, then, is the intellect? What is the role of *dreaming functions* in continuously creating the mind into its own exceedingly complex structure, its ever changing qualities and its defeatingly complex workings? It is in this both continuous and unending process of *dreaming* the human mind into its own existence that the mystery of all things seems to be given life to. *Pathology* is the name this book has been suggesting for all that thwart, and eventually destroy, the continuous *dreaming* the human mind into all its own potential qualities.

Dreaming functions have extensively been argued in this book to continuously create the inner world, unendingly enriching it and branching it out into ever new qualities of both its own structure and qualities. This "affection of the soul," as Aristotle named it in his slim treatise *On Memory* (cf. Chapter 7) – this highly elaborated "affection of the soul" – not just the new psychical elements that "the stone," through the workings of the *dreaming functions*, the creative strength of the unreadably complex dynamic of psychic reality has been given different forms and *new lives* to within the mind – it is this affection of the soul that are seen here as the changing qualities of this new psychical elements, these *real* transformations of the mind is what I have been calling *knowledge*.

Note

1 My translation from the complete French edition of Aquinas' *Somme Théologique*. Cf. Bibliography.

Chapter 17

Still Unregistered Disorders

1 How Many Mental Disorders Still Lie Unregistered in the Canonical "Roster" of Pathology?

I will now go briefly back to Bion's remark:

> A felt need to convert the conscious rational experience into dream, rather than a felt need to convert the dream into conscious rational experience. The "felt need" is *very* important; if it is not given due significance and weight, the true dis-ease[1] of the patient is being neglected; it is obscured by the analyst's insistence on interpretation of the dream.
>
> (Bion 1992, p. 184)

How upsetting is the psychical disorder consisting of not feeling the need to convert the conscious and rational experiences into *dreams*, that is, to *dreaming* them into new, hopefully creative psychical elements, possibly implying new experiences of meaning? How best should we approach, in the concreteness of the clinical hour, this as yet unnamed disorder? How the analyst, who may not himself have often experienced this key urge and may have never seen the absence of such need as "the true dis-ease," in Bion's own words, can be expected to deal with this form of psychical disturbance in both himself and the analysand in the course of the analytic hour? In what form or forms may the conscious or rational elements which have never been touched by the urge of converting them into *dreams* may emerge in psychical life? Have they ever emerged in psychical life? What is the fate of each of these rational and conscious experiences which have resisted or have never been touched by the need

DOI: 10.4324/9781003375159-19

of being *dreamed* into new emotions, unconscious phantasies, thoughts and generally into psychical elements now made capable of operating themselves as new *dreaming functions while keeping the qualities inherent in conscious and rational pieces?* What is the fate of such conscious and rational pieces which have continued their unhappy journey through the analysand's mental life on the sidelines of the psychical, perhaps injured by the unfelt urge of having them reshaped into the experience of meaning? In what forms may the voices of such scraps of mental life make themselves heard outside the clinical hour? May these untransformed pieces take the form of basic assumptions, or psychosomatic symptoms, or "undigested facts" (cf. below)? In how many different forms may this still unnamed disorder travel, unrecognized, throughout a whole analysis?

Perhaps the worst form that the unfelt need to *dream* conscious or rational experiences into psychical life may take is the frightening form of neglect and indifference. Who would ever be prepared to guess the damages inflicted upon one's own internal life as well as upon so many others' by responding with neglect and indifference to the wonder of creative thought, to the discovery of the inspiring experience of uncertainty, to the merits of living beyond the edge of the unknown, the unknowable and the unthinkable? How often such response to the world has emerged in the course of an analysis evading the analyst's eye who may himself have never been touched by the tumultuous experience of passion? How often has this unfelt need to *dream* conscious and rational material slipped away unnoticed throughout the many years of an analysis? How often have such clinically critical phenomenon travelled, unseen, throughout the many years of an analysis?

How many other disorders may have never been given a name, having therefore never joined the official roster of pathologies? I would tentatively believe that the parts of the personality that do not feel the urge to convert conscious and rational material into *dreams* have never been touched by the experience of mother's passion.

2 "Life Will Always Be a Wonder"

On the 21st of June 1962, in his inaugural address to the Institute of Genetics at the University of Cologne bearing the title "Life and Light Revisited," Niels Bohr stated the following:

I think that the feeling of wonder which the physicists had thirty years ago has taken a new turn. Life will always be a wonder but what changes is the balance between the feeling of wonder and the courage to try to understand.

(cf. Pais 1991, p. 444)

What Bohr stated here about the new developments in physics evidently apply to all domains of thought. The key question seems the same in all fields: *"What changes is the balance between the feeling of wonder and the courage to try to understand."*

How then should we name this other disorder consisting in cowering before new experiences of wonder? What, then, is the place, among the many others in the roster of mental disorders, of our recoiling shunning the trial inherent in facing a catastrophic change even if this refusal would imply being deprived of new experiences of wonder and a shift in our way of seeing the world? How often does the emotional turmoil of passion and wonder go unnoticed or are shunned by the analyst who has never been swept by any of these fundamental experiences of the psychical life in the course of the clinical hours, even of an entire analysis? How often does this cowardly avoidance come from the chair rather than from the couch? How hurtful may this unrecognized disorder of the analyst's, consisting of having lost the capacity for fascination and wonder, be to the analysand's experience of himself, of his internal life and of his own experience of analysis? How often are the silent, unvoiced scars inflicted on the analysand by this mental disorder of the analyst allowed to travel throughout the whole analysis, misguiding the analysand, and even throughout his entire life? How unfortunate is the analyst's shunning the threat of catastrophic change even though this would imply sacrificing the possibility of new insights and new experience of wonder? How sad is the analyst's dullness? How unfortunate is the analyst who, in the concrete course of the clinical hour, cower before the fear of shifting his own understanding when put right before new experiences of wonder which would operate such shift in him? I will just recall a key remark that Bion put in audible words, in the course of a seminar, which had always been silenced in psychoanalysis: "Such a lot of analysts seem to be bored with their subject; they have lost the capacity for wonder" (Bion 1987, p. 15, Brasília, 3rd Seminar, 1975). What parts of the analyst's personality may have gradually withered away his own capacity for marvelling "the extraordinary nature, [and] the mystery of psychoanalysis"? Have they ever experienced the rare privilege of their own precious job any close to Bion's transparent words? Have they ever seen psychoanalysis to come any near Bion's way of experiencing it? How is it that so many analysts, who have the privilege of working every day with the endless wonders and enigmas weaving the human mind, may have drowned their capacity for wonder into boredom and dullness? How is it that all that defeats the analyst's understanding in virtually every clinical hour may be allowed to so easily triumph over his capacity for passionate feelings before the marvel of the human mind, persuading them to cower into dullness and the shabby gratifications of routine and hierarchy? To what extent should this as yet unnamed disorder be seen as an unfortunate child of years of the analyst's own unnoticed failures in *continuously* converting into ever new *dreams* both conscious and unconscious, and rational and irrational, pieces in his thoughts? To what extent has this disconcerting failure to respond passionately to the wonders of the human mind already been at work in him since he was a foetus? And yet these continual failures to *dreaming* may perhaps leave a deep, silent and yet lasting trace on his patients.

How serious is such a disease? How puzzling is its absence from the very long list of mental pathologies? Why the silence?

What impact has this repeatedly unfelt need to continuously convert both rational and conscious, as well as irrational and unconscious pieces crowding his thoughts, into ever new *dreams* may have had in tipping over the balance between the feeling of wonder and the courage to understand, ending by placing the final choice on the side of cowardice?

The analyst's focusing on interpretating dreams rather than on what each new *dream* may teach him about the presence or absence of this unfelt need in both his analysand and himself may drive the analyst to focus on what he thinks he knows rather than on what he does not.

This book takes the stance that psychoanalysis is primarily about the experience of passion and wonder and the capacity for making life and the world scintillating with meaning rather than curing symptoms.

Meltzer believes that passionate emotional experiences play the most central role in shaping the qualities of the mind (cf. 1988, p. 562). This book puts a firmer emphasis on Meltzer's view believing passion to be the fundamental force leading us to live in and research into the unknown, the unknowable and the unthinkable as the source of mystery.

The felt need to convert every conscious and rational experience, as well as every unconscious and irrational one into new *dreams*, that is, *to always dream them into new dreams*, seems to be a key piece of evidence of the vitality of mental life witnessing the strength of passion breathing this urgency into us.

"[Poetry] awakens and enlarges the mind itself by rendering it the receptacle of a thousand unapprehended combinations of thought" (Shelley 1821a, Harvard p. 10; and Shelley 1821b, Oxford p. 680). This line is both an inspired and inspiring way of getting the nearest meaning of *dreaming* and of what "forces" us to continuously convert both conscious and unconscious experiences into ever new *dreams*.

Note

1 In his edition of *King Lear*, Oxford Shakespeare, Stanley Well offered a note to line I. i. 163: "To shield thee from dis-eases of the world." Lear had just banished Kent from his kingdom, adding: "Four days we do allot thee for provision/To shield thee from dis-eases of the word." This is what Well gave the word *diseases* in this particular line: "discomforts, misfortunes – closer in meaning to F's 'disasters' than the modern sense of the word" (cf. Well 2000). Although I cannot substantiate my feeling, Bion's "disease" seems to near this shade of meaning, particularly "misfortune" and "disaster." This is important in the argument of this book.

Chapter 18

I Don't Know

1 Introduction

> The division of the psychical in what is conscious and what is unconscious is the fundamental premise of psychoanalysis; and it alone makes it possible for psychoanalysis to understand the pathological processes in mental life.
>
> (Freud 1923, S.E. 19, p. 13)

As it is so characteristic of the many strengths of Freud's genius, this short statement is once again remarkable in bringing together both clarity of purpose and impact. His fundamental premise of psychoanalysis has, of course, made history.

If, however, we now tentatively move Freud's premise under the light of both Bion's theory of dreams and his visionary model of the mind, we may perhaps soon be lost in perplexity, feeling at odds to closely follow Freud's famous formula.

The riddle that we may be first forced to face in Freud's formulation of the fundamental principle of psychoanalysis is what appears to be Freud's unuttered assumption that he is prepared to decide what is conscious and what is unconscious in virtually everything in the human mind.

Inherent in this first assumption, and again moving it under the light of Bion's visionary model of the mind, a second one may invite irresolution: the assumption that the dividing line between conscious and unconscious may trivially be always possible to be drawn.

Both assumptions live in Freud's lines as if outside the reach of questioning.

Seen, however, in the light of what I have tentatively described as Bion's theory of dreams, the psychical does not seem to be divided in what is

DOI: 10.4324/9781003375159-20

conscious and what is unconscious. The psychical would rather emerge more as a defeatingly complex web of functions and processes assisting us to continuously *dreaming* the psychical itself and therefore also the structure, the qualities and the workings that we tend to associate with the human mind.

In other words, the psychical would come into life more as the overwhelmingly complex dynamic the most crucial quality of which is believed to be its capacity for continuously creating itself into existence or, more specifically, to continuously *dream* itself into existence. Furthermore, as the psychical creates itself, it is also believed to continuously create the group of qualities, functions and processes that we tend to associate with the term *conscious*, or *being conscious of something*, as well as a very different group of qualities, psychical functions and processes that we tend to associate with the term *unconscious*. However, the processes involved in creating both psychical configurations – say, *conscious* and *unconscious* – are believed to be both continuous and unending. Moreover, no one seems to know how many psychical functions and processes are involved, and no one seems equipped ever to come to know it. Besides, *being conscious of something* may itself be endlessly enriched, and once again, no one seems to know how complex – or indeed how inspiring may this so common and yet so immensely complex process may eventually reveal itself to be. The inspiring strength of *any* object that we may become conscious of by having *dreamed* it and endlessly *redream* it into ever new psychical elements cannot possibly be controlled. This inspiring strength seems to greatly depend upon both the wealth of the unconscious elements woven together into each one of the apparent trivialities usually described as *becoming conscious of something*. If we tentatively side with the view that one of the most extraordinary qualities of the human mind is the creative strength of the unreadably complex dynamic of psychic reality, we should be expecting that virtually all psychical elements may be *continuously dreamed* into ever new, hopefully more creative psychical elements. We can watch it everywhere both inside and outside the consulting room but perhaps with the clearest evidence in every instance of our making life and the world glittering with meaning. We all may become conscious of the same object in countless many different levels of depth depending on how often, or deeply, or both we *redream* it into new, hopefully more creative psychical elements.

2 What Is Understanding – A Preliminary Note

Another source of perplexity living in Freud's lines and perhaps slightly disturbing the careful reading of his meaning is the way Freud brings in the word *understand*. The overtone of confidence and doubtlessness that his premise largely concentrates on this particularly sensitive word, "and it alone makes it possible for psychoanalysis to understand the pathological processes in mental life." Freud evidently believes that psychoanalysis is equipped to understand the pathological processes of the human mind. Here again, however, the idea of understanding, when the object of understanding is the human mind, is a key point of extensive debate in both Bion's theory of dreams and his visionary model of the mind, as well as in Meltzer's view of this defeatingly complex object of research.

Moreover, "confronted with the complexities of the human mind the analyst should be circumspect in following even accepted scientific method; its weakness may be closer to the weakness of psychotic thinking than superficial scrutiny would admit" (Bion 1962, p. 14). Bion's remark falls upon us as a warning.

This sea of uncertainties is believed to speak far more truly and far more illuminatingly of the human mind than any psychoanalytic theory. And they are the fundamental subject-matter of every clinic hour and a far more inspiring light for us in each clinical hour.

3 I Don't Know

The problem of clearly determining what is conscious and what is unconscious in each single moment of psychical life seems a daunting one. It very often drowns us in complexity and doubt.

As we attempt to closely examine Freud's fundamental premise rather than just take it as a principle not exposed to questioning, we may perhaps begin to realize that although we all have been invited to take it as a trivial claim, it may soon begin to defeat us in every single little inquiring step into its meaning. The concepts of conscious and unconscious have both been brought to detailed question in all previous chapters. I will continue to proceed along this same tentative line of inquiry to the conclusion. In view, however, of the crucial role played by what we used to call *unconscious* in the unending complexity of the workings of the cluster of *dreaming functions* continuously creating the structure, qualities, functions and the workings of what we used to call *conscious*, no one seems prepared to clearly determine how unconscious is all that we see as being conscious.

In other words, conscious material is both *essentially* conscious and *essentially* unconscious. The concepts of *conscious mind* and *unconscious mind* were both introduced in Chapter 3 and discussed in detail in Chapter 4 as auxiliary concepts in my tentative reading of Bion's theory of contact-barrier. These concepts are believed to play a role in arguing that it would seem virtually impossible to clearly determine what exactly is conscious and what unconscious in each non-psychotic psychical element that we are equipped to observe and even in each – or perhaps in virtually *any* – moment of psychical life.

Bion has forced psychoanalysis to sway very unsafely on the lure of knowability and understandability and, therefore, on the illusion of having control over the unreadably complex dynamic of psychic reality. Bion and, shortly after him, Meltzer have both began to extensively expose psychoanalysis to the fundamental fragility seen as a precious source of inspiration and vision of the human mind. In their hands, the best psychoanalysis would ever be prepared to achieve would be to grope its most uncertain way behind what essentially pulsates beyond the edge of the unknown, the unknowable and the unthinkable. Unexpectedly, as they tentatively walked their as yet untrod way, both Bion and Meltzer also suggested to psychoanalysis that the shining light of uncertainty is one of its most precious guides. This profound shift of direction brought with it an equally profound shift of its conceptual frame.

The idea of a clear dividing line between conscious and unconscious was drowned in the sea of enigmas and unknowns holding us the mirror of how lost in both perplexity and yet in wonder we stand before the defeating complexity of the psychical dynamic governing the connections between elements, processes and functions, requiring endless scrutiny.

If this view of the defeating complexity of the human mind in both its genesis and workings invites plausibility, how could we ever expect to meet such a dishearteningly simplified picture of vision waiting for us in everyday consulting room? How is it that we can possibly believe that what expects us in virtually every clinic hour is an alarmingly simplified version of the human mind. If, however, we would nevertheless still feel inclined to keep a fundamental premise of psychoanalysis, I would more clearly suggest that we might perhaps better select one of the following: "we always feel deeply lost in both perplexity and awe," or, in alternative, "I don't know."

Chapter 19

What Is *Hearing?*

1 "I Don't Know What I Mean; I Don't Know What I Mean"

At a certain point of his analysis with Bion, a man went on repeating "I don't know what I mean; I don't know what I mean." Bion shared with us a first thought about this man's claim: "Now, here again I just listened to it, and I suppose I must have listened to it for a matter of months, and then something happened" (2013, p. 18). So Bion kept listening to his patient repeating, for months, the same claim: "I don't know what I mean; I don't know what I mean." Although Bion seems to have *listened* to his patient quite attentively, he might have failed to *hear* him, to *hear* what exactly his patient was struggling to tell him, to convey to him. For months, he was unable to read his meaning, to *receive* it, to really *hear* what this man has repeatedly projected into him in such earnest. And yet very much like a foetus or an infant who may have been able to learn to wait for mother's demurring understanding his meaning – waiting for the unique privilege of the experience of revelation of meaning that mother's reverie would hopefully spark in him while he keeps, for a certain time, clinging to his own previous experiences of hope (character 7, section 2); very much like the foetus and the infant who have been able to learn to tolerate mother's difficulties in reaching his meaning, Bion's patient also waited for months for the privilege of Bion's *dreaming* the source of his unassuaged anxiety, *dreaming* his emotional conflicts into a revelation, clinging to the hope of being *heard* by Bion, clinging to the hope of being offered the piece of light that continued to evade himself and Bion, though still being capable of tolerating the uncomprehending mother – the uncomprehending Bion,

DOI: 10.4324/9781003375159-21

keeping on entreating Bion, very much as Kent, Lear: "See better, Lear" (I. i. 159).

2 On the Rush to Interpret

Instead of rushing to interpret, the uncomprehending Bion listened. And he kept listening until something happened, as he himself puts it. Bion's description of this short piece of his own clinical experience somehow brings back to mind his own key fragment on the wisdom of waiting:

> Drugs are substitutes employed by those who cannot wait. The substitute is that which cannot satisfy without destroying the capacity for discrimination the real from the false. Whatever is falsely employed as a substitute for real is transformed thereby in a poison for the mind.
>
> (Bion 1992, p. 299)

Each of these lines seems to largely hold to smugness so often resorted to against the unbearable pain of uncertainty, the illuminating experience of perplexity and the demanding wisdom of waiting for the meaning of what we listen and observe to gradually shape at the deep level of our internal characters in *every* clinic hour.

Then, commenting on his forbearing patient, Bion added the following:

> You listen to it, and you listen to it. And [one day] I drew his attention to the fact that he was lying on the couch, and I said to him 'I think that you are feeling that you are really just a little baby, lying there on the couch. And nobody knows what that means. But of course what it means is that your parents have been having intercourse.
>
> (Bion 2013, p. 18)

Then, looking back to the whole scene he has just described for us, Bion himself was taken aback by his own interpretation, again generously sharing his thoughts with us: "I really don't know how one is to put up with this kind of thing."
And yet, though experiencing the discomfort of his own interpretation, Bion went on:

> At the time it is so obvious, that you wonder how on Earth you can listen to a patient for months without seeing that point. Because when the point occurs, it has got this absolute unmistakable clarity, which just

carries conviction absolutely. And it carries conviction in the patient;
there's no doubt about this interpretation to the patient or to myself.

(Bion's 2013, p. 18)

"At the time it is so obvious, that you wonder how on Earth you can listen
to a patient for months without seeing that point." This line grounds the
differentiation that I am trying to establish in this chapter between *listening* and *hearing*. We all, indeed, usually *listen* to the same analysand for
years, and no one of us is equipped, or will ever be, to vaguely assess how
often we have missed the analysand's meaning, how often one has failed
to *hear* him for days, months, even years, missing, time and time again,
the very core of some entangled lump of emotional conflicts, unconscious
phantasies and thoughts that keep being dragged along the analysis, even
the whole time of an analysis without one being capable of *dreaming* them
into an experience of revelation so inherent in the unique experience of the
creation of meaning by introjecting the qualities of mother's reverie. One
may, therefore, be depriving the analysand, even for the time of an entire
analysis, of this sweeping experience of not being able to *hear* him. This is
not a minor deprivation. For each experience of the creation of meaning is
believed in this book to be yet a new concrete step in continuously *dreaming* our own mind into life – in perhaps enriching its structure, adding a
new light to its qualities, and in succeeding to perhaps gain a new insight
into its defeatingly complex workings.

This seems an immensely sensitive matter, that it seems to emphasize
the key importance of waiting, no matter how long, for the unavailable
meaning of the analysand's emotional conflicts to gradually shape in our
mind, that is, to be *heard* by our own internal characters.

The depth of our *hearing* the patient is a measure of the depth of our
respect for him.

3 Aesthetic Experiences as a Key Guiding Light to the Truth of Our Hearing – A Note

We usually listen to the same analysand for years. We may, however,
keep listening to him, keenly focusing on all that we are able to carefully
observe coming from both the couch and the chair all along these many
years. And yet no matter how much care we may have put on *listening*,
and no matter for how long we have *listened*, it would seem reckless of us
to assume that there have not been emotional conflicts, even fundamental

emotional conflicts coming from the analysand's earliest days, that have not been allowed to travel unnoticed through the sessions, right before our uncomprehending eyes or *unhearing* ears, being lost to the history of the transference-counter-transference all along these many years of any particular analysis. We may, indeed, put all our effort on *listening* to both the analysand and ourselves, though being incapable of *hearing* the analysand in some of his earliest, perhaps more crucial emotional conflicts – even if we would see this analysis greeted by the label of a successful analysis, unanimously credited by the official voices setting on judging, and even by the analysand himself, who may genuinely experience his analysis as a really rewarding experience. Even in this propitious landscape, nothing ensures us that the analysand has really been *heard* in most of his earliest and perhaps most crucial emotional conflicts. We seem unequipped to confidently believe that we have *dreamed* most of the analysand's earliest emotional conflicts into new instances of the momentous emotional experience of the creation of meaning (cf. Chapters 6 and 7). Nothing can ensure us that by the end of analysis – by the end of *any* analysis – nothing in either the analysand or in us no longer echoes the same complain: "I don't know what I mean; I don't know what I mean." As I would tend to see it, however, there seems to be a key guiding light showing us a way to our hope that perhaps not too many entangled lumps of severe emotional conflicts, unconscious phantasies and thoughts have been left behind unconverted into the sweeping experience of meaning. This is when the analysand and the analyst are both touched by a lasting aesthetic emotion about their experience of the analysis. For this is believed to be the language in which *dreaming* emotional conflicts into the awestruck experience of the creation of meaning is thought to best speak. When we observe that the analysand's gratitude begins to mature into aesthetic experience, this is tentatively seen as evidence of the analysand's recognition of the awestruck experience of mother's reverie.

4 On the Role of the Internal Characters in the Session – A Note

Why exactly is it that, quite suddenly, what is so unmistakably evident now had, however, been resisted for months, often even for years, or indeed for the entire time of an analysis to come out in the form of a revealing insight? How often is a key emotional conflict which has been listened to with devoted attention, and even discussed with equal involvement and detail with the analysand himself, may keep resisting to be really *heard*? How often has the meaning of such key emotional conflicts evade the analyst's uncomprehending eyes? How may these unheard emotional conflicts travel their uncertain ways all along the patient's analysis, even to travel untouched by the revealing strength of *dreaming functions* throughout his entire life? How many emotional conflicts may simultaneously pulsate within the same so-called *key emotional conflict*? How fragile is our capacity to find our way to *hearing*? How uncertain does this way really seem to be? How enigmatic is this fragility?

> We tend to think that the transference is directed toward the [analyst's] self. . . . I think that it is not . . . one's functioning in the countertransference is really . . . our identifications with one's [internal] characters. . . . It is our internal characters that are the object of the transference. . . . I think that the realization of this makes a very great difference.
>
> (Meltzer 1989, p. 5, cls. 1–2; unp.)[1]

As I would tend to see it, the enigma of our disconcerting fragility to find our own way from *listening* to *hearing*, the enigma that hovers over why it has taken Bion months to reach the meaning of his patient's desperate claim: "*I don't know what I mean; I don't know what I mean*" – as it might as well have taken him years or even never have happened – this enigma would seem to lie in this that who *listens* to the patient is the analyst, but who *hears* the patient's meaning are his own internal characters. While the *listening* goes to the analyst, the *hearing* goes to his internal characters. The analysand's internal characters are believed to address the analyst's through the transference. And the analyst's internal characters are believe to address the analysand's own internal characters by *dreaming* the transference into hopefully new, more creative psychical elements. The analyst's *dreaming* should somehow echo the voice of mother's reverie – if it has been deeply cared for and greeted with ever deeper gratitude and awestruck fascination. That Bion had to wait for months to suddenly *hear* the patient's meaning, *surprising* Bion himself as well as his patient, that it has taken him months to suddenly meet the missing meaning would seem to suggest that it may have taken him that long to tune his own internal characters with the analysand's so that the analyst's internal characters *directly* address them. It may no longer be the analyst's task to do it. He would not be equipped to. This shift from *listening* to *hearing* in virtually every session, this shift from the *person* of the analyst to his own internal characters, and from the *person* of the analysand also to his internal characters so that the analyst would perhaps be at last prepared to meet the analysand's meaning, may perhaps take quite a long time or even never happen. This crucial shift may also be formulated as the shift from psychotherapy to psychoanalysis. The former runs between persons – the patient and the analyst. The latter between internal characters.

We may recall Milton's lines speaking of how his unseen Muse has once again just *dictated* to him, during the night, her own new verses, expecting him to just write down his unpremeditated verses:

> Her nightly visitation unimplored,
> And dictates to me slumbering, or inspires
> Easy my unpremeditated verse
> (Milton, *Paradise Lost* IX, 22–24)

In light of Meltzer's insight, essentially the same may, I believe, be said of Bion's insight into the meaning of his faithful patient's mysterious claim: "*I don't know what I mean.*" It was his muse – his good internal characters, I would take it – that *dictated to him*, while "sleeping," the recalcitrant, though much searched-after meaning of his anxious plea.

But Meltzer has even gone deeper in his own insight, I believe. For he has offered Bion an insight which is his own, not Bion's – the insight, that is, which would bring to an end the myth that the mind thinks. Meltzer takes the view that it is not for the mind to think. The thinking is the job of the internal characters, not – rather lumpishly – the mind's. If Meltzer's insight invites plausibility, the demands burdening the function of both *hearing* the analysand and *dreaming* his clinical material in the course of virtually every session seems more subtle than when we used to hold to the relatively coarse belief that it is the mind what, in us, thinks. The task of discriminating the many voices that may, in this light, be speaking to us in the course of the same session may grow defeatingly demanding even though gratefully rewarding.

If, furthermore, we refuse to entrust the lie of certainties with the task of sparing us some of the work of very closely follow the analysand along most clinic hours, we may gradually discover uncertainty as an illuminating guide in both research and clinical work and that *dreaming* is, again, primarily the work of the internal characters. We may perhaps then learn the importance of waiting for the internal characters to find their ways into the consulting room. This really makes smugness burst with stupidity.

The closer we live to our own good internal characters, the more we seem invited to watch the way we live our lives.

5 New Notes on Not Hearing

For months, then, Bion listened to his patient repeating the same rather desperate plea: "*I don't know what I mean; I don't know what I mean.*" Bion might well have listened to him many months more, even years, and might as well have never been able even to touch the periphery of his patient's meaning. He, of course, might well have never been able to *hear* him, regardless of the degree of attention he may have put in follow him. More troubling even is the rather disconcerting fact that we do not seem to have any means to access how distant we may all possibly be to touch the analysand's always evading meaning. How often we may really have failed to *hear* the analysand even for the *entire* time of a whole analysis.

Bion must feel both lost and helpless because no model of the mind will ever offer him – or us – a road map for how best he should move from *listening* to *hearing*. Most of the time we are all, indeed, both lost and helpless though unaware of being both. It is extremely puzzling that such exacting quality so crucially inherent in everyday clinical has mostly been greeted with such neglected silence and indifference by analysts. Analysts are so often shown how to best manage smugness to hammer away the keen awareness that are both lost and helpless. Again, the brutality of certainties smooths that too demanding way for us.

However, in the light of Meltzer's claim that the transference addresses *directly* the analyst's internal characters, not his self, and that counter-transference is the voices of his own internal characters speaking through him to his analysands' internal characters, we seem better equipped to realize how crucial the question of the fundamental difference between *listening* and *hearing* really seems to be. Meltzer's insight puts things on a new level of psychical depth. There are no known rules governing the activity of the internal characters. And yet without them, no creative ideas or thoughts or dreams seem possible, beginning by mother's reverie as well as the awestruck introjection of mother's reverie qualities by the foetus and the infant. These are all prodigies of creativity. This is another reason why Meltzer's insight puts a new, critically important emphasis on learning to wait for the internal characters to do their job and hopefully come up with some new revelation about the meaning of what we have been unprepared to *hear*.

6 "Now, Here Comes the Difficulty"

> Now, here comes the difficulty. We must be rigorous, we must be critical of each other's work. It is a hopeless situation really, when one is allowed to proceed on the basis that one is doing analysis correctly, when one knows that it is very unlikely without the assistance of a critical comment from our colleagues. So that is really necessary; we cannot do without it. And at the same time, it is very difficult to put over any evidence for such an interpretation. . . . On what grounds have we been driven . . . to give the interpretation?
>
> (Bion 2013, p. 19)

During a coffee break in a clinical seminar held by Donald Meltzer in Lisbon, and without knowing of Bion's remark, Meltzer, a colleague of mine, and myself stayed in the seminar room talking about several topics. One of these topics, raised by this colleague was whether senior analysts should ask for better prepared advice about particularly difficult moments in the course of their analysis. To this Meltzer answered, in a surprisingly quiet, and as a matter of fact tone of voice:

"Oh, you see, but an analyst who has stopped asking for supervision is finished, really . . ."

"*Finished?*" asked the colleague who put the question.

"Yes . . . I mean . . . he is just finished. . ."

One of the deepest reasons why analysis is such a fragile and profoundly sensitive task, I would believe, is because of the key role of the internal characters – the analysand's and the analyst's – are *continuously* called to play in the course of virtually every session. The analyst's *hearing* seems so very crucial if analysis is to be taken for what it is. Again, analysis seems a job for internal characters, not for the analysts' selves. They may not be prepared to take such responsibility on their less sensitive hands.

But the difficulty invoked by Bion has many faces. It is not only about the frightening fragility of our capacity for *hearing*, or more precisely, to regularly find our way back to our own good internal characters' voices in the normal course of every session. It is not only this but the strength of the unreadably complex dynamic of psychic reality making things unmeasurably fascinating, even if also unmeasurably more complex.

7 "This Sense of Helplessness"

During a supervision session with Donald Meltzer, I confided to him yet another apprehension about my analysand:

JSM: I have recently noticed that I have often been worried with her, perhaps feeling her new steps so fragile, worried with the extreme complexity of this process and its extreme fragility . . .

DM: Well . . . yes . . . worrying about your patient is terribly important . . . In fact, the only way we have of keeping the patients safe is to be worried about them. Because when we're worried about them it's always because they have evacuated into us their own worry, and then to accept it, and not to try to analyse it away . . . to accept it along with our helplessness . . . I mean, we are *very* helpless, really . . . we're very helpless and that's how we help our patients . . . it's by being helpless . . . *(smiling thoughtfully)* . . . it's extraordinary . . . (in: Monteiro 2019, p. 148)

This sense of helplessness is believed to create a way of *hearing* better prepared to closely following the music of the analysand's many voices which would otherwise not easily come to the analyst's ear. This sense of being both helpless and lost also smooths the way for us to sharpen our ear to the many voices in which the analyst's own internal characters speak to him in the session, and through his own voice, to the analysand's internal characters. *Being helpless* – and being true in our being *helpless* – being truly helpless and truly lost and yet not scaring our helplessness away into the brutality of certainties and of smugness is believed to gradually shape a feeling of intimacy with the analysand at deep levels of emotional experience. Certainties, the language into which interpretations are so often couched, are largely the language of smugness as well as of cowardice before paranoid-schizoid elements. Certainties are so often carried right into the analysand's mind, being *heard* by the foetus' and the infant's parts of the analysand's personality, lying on the couch, at the earlier levels of communication with the mother. At that key level of psychical life, certainties may well be heard as mother's fiercely hostile responses to her foetus' or her infant's. And we may not be prepared to see the defence strategies that may unconsciously be set in train by the *adult* analysand in response to the chilling sound of the analyst's certainties heard by the earliest parts of his personality. The language of certainties may be heard by the foetus and the infant parts of the personality as a squeaking rejecting voice coming from the mother. The language of certainties seems a dangerous language in psychoanalysis.

8 "Thought Is Only a Flash"

"At the time it is so obvious, that you wonder how on Earth you can listen to a patient for months without seeing that point." Bion's line invites the same question as before: exactly why, then, has it taken him months to reach his patient's meaning? Why exactly did it take *months* of failed attempts to get hold of his patient's meaning? How often have we all allowed emotional conflicts – sometimes rather critical emotional conflicts – to travel, unheard, through the sessions, during weeks, months, years, and even for the whole time of an analysis? Why? How can this ever happen? And yet it happens. Perhaps it happens often.

Bion's description leads us back to Poincaré's line: "Thought is only a flash between two long nights, but this flash is everything" (cf. Bion 1992, epigraph). As suggested before (cf. Chapter 15), Poincaré's statement should perhaps be reversed. For thought is believed, in this book, to be the immensely complex work of *dreaming functions* operating outside the reach of observation, consciousness and the grip of reason, between two brief bright blows of light. The two long nights hide from Poincaré's uncomprehending eyes the prodigious labour of the *dreaming functions* in finding the analyst's much uncertain way towards the mystery of the revelation of meaning. Poincaré's *selected fact* was first seen by Bion, as the *discovery of the experience of coherence*. In Chapter 16, I suggested an alternative reading of *selected fact* as the *creation of a new passionate link to the world*. In this alternative reading, the dynamic of PS↔D is therefore seen as the creation of that new link. So the work required for Bion to quite suddenly meet his faithful patient's meaning, experiencing it as a revelation, would then seem to correspond to Poincaré's two long nights. The unobserved work done all along these two long nights is everything, not the moment of revelation which so impresses Poincaré.

9 Why the Months? Why Never?

Meltzer's insight into the psychical meaning of the transference and the counter-transference – that the transference addresses the analyst's internal characters, not his self, and the counter-transference is the voice of his own internal characters speaking through his throat to his analysand's internal characters – if Meltzer's view invites plausibility, we may feel even more pressed to consider the rather disquieting question: why was it that it took Bion months of listening to his patient repeating the same plea to at last *hear* him and therefore reach his meaning? Why months? Why years – if it had been years that would have taken Bion or any one of us to finally touch the defiant meaning? Why never – as it so often surely happens with all of us, regardless of the keenness of the analyst's attention to all that the analysand had said? Why the time? Why the uncertainty concerning the extension of the wait?

10 What, Then, Is Hearing?

"On what grounds have we been driven . . . to give the interpretation?" Bion's question may perhaps be greeted with a first, brief, though insufficient answer: on exactly the same grounds, I would believe, that a mother is instantly and unmistakably moved to set the exact tone of the music of her voice in response to the slightest sign of unrest that her foetus or her infant sends her. This also seems essentially the same grounds upon which it is suddenly *shown* to the poet the unmistakable evidence that this precise word and no other is the right one for him to bring into this particular point of this particular line, just like Milton (cf. above); or to the composer who is unexpectedly *taken* by the unfailing evidence that he had not thought of before and takes him by surprise that this beat of a phrase is particularly beautiful; or that which moves the painter to suddenly *see* what he had failed to see for days, weeks, months: that this is the *exact* patch of paint and no other that was missing in his unfinished canvas. All these pieces of evidence would seem to share the same mysterious quality: "when the point occurs, it has got this absolute unmistakable clarity, which just carries conviction absolutely. And it carries conviction in the patient; there's no doubt about this interpretation to the patient or to myself."

So what mysterious grounds are exactly these? Here again I am entirely unprepared to venture any answer, however drafted. Nevertheless, it would seem that Meltzer's insight that the widely accepted view that the mind thinks may indeed be an unconvincing myth and that what does think in us are primarily our internal characters whose workings are untouched by all our common ideas of rational control. To *hear*, then, would seem to imply *directly* hearing the language of the internal characters, not the one of theories or argument. This would seem to be the language of what we tend to call *intuition*. Why is the *immediacy* of this language so often so imposing carried by the strength of evidence? And so often almost impossible to reach, it seems, yet another unreachable enigma of the human mind. I would, nevertheless, believe that a close, *careful*, indeed loving closeness with our own internal characters – less far off, less aloof from "their" exceedingly sensitive world, less deaf about their voices – would make much to ease our way to *hearing* the analysands' words as carriers of the music of their internal characters' voice as well as our own's.

If this tentative understanding invites any plausibility, the importance of learning to wait for the meaning of what we listen to gradually ripens from *listening* to *hearing*.

11 On the Threat of Being Sure and the Experience of Respect

But Bion went on further commenting on his patient:

> When it comes to the kind of interpretation that I have just made, it's very difficult to justify, and very difficult (even to oneself) to begin to say how one came to it, because it's this whole series of subliminal things.
>
> (Bion 2013, p. 19)

If, however, we now reread Bion's lines in the light of Meltzer's insight into the role played by both the analysand's and the analyst's internal characters in tightly weaving the transference and the counter-transference, Bion's qualms may perhaps be more clearly followed. His *this whole series of subliminal things* might, perhaps, be fruitfully seen as the analyst's internal characters at work and, at times, making it *so obvious, that you wonder how on Earth you can listen to a patient for months without seeing that point.*

So I would now tend to see the waiting even more important *for the analyst* to fully allow his own internal characters to work out the meaning of what the analysand has projected into him, addressing his internal characters, than for the analysand to be prepared to listen to the analyst's interpretation. In the light of Bion's description of this key piece of a session with his patient, and of Meltzer's view of the role of the internal characters, it seems more important that the analyst be himself well prepared to interpret than the analysand be prepared to listen. For this decides the value of the interpretation. It may determine its truth, its depth and, crucially, the music of the analyst's voice into which he would couch it.

In this light, the stupidity of smugness as well as of the analyst's resorting to certainties to shield himself away from the pain of being both lost and helpless swells even further into hurtful breaches of respect for the analysand. If, again, transference *directly* addresses the analyst's internal characters, and the value of interpretation crucially depends on the depth and truthfulness of the analyst's interconnections with his own internal characters, the fragility and the sensitivity of the psychoanalytic process in each session goes well beyond any reasonably weighed measure, and it shapes a new understanding of *respect* – of the psychical meaning of *respect* – that is due to the analysand. This sense of respect demands from us to learn to wait for the meaning to truly shape in our mind, which seems to mean to make way for our internal characters' voices to be *heard* in the session, surprising both the analysand and the analyst, as it evidently happened with Bion and his patient.

In this light, smugness – the analyst's smugness – now emerges as a hurtful disrespect for the analysand. Who is the analyst to pretend to be sure of anything whatsoever on the face of such unmeasurable sensitivity and fragility of each single step of the psychoanalytic process? Who are we to put certainties forward and stick them into the session so woven by perplexity and unknowns?

12 On the Wisdom of Uncertainty and the Concept of Respect – A Note

Bion's remark leads us once again to the idea of reverting Poincaré's view of thought as a flash between two long nights, the flash being everything. For thinking – the unreadably complex labour of the *dreaming functions* entrusted with working out new paranoid-schizoid pieces of the personality into new passionate links to the world – now seems to be described by Bion as "this whole series of subliminal things." In my tentative reading, this *whole series of subliminal things* is how Bion seems to describe the concrete operative processes of the cluster of the *dreaming functions* hopefully leading the way for us to *hear* what we were unable to do before. Once again, the concrete workings of this cluster of *dreaming functions* are believed to operate essentially beyond the edge of the unknown, the unknowable and the unthinkable. It therefore seems hardly possible to describe how exactly we may come to the experience of *seeing* it with *absolute* conviction for both the analysand and the analyst after days, months, even years of *dreaming* – or resisting *hearing* – that which one has been projected into. This long, trying, mostly unworded internal labour seems to create, in both the analysand and the analyst, an experience of intimacy. This intimacy seems to feed in both the analysand and the analyst a new experience of hope (cf. Chapters 7 and 13). The experience of intimacy, gradually shaped in the truth of the analyst's experience of being deeply helpless and yet of forbearing his own uncertainty and unrelenting work, seems to assist lending firmness to the analysand's discovery of the experience of respect.

13 On Nightmaring Emotions Into Certainties – A Note

This long thinking journey somehow calls back to the mind Meltzer's view of the most important quality of the setting: to offer the analysand *the concrete experience of a thinking mind in the room*. The analyst, I would believe, seems under the duty of making the truth of this key experience available to the analysand at any time. This central piece of the setting greatly assists cleaning the room of the analyst's unwelcome feelings of being sure of anything. Every time the analyst feels sure of something, he seems to be just nightmaring what he is told, or more precisely, by scaring his anxiety away through nightmaring it away into being certain.

I would believe that the analysand crucially needs the analyst's uncertainty to experience the truth of his being uncertain about virtually all that goes on in the clinic hour. This seems crucial in the shaping of the sense of respect. The analyst's uncertainty seems a key condition for the possibility of ever reaching the analysand's meaning by *hearing* him. The analyst's uncertainty – his *being* uncertain of everything that really goes on in the analysand's mind – his feelings, his emotions, his unconscious phantasies, his thoughts – comes through into the analysand not only in the syntax and semantics of all that the analyst says but also in the *truth* of his many silences, as he endeavours to reach the truth of all that the analysand conveys to his internal characters who more closely follow the analysand's voice, particularly the music of his voice. This would be the fundamental language in which the analysand can *hear* the analyst really *listening* to him and, as he listens to him, is also trying to *hear* him at the level of the mother-foetus and mother-infant relationship. A mother who is always sure of everything that is going on with her foetus or her baby is a very frightening mother. The analysand will immediately be deprived of *the concrete experience of a thinking mind in the room* as the key piece of the setting and, crucially, of the analyst's hopefully deep focus on *the meaning of being human*.

If, however, some of the analyst's internal characters are still invaded by split parts of his personality, the analyst can of course no longer trust their voices.

Bion's struggling with the unanswered question of how was it that, after months of feeling lost and helpless, incapable of reaching the analysand, he suddenly *hears* the meaning of the analysand's painful feeling himself lost "has got this absolute unmistakable clarity, which just carries conviction absolutely. And it carries conviction in the patient; there's no doubt about this interpretation to the patient or to myself." Bion's double predicament seems to somehow meet Wordsworth's claim: "Poetry does not have to invoke a god to sanction its working: its truth . . . does not stand upon external testimony but carried live into the heart by passion" (in: Heaney 1995, p. xviii). This, I would believe, is again the unfailing voice of the good internal characters. But perhaps it is the only way to *be sure* of anything in psychoanalysis, just, perhaps, as in every creative process and, most crucially, in governing the truth of the mother's link to her foetus and her infant.

How many vignettes and clinical reports crowd the shelves of institutes though not offering a single word on the crucial importance of *hearing*?

14 On the Key Importance of the Music of the Voice – A Note

A number of other factors seem to crucially add up to the view of the *essential* uncertainty of everything in psychical life and, therefore also, to the immense fragility of the concrete practice of psychoanalysis.

I think that the music of the human language and human voice is very primal. It is the link between mother and baby while it is still *in uterus*: the music of the mother comes through to the baby. I think that the deepening of the analytic transference is very dependent on this music and much less dependent on the intellectual insight that you can communicate by interpretation. I don't mean that interpretations don't have some importance, but the importance they have is mainly that they confirm for the patient that you really are listening and thinking. The patient does not know anything about whether they are right or wrong, any more than you as analyst know whether they are right or wrong. Either they fit the material or they don't fit the material. Things can be utterly wrong and fit the material; but that is just the intellectual content, and relates to our theories of emotional development and so on, which are very flimsy and deal more or less just with the surface of mental phenomena.

([457], Meltzer 2005, pp. 456–457)

Meltzer's insights unveil a new dimension of the defeating complexity of psychical life as well as of its awestruck beauty. His vision adds a surprising weight to seeing the bright light of uncertainty as a unique guide in researching into the unending enigmas tightly weaving the human mind. One really wonders how much rubble we stuff the sessions with, uncomprehending the analysand, incapable of *hearing* his many voices, incapable of reading the evidence of his meaning in what one listens, incapable of closely following the music of his many voices as well as of those still hopefully coming from the analyst's own internal characters. How much clatter, coming from the chair, does the analysand have to listen to without fully realizing it? And yet we're busy "teaching" the analysand, in the form of our ready interpretations, the evidence of our being incapable of waiting for their non-evident meaning to come through the noisy web of our own unable thoughts. With how much clatter we often fill the sessions with reaching the analysand in the voice of our being lost and indeed helpless, though still clinging to interpreting both these feelings away being unprepared to understand, sticking it out in the voice of smugness that is carried right into the analysand's mind?

Bion's fragment favours the importance of reverting to the same dream over and over again (Bion 1992, p. 184; cf. previous chapter). Nevertheless, it should perhaps also be seen as an attempt to address the question of the analyst's struggling – and so often failing, or not even really struggling – to *hear* the analysand's, to perhaps reach his meaning, being aware of how unprepared he is to take this step.

How aware are we of the question, raised by Meltzer, of the crucial importance of the analysand's earliest experiences of the changing music of mother's voice to be closely followed in the sessions in the earliest levels of the transference? How critically important, in virtually every analysis, that the analyst is prepared to *dream*, in the session, the emotional experiences of the foetal parts of the analysand's personality into the experience of meaning. How crucial for the rooting and the development of the transference are the analyst's internal characters' many voices assist us in carefully reading the meaning of the foetus' and the infant's earliest emotional conflicts vividly present in the transference.

15 On the Futile Concern About Being Right or Wrong

Meltzer's "the patient does not know anything about whether [your interpretations] are right or wrong, any more than you as analyst know whether they are right or wrong" invites the view that what is right and what is wrong should not be a main theme in the course of the session. The truth of the voices of the analyst's internal characters seems to be the core of counter-transference and the core of what the analysand indeed *hears* in both the music of the analyst's voice as well as in the music of his silences, although no one seems to know at what levels of the analysand's mind he does really *hear* the music of the voice of the analyst's internal characters, nor what exactly he really does *read* in them at each moment of each session. This, at least, would seem plausible: the analyst's voices are certainly *heard* by the analysand at deep levels of his emotional links to the mother, and this should be a key guiding light for him about the truthfulness of mother-analyst and of her passionate interest for the analysand's psychical life. I return to Wordsworth's inspired line: what is true is what is carried into the heart by passion, regardless of whether it is right or wrong.

Furthermore,

> [psychoanalysis is] all based on counter-transference: on the [analyst's] emotional response, and the ability to recognize the emotional response, and . . . the ability to find a language with which to express it. Counter-transference is everything in psychoanalysis. . . . You are communicating [your counter-transference] in the music of your voice all the time.

(Meltzer 2005, p. 458)

What, in the analyst, seems to better *hear* the analysand's earliest and perhaps more truthful voices is the analyst's own good internal characters. I would believe that the analyst's best guide through the minutes of every session is his good internal characters' voices revealing to him, analyst, something of the truth of what he is listening though still uncomprehendingly. It sems important and, I would believe, inevitable that the analyst goes through Sidney's visionary line: "O how the soule, apt for all impressions transcending reason, can comprehend unapprehensible things!" (*Arcadia*, 1622, p. 333). The analyst may eventually learn to very carefully listen to his own internal characters hopefully guiding how to best redirect his focus to much of what he has not yet been able to *hear* – to the unapprehensible things. These internal characters may also know something precious that the analyst may still have no access to. Again, I would think, we should perhaps entrust our good internal characters with the *hearing*, rather than, lost and desperate, imprudently rush to soothe our anxiety by thrusting into the session the voice of unmastered theories. Good internal characters may not really need to search for the evidence that was lacking Bion to ground the interpretation he offered his patient. For it is his own good internal characters who *know* it and have imparted it to Bion himself, taking him by surprise – as well as all of us each time we just listen to ourselves *repeating* to the analysands what these internal characters know is *their* evidence coming from the heart stirred by passion.

16 The Futile Concern About Being Right or Wrong – New Remarks

At the end of a supervision session with Donald Meltzer, during which the question of the key role played by the music of the voice of both the analysand and the analyst was discussed, I asked him how much of each interpretation should be entrusted with the music of the voice rather than to the immediate guidance of theories and articulated speech. This was Meltzer's answer:

> This is Bion's idea that communication is only very partially linguistic, but that the *substance* of it is musical, and operates by projective identification in transmitting the mental state. This is why it's very important to try to interpret as poetically as you can, and not in a dry and factual way; projective identification as a more primitive form of communication of states of mind.

This was yet another instance of Meltzer offering Bion an illuminating insight which is largely Meltzer's, not Bion's.

Much of our concern about being right and wrong seems both persecutory and very narcissistic. The concern suggests that the analyst's focus has just once again fallen on himself rather than on the analysand. The key question of *hearing* the analysand seems again shadowed by the analyst's swelled concern about himself. The passionate link with the analysand may have been disturbed.

17 Again the Question of Being Right or Wrong – Further Remarks

In a clinical seminar held in Brasília, a young analyst, worried whether the interpretation he had offered his patient was the adequate one, has stirred Bion to interrupt him:

> [Bion]. If you had been practising analysis as long as I have, you wouldn't bother about an inadequate interpretation – I have never given any other kind. . . . I would be rather bothered if you felt it was adequate. The practise of analysis is an extremely difficult occupation which hardly provides space for dogmatic statements.
>   M.[analyst] What [then] remains for the analyst? Only feeling?
>
> (Bion 1987, pp. 43–44. Sem. 9)

M.'s is a key question. It relocates the problem of the role of the analyst in the psychoanalytic process and, therefore also, the question of what exactly psychoanalysis is about. Apparently, Bion drifted away from M's question, getting himself lost in rehearsing what appears to be an unconvincing chain of thoughts leading himself – and us – nowhere.

What exactly, then, is the role of the analyst in an analysis? "Only feeling?" – M. asks. In Meltzer's view, the best an analyst can ever offer the analysand are two closely connected things: a passionate interest in his mental life and *the concrete experience of a thinking mind in the room*, the latter lending concrete substance to the former.

Bion's *I have never given any other kind* of inadequate interpretations seems a crucial claim. Would it *ever* be possible for anyone to offer the analysand an *adequate* interpretation? What exactly is an *adequate interpretation*? Underlying this understanding lives the canonical view hanging on the idea of being right or wrong.

I would briefly recall Bion reading Poincaré's concept of *selected fact* as "the name of . . . the emotional experience of a sense of discovery of coherence" (1962, p. 73). I tentatively take the view that the epitome of the emotional experience of the discovery of coherence is the creation of new passionate links to the world. This is how *the sense of discovery of coherence* is believed to perhaps be best translated into our observable relationships with the world. Furthermore, I suggested before, every concrete instance of the sense of discovery of coherence is believed to play a key role in the genesis of the meaning of hope, this is believed to be an unending process. My belief is that an interpretation is a new passionate link to the world for both the analysand and the analyst. In this exact measure, every interpretation should add a new word to the sense of hope in both the analysand and the analyst. Every interpretation should be a revelation for both the analysand and the analyst. It should *surprise* the analyst as much as the analysand.

Bion's puzzling answer to M.'s key question by just drifting away into nonsense, I take it, was a way of suggesting him – and us – that the complexity and sensitivity of the human mind shows that the canon is such an unmerited guide for us for both research and clinical work. Bion's *I have never given any other kind but inadequate interpretations* could hardly be wiser and more insightful.

18 On the Defeatingly Complex Fragility of the Human Mind – A New Note

Apparently, however, the interpretation that Bion offered his faithful patient – "*I don't know what I mean; I don't know what I mean*" – seems to contradict his own claim in this piece of a seminar: *I have never given any other kind of inadequate interpretations*. And yet it seems that Bion's claim addresses the widely assumed understanding that interpretations are statements directly borrowed from theories, sanctioned by theories, and therefore endowed with unfailing authority. And yet Bion – just as Meltzer – thinks that psychical life is so defeatingly complex and so immeasurably sensitive that the assumed authority of theories assists soothing the impact of perplexity. By achieving that purpose, however, analysts put on sale the gloomy assumption that the source of their knowledge which they are supposed to replace their *hearing* in the sessions is theories. And yet it is a permanent view in this book that perplexity is a treasured guide not only in virtually every clinic hour but also in every new step in research.

I would believe that psychoanalysis should closely follow Shelley's view in emphasizing the power of poetry in "rendering it [the mind] the receptacle of a thousand unapprehended combinations of thought" (Shelley 1821a, Harvard p. 10; and Shelley 1821b, Oxford p. 680). The best interpretations we may ever be prepared to suggest the analysand, I would believe, should perhaps be as much closer to Shelley's line than to the often unprepared voice of theories: that our interpretations may somehow assist rendering the analysand's mind something nearing the receptacle of a thousand unapprehended combinations of thoughts.

The time that it may have taken the analyst to open the way for his own internal characters to speak to his puzzled patients may somehow invoke in him, in the session, the time that it might often have taken his own mother to convert his own projections as a foetus and an infant into the unique experience of the discovery of meaning, thus perhaps bringing to life, *in the session*, something of his own earliest emotional experiences, hopefully giving him a deeper understanding of the analysand's *concrete* experience there, on the couch. This seems all so complex, so fragile and sensitive that we may perhaps never be prepared to find an answer to Bion's question: "on what grounds have we been driven . . . to give the interpretation." We may never succeed in describing the journey that our own internal characters have to go before we are prepared to allow their voices to be *heard* by the analysands and by ourselves as we just listen, in surprise, to what they had to say, exactly as happened to Bion himself.

This once again speaks for how immensely complex and sensitive psychoanalysis really seems to be at virtually every moment of virtually every session.

Yet another challenge making the practice of psychoanalysis so defeatingly complex and fragile is for the analyst to *dream some of* the analysand's paranoid-schizoid elements into new passionate links to the world, this being a key way of keeping *dreaming* the human mind into its own structure and its own ever-changing qualities. Such *dream* – such new passionate link to the world – is what I mean by *intuition*.

19 On the Psychical Meaning of Kindness – A Note

Meltzer claimed that the first and foremost single quality for anyone to qualify as analyst is his capacity for *kindness*. He inherited this understanding from Roger Money-Kyrle. What Meltzer exactly means by *kindness* may not, however, be trivial. By *kindness* Meltzer seems to mean one's capacity for passionate interest for the analysand's mental life, forbearance, capacity for devotion and generosity.[2]

In one of his most famous plays – *The Wild Duck* – Ibsen discussed the potential conflict between kindness and honesty. In his most famous novel, *A Passage to India*, Edward Forster worked out Ibsen's view suggesting that kindness may even enhance truth, arguing that "kindness is as important as truth – not only to mitigate the harshness of truth but to make it more true" (In: Steiner 2016, p. 434). More recently John Steiner rephrased Foster's view into the line: "Forster's point is not just that truth without kindness can be cruel, but that truth without kindness is not fully true" (Ibid). Now, how exactly is it that kindness may not only enhance truth, therefore making the truth a better truth, but it may even make it *fully true*? What does this exactly mean? How exactly is it that, in Meltzer's understanding, kindness is so crucial in everyday psychoanalytic clinic? How exactly is it that the analysand's experience of analysis will be *profoundly* different if kindness has always been a key issue in the analyst's thoughts and feelings and, therefore also, in the music of his voice?

I tend to believe this enigmatic effect of kindness in analysis is closely related with the qualities of the music of the mother's voice speaking to her foetus and her infant and its mysterious impact in both. The mysterious qualities of mother's voice must be central in the foetus' and the infant's sweeping experience of her passion as, perhaps, *the* most crucial emotion in having one's mind being *dreamed* into life. Furthermore, it seems that the qualities of the music of mother's voice as she speaks to her foetus and her infant may have another mysterious effect on the adult's faculties of clustering around understanding.

Take the plain text of an interpretation, say, of a dream, and then listen to two versions of that interpretation: one couched into a language that carries into the analysand the analyst's passionate interest in his mental life, his kindly sharing with his analysand the truth of his uncertainty about *all* his own thoughts, together with his awareness of the exceeding sensitivity of all sides of psychical life. The alternative version of exactly the same text of the interpretation would, on the contrary, be uncaringly imposed upon the analysand carrying into him the harshness of certainties and inevitably echoing the analyst's smugness and uncaring about him. Though the text may be exactly the same, the interpretations could hardly be more hurtfully different. What, however, is the *essential* difference between both? The second interpretation is primarily an assault on the link between the analysand and the analyst at the level of the mother-foetus and mother-infant relationships of which the analysand has to urgently defend himself from. The emotional turmoil forced into the analysand's mind in the session must be very difficult to support and deal with. Mother-analyst is *no longer* experienced by the analysand as if talking about a dream but rather as filling him with nightmares and other terrorizing experiences of the mother-analyst himself. This does communicate to the analysand, particularly at the earliest level of the foetus and the infant, a highly disturbing view of his dream. The truth has been so brutally assaulted on and nightmared that it hardly keeps much of what it was. It is, primarily, an unreadably confused emotional turmoil peopled by paranoid-schizoid elements which the adult has to wrestle with filtering the experience down to a highly distorted view of what is true and what is not.

The same seems to hold to every other piece of clinical material along any entire analysis.

I take kindness as a language – a particularly important language, an internal language into which emotions and thoughts may and may not be couched into. Its importance lies, I would believe, in this that it is *heard* by the foetus' and the infant's parts of the personality to be closer to the music of the passionate mother's voice speaking lovingly, tenderly, in a sweet singing rhythm to her loved foetus and her much loved infant. I would believe that interpretations should be close to the language of mother's reverie. I would believe that the language of kindness, in wording interpretations, should even be close to that of mother's reverie in the sense that Bion took it in its deep connection with the psychical meaning of love: "When the mother loves her infant, what does she do it with? . . . my impression is that her love is expressed by reverie" (Bion 1962, pp. 35–36). The language of kindness in conveying a truth does not add to the truth a judgement – any judgement. It rather conveys a sense of tolerance, perhaps also of forbearance. If the analyst is false in his thoughts or feelings, the analysand may develop a silent hatred of him, even if he would eventually divert his hatred to someone else, or some parts of himself, or some side of life or the world. Or he may soon learn the unfortunate language of cynicism and of compromise. The analyst's falsehood and cunningness in his efforts to misconstrue it as care and concern may be severely damaging for any true development of transference and therefore for analysis. If the analyst is really not passionately interested in the analysand's mental life, it may go right into the earliest parts of the analysand's personality. The foetus and the infant parts of him unfailingly *hear* it. From that moment on, a complicated web of manoeuvres may be set in motion. Both the analyst and the analysand will start lying to one another in whatever ways. Seduction, I would believe, may be the most common language of untruthfulness coming from the chair. Obviously, hardly anything like an analysis may ever succeed and result from it. And yet, we may really wonder how many such "analysis" have so often been sanctioned by Institutes.

Now, it is of course crucial to differentiate kindness from seduction. Seduction seems so often resorted to as a means to outwit the analyst's incapacity for passionate interest for the analysand's psychical life as well as his cowardice before his feeling both lost and unprepared to face the demands imposed by the clinic hours. The lie of seduction poisons the analysand's mind, and it is a betrayal of the analysand's trust at several levels of the transference. The analyst's seduction invites the analysand to join in a degrading affair based on unuttered compromises destroying any possibility of intimacy, perverting the evolution of the transference and therefore of analysis.

20 On Kindness and the Experience of Mystery – A Note

The sea of enigmas and of mysteries believed to tightly weave the human mind is believed to demand the key assistance of the voice of kindness. For these enigmas and mysteries try us all the time with perplexity and wonder. Feeling deeply lost and yet marvelled may at times leave us on the verge of new catastrophic changes. The extreme sensitivity of all psychical processes is, once again, so emotionally trying, so demanding, so often so exacting and at the same time so awestruck that any language other than the language of kindness could be so disruptive and so damaging that it may at times be hardly bearable. The harsh language of smugness and omniscience may alarmingly disrupt our fragile understanding of the meaning of *being human.*

The history of the evolution of the passionate feelings coming from both the couch and the chair in the course of an analysis seems a key guiding voice speaking of the growth of the experience of intimacy. The unending deepening of this enigmatic emotional experience holds the mirror for both the analysand and the analyst showing them the key and yet elusive links between the experience of intimacy and the sense of the mystery of things.

Every interpretation should be a piece of passion and of kindness.

21 The Key Role of Passion in the Enigma of Hearing – A Note

The moment we begin to see theories, formulas and certainties strutting through the room as we listen to the analysand instead of listening to him, we may be quite sure that we are just nightmaring what we have been told, right there, in the session, and cowering away from the unbearable pain of uncertainty and the feeling of being lost.

The moment theories and formulas and certainties storm the room, anxiously summoned by the scared and coward analyst, he is believed to be just nightmaring the session. The moment perplexity and wonder have both left the room, we may be sure that we ourselves have left the room, not really being back again and not even wishing to be there anymore.

It does not seem to matter what we listen in the session but whether the way we listen translates itself into the analysand's experience of the session. If the way we listen to him reaches him in the form of *a concrete experience of a thinking mind in the room*, together with the experience of truth of our being passionately interested in his mental life, the analysand is believed to have been *heard*. This way of listening may also mean that, while listening to the analysand, we actually seem to be *dreaming* what we listen into new experiences of intimacy. This also seems to mean that we have somehow closely followed what the analysand's internal characters may perhaps have confided to us. The way we listen to the analysand is believed to be the essential of all we may have to communicate to him.

As soon as perplexity is no longer with us in the room, it seems a warning that we may have slid into a state of mind close to the mother who has just lost the thread linking her to her foetus and her infant and not even aware of the broken link, thus somehow putting her foetus' and her infant's mental survival at risk. We may, indeed, have also lost the thread of the session and later hopefully realize that nothing in us is caring about this broken link. This lost thread may, however, grow in us and remain in us even for a long time in the form of a feeling that we have lost a passionate link to the world. This feeling, I would think, may perhaps near mother's disturbing experience of having lost a baby from her now sadly barren inside. I again recall Meltzer's remark in the course of a supervision session:

> If she lowers the passion, she lowers the value of everything, and then abandonment is so much easier – to abandon this, to abandon that, if their value has been brought down. So I think that it is very important

to bring out how it comes about that she is able to lower the value of the analysis, and then just vomit it out, lose the session, lose the babies.

(Meltzer in: Monteiro 2019, pp. 57–58; cf above)

And we may once again ponder over Bion's remark about what he believes is "the extraordinary nature, the mystery of psychoanalysis": "Such a lot of analysts seem to be bored with their subject; they have lost the capacity for wonder" (Bion 1987, p. 15, Brasília, 3rd Seminar, 1975). Inevitably, the clinical hour would grow itself boring. The analyst may then succeed in making the hour shuffling along its too heavy minutes until the watch signals to him the time to continue shuffling along though now with yet another patient, the shuffling being basically the same.

What, once again, is the name of such serious disorder? Why is it that no analyst has ever given it a clear name? Why have analysts resisted so far to move it into a central place in the psychoanalytic "roster" of mental troubles? Why is this disorder so alarmingly silenced in both the psychoanalytic literature and in the conference rooms? A bored ear cannot possibly hear the music of passion in the voice of his analysands. Such sad ear can also never be touched by the experience of intimacy. Only a passionate ear can *hear* what is really important in the human mind, that is, what is passionate, awestruck, deeply creative, perplexing and out of measure – *out-of-measure* being, in this book, the best measure of what is human.

I do not think that analysis is about symptoms but about passion and the destruction of passion; it is about collapsing "mother's beauty" – collapsing "the *dazzle of the sunrise*" (cf. Meltzer & Williams 1988, pp. 28–29).

Passion and its mysteries is perhaps our wisest guide to *hearing* the analysand. Analysis is about the meaning of *being human*.

Hearing is an act of passion and of intimacy. It should perhaps be the core of every clinic hour.

Notes

1 Meltzer kindly gave me an unworked copy of this paper. The paper is a rough transcript of a lecture that he delivered in Munich in 1989. To my best awareness, the text of this lecture still remains unpublished today.
2 Personal communication. For a slightly different version of Meltzer's view of *kindness*, cf. Meltzer's 1997, p. 182.

Part 2

The Human Mind as the Celebration of Unmeasure

Chapter 20

The Fundamental Basic Assumption[1] of Psychoanalysis

1 Introduction

For the sake of the clarity of the argument, I will next call *the foundational structure of psychoanalysis* the group of both acknowledged and unacknowledged beliefs, assumptions, principles, values, ways of thinking and views of the world that play whatever relevant role in determining the substance, purpose, form and main guiding lines of psychoanalysis in both its research and clinical areas. Although many of the elements in this foundational structure may not be easily identified and given a clear name to, many others can. As we very closely examine on what exact merits have many of these elements been trusted to play key roles in this exceedingly complex foundational structure, we may at times find reasons to wonder how carefully these merits have been assessed and what exactly speaks for the selection of some of them. And yet all these foundational elements are, by definition, entrusted with directing all our steps in both research and everyday clinic practice. Irrespective of differences of major schools and of clinical orientation, some of the most important elements ensuring the foundational structure of psychoanalysis cluster around Freud's conceptions of knowledge, understanding and thinking. Furthermore, the key role that Freud has always entrusted reason with assisting him in researching into the human mind and guiding him all along virtually every clinic hour has long put reason side by side with the previous three key epistemological concepts as foundational factors of psychoanalysis. So reason too has from the beginning of psychoanalysis been entrusted with crucially guiding Freud – and us all – in both research and clinical work. And yet, if we now carefully re-examine many of these elements though in the light of Bion's theory of dreams and his visionary model of the mind, the foundational merits of many of these elements seem surprisingly questionable.

DOI: 10.4324/9781003375159-23

Furthermore, under this same new light as well as under the light of many of Meltzer's insights and findings discussed in this book, some, or perhaps even many of these key foundational elements are now surprisingly seen to have been operating as *basic assumptions*. Among these basic assumptions, I will particularly examine the one that takes for granted that the group of beliefs, principles, values and way of thinking clustering around the classical concepts of knowledge, thinking, understanding and reason can alone fully equip us to gratifyingly research into the human mind and even lead us ever closer to the truth of psychic reality. This assumption, moreover, carries with it the proud belief that psychoanalysis, grounded upon these unexamined foundational pieces, is confidently prepared to lecture history on the unending enigmas and mysteries argued in this book to tightly weave the human mind, even to *be* the essentials of the human mind. Many of Meltzer's insight and findings studied in this book are believed to lend Bion's visionary ideas a new dimension. The closer we follow both Bion's theory of dreams and all these Meltzer's insights, the clearer it emerges that the uncounted enigmas and mysteries so inspiringly weaving the human mind keep us all drowned in its unending complexities and lost in ever deeper perplexity and wonder.

This fundamental assumption – that the foundational elements of psychoanalysis clustering around Freud's concepts of knowledge, understanding, thinking and reason can alone equip us to keep researching into the human mind under the disconcerting belief that this research could lead us ever closer to the truth of psychic reality as well as to confidently guide us along most clinic hours – this assumption is called in this book *the fundamental basic assumption of psychoanalysis*.

It therefore is this assumption that most spreads the rather reckless belief that classical psychoanalysis is equipped to lecture history on the unending enigmas and even mysteries believed in this book not only to tightly weave the human mind but to fundamentally *be* the core of the human mind.

The question seems to stand on our way to closely re-examine the too confident belief that I am calling *fundamental basic assumption of psychoanalysis*: what human mind is the human mind of which psychoanalysis believes is fully equipped to extensively lecture history on? How human is this human mind? How human is the human mind of which psychoanalysis believes to be equipped to reveal virtually every one of its many secrets, remaining unprepared to contemplate the view, so crucial in Bion's visionary model of the mind, that what seems most human in the human mind is what in it is so profoundly enigmatic and so profoundly mysterious, as well as what in it is so awe-inspiring?

What exactly, then, is the object of research of psychoanalysis? What exactly, then, is psychoanalysis about?

2 The Fundamental Basic Assumption of Psychoanalysis – New Remarks

So on what exact grounds has Freud, as well as all those closely walking behind him, built up such firm belief which still remains so central in psychoanalysis today? What massive clinical evidence, assisted by the thoroughly re-examined argument have been emboldening us to back such apparently imprudent, even perhaps reckless claim, implying such a frightening amount of both clinical and theoretical far-reaching implications? What exactly is it that fully sustains the credo that such large group of unexamined both acknowledged and unacknowledged beliefs, assumptions, values, principles and ways of thinking closely clustering around the classical concepts of knowledge, understanding, thinking and reason would alone equip us to extensively research into the awestruck complexity and beauty of the human mind and even to perhaps take us near the truth of psychic reality? What exactly sustains the widely shared unexamined assumption that these foundational elements fully prepare us to proudly lecture history on the unending enigmas and mysteries not only weaving the human mind but again *being* the core of the human mind? How could such unexamined means qualify psychoanalysis to shed such a revealing light over these uncounted enigmas and mysteries and to at long last reveal all its unyielding secrets? How could this little assumption, believed in this book to swell with pride, ever bring us the promise of preventing us from being ever again lost in both perplexity and wonder before the awe-inspiring complexities crowding the human mind? How could such proudly reassuring little line could ever lay bare all that which, in the human mind, has always kept buffeting us all so painfully and so uncomprehendingly for as long back in time as history is equipped to glance? Puzzlingly, furthermore, how could such pedestrian assumption ever prepare us to account for all the awe-inspiring qualities of the human mind constantly unsettling us with the uncounted marvels the human mind so continuously creates and crowds life and the world with?

This disconcertingly simple assumption – the fundamental basic assumption of psychoanalysis – seems to bring with it an odd dilemma. Each branch of this dilemma seems to lead to an extraordinary end. For either the human mind has little or nothing to do with a sea of defeatingly complex enigmas and mysteries that this book believes *is* the heart of the human mind, and then psychoanalysis can indeed be confidently said to be about the human mind and believe itself to unravel all its secrets as Freud had always been so keen on, or what is most crucial in the human mind is precisely this sea of defeatingly complex enigmas and mysteries and awe-inspiring qualities as this book so extensively argues it is, and then psychoanalysis has really nothing or little to say about the human mind.

This book can also largely be said to be about this dilemma. The dilemma was forced out into the open by the illuminating strength of Bion's theory of dreams and his visionary model of the mind, as well as by Meltzer's many new insights and findings lending many of Bion's views a whole new dimension.

3 The Conflict Between Means and Ends – A First Note

The fundamental basic assumption of psychoanalysis carries with it, right to the heart of psychoanalysis, what seems to be an irreparable conflict. This is a conflict between means and ends – the conflict between the means and the ends of classical psychoanalysis. The means that Freud believed were best to assist him to both extensively research into the human mind and direct him – and us all – through virtually every clinic hour carry with them the unseen seed of this conflict: to what exact extent do the means Freud has summoned and entrusted with guidance gratify him in both these ends? If these means are believed to answer this double call, the previous question again forces its way into our perplexity: what exactly human mind is this human mind? How human is the human mind of which psychoanalysis, assisted alone by these unmerited means, is simultaneously sure to know so much about and be equipped to successfully work out most of its disorders?

In still other slightly different words: how far do the means that Freud has summoned to best guide him – and again us all – to research into the human mind and very perceptively address so many really piercing, even tearing emotional conflicts that have so anxiously waited for him, and now for us all, in everyday consulting rooms – how do these means equip us to offer all of psychoanalysis' heralded promises? How, again, do these means prepare us to fully answer their expectations? It would, however, seem that both the means that Freud has always entrusted with best assisting him in both purposes – research and clinical – and the heralded ends of psychoanalysis have both been allowed to travel throughout psychoanalysis in the form of a swelling lump of a blurred bunch of generalities leaving all doors open to confusion. So the key conflict between means and ends continues to be allowed to travel along the history of psychoanalysis entrusted with the inept labour of inept hands. What, then, is the clear answer to the clear question: what is the object of study of psychoanalysis? What exactly is it that psychoanalysis researches into? What exactly is it that psychoanalysis really and finally wants?

4 The Conflict Between Means and Ends – A New Note

Until relatively recently, this potential conflict between means and ends – that is, whether and to what exact extent do the means of psychoanalysis make it possible for it to fully meet its own ends – so this potential crucial conflict has been allowed, again, to elusively worm its way through the countless pages of psychoanalytic literature and, far more upsettingly, through countless many clinic hours, not exactly as a conflict but rather as an undisputed and unexamined claim. So for decades, the assumed accord between means and ends has, again, been dragged along undiscussed. Bion and, soon after him, Meltzer have however both brought Freud's means and ends under scrutiny. Gradually, and through different paths, they have extensively questioned even the meaning of both as the best approach to research into the human mind and, therefore also, to consistently serve clinical purposes. If, however, we carefully reread this very claim, we may soon recognize it speaking in the voice of what I am calling the *fundamental basic assumption of psychoanalysis*.

So at every turn of the road – at every unexpected turn of countless unexpected roads in the unreadably complex map of clinical experience – we are again and again met with uncounted pieces of evidence defeating the belief that we know and constantly pressing us to deeply review the role that psychoanalysis has always entrusted knowledge, understanding and thinking rationally with lecturing history on the human mind and dangerously feeding our as proud as vain belief of being equipped to direct every clinic hour, arguing the pathetic show of analysts' famous smugness seems to be.

5 How Human Is the Psychoanalytic Human Mind? – A New Note

So Freud believes that he knows virtually everything about exactly the same object of extensive clinical observation and research about which both Bion and Meltzer believe they ignore virtually everything. And yet they have both gone so deeply into the human mind that they came to the belief that the concepts of knowledge, understanding and thinking, together with the host of assumptions, principles, values and ways of thinking clustering around these concepts, are inept means to guide us more insightfully along every clinic hour as well as in further deepening our research into the human mind than what classical psychoanalysis has already succeeded to take us. For both Bion and Meltzer are believed in this book to have opened the way, leading us to see the inspiring strength of uncertainty as a fundamental guiding light in both research and clinic. Furthermore, particularly Meltzer, but also Bion in his latest days, have again been first in quite remarkably intuiting that the human mind is tightly woven by a host of enigmas and even mysteries which were slowly seen, again in the light of Bion's visionary model of the mind, as the most inspiring and faithful voice speaking for the essence of the human mind. Moreover, the fundamental intuition that this book has been given to Bion from its outset that all that is really interesting in the human mind is both born and pulsates with its best life beyond the edge of the unknown, the unknowable and the unthinkable is also argued here to be shared and further deepened by Meltzer. So what exactly it is that Bion and Meltzer can be said to know about the human mind is something I am unprepared to guess but so are they. For in the light of what I have been calling Bion's visionary model of the mind, the meaning of the classical idea of knowing anything about the human mind has gradually been edged away from its former condition of the undisputed guiding voice in both research and clinic.

So again, their differences seem not only unbridgeable but to grow irreconcilably divergent at each new step into the human mind. For Freud firmly believes the human mind is a plain object of thought, understanding and knowledge; that, by extensively observing it, thinking about it, understanding it and knowing it we are all granted a firm grip on virtually all its secrets. Freud is as confident about what he believes he knows of his patients' minds as Bion and Meltzer are of not even knowing the very meaning of knowing anything about the human mind. So again, Freud feels as sure about what he believes he observes in his patients' mind and indeed in virtually every mental process, as Bion and Meltzer feel lost and uncomprehending about exactly the same object of observation and research.

Freud's famous claim of having grasped virtually everything about the structure and the workings of the human mind should have been received with untold relief by uncounted harrowed minds who have suffered from so many of the unyielding enigmas and mysteries believed in this book not only to tightly weave the human mind but once again to *be* all that is essential in the human mind.

Freud's overconfident voice about the human mind still resonates today in countless pages of the psychoanalytic literature, in countless hours in the conference rooms and, far more unfortunately, in countless clinic hours. Freud's credo still remains today the commanding voice in the psychoanalytic canon and the main source of analysts' unfortunately famous smugness.

6 The Conflict Between Means and Ends – A New Note

Characteristically, the conflict between means and ends leads to an odd turn: if the means do not accord with the ends, we may tend to force the ends to accord with the means. For as long as these means would continue to somehow gratify analysts both for the often positive results flourishing from their honest efforts, but also often for further feeding their smugness, psychoanalysis would live largely happy with the lumpish compromise silently negotiated between its unclear means and its unclear ends. This compromise may perhaps be better described to consist in allowing their means to largely shape their ends, even to warp their ends.

This is exactly the case of having the ends of psychoanalysis framed by its means, that is, by the unexamined group of both acknowledged and unacknowledged beliefs, assumptions, principles, values, ways of thinking and views of the world and, crucially, by the fundamental basic assumption of psychoanalysis. To warp the ends down to the limits and other requirements of the means entails forcing every conception of the human mind into the model previously determined by the limits and again other requirements of the means. Submitting the ends to the requirements of the means may severely warp the scope, reach, depth and meaning of psychoanalysis. This compromise would, however, ensure analysts the proud illusion of knowing everything about the human mind. And yet the human mind that emerges from this compromise is irreconcilable with the one gradually emerging from Bion's theory of dreams and his visionary model of the mind, as well as from so many of Meltzer's illuminating insights and findings crucially enhancing Bion's vision and redirecting it in new uncharted paths. One direction of thought privileges the means over the ends, the other, the ends over the means. In perhaps clearer words, if what both Bion and Meltzer repeatedly observe lead them to challenge and even openly dispute the ever accepted means, no matter for how long and no matter how firmly previously accepted means, they would certainly blow the means away to be true to what they believe they watch, thus serving the ends by reshaping the means defeating no matter how firmly accepted elements of the foundational structure of psychoanalysis.

They both followed along irreconcilably different directions and met irreconcilably divergent ends. Crucially, each direction returns irreconcilably conflicting views of the human mind and, therefore also, of the meaning of *being human*.

Inevitably, these differences dramatically weigh on the course of each single clinic hour. These differences profoundly reshape the qualities of our *hearing* (cf. Chapter 20), insensibly leading us from *listening* to *hearing*, as well as to hand over the session to our internal characters rather than to our own conscious thoughts. These difference also profoundly reshape the music of the analysts' voice, the depth, the wealth and the truth of the transference and of the counter-transference, and therefore also, of both the analysand's and the analyst's experiences of analysis.

7 Two Irreconcilably Disparate Human Minds

If we now focus on the human mind that gradually comes out of Bion's theory of dreams and of his visionary model of the human mind as well as from Meltzer's insights and findings adding to Bion's vision, the means that classical psychoanalysis has always entrusted with best guiding us all in both researching into the human mind and guiding our steps along every clinic hour, classical psychoanalysis would seem dramatically unqualified to meet the new ends. If, for instance, we would side with Bion's viewing the human mind to essentially pulsate beyond the edge of the unknown, the unknowable and the unthinkable, virtually all the means of classical psychoanalysis would require dramatic revision. The same if we succeed to gradually convert uncertainty as a persecutor into uncertainty as a precious source of inspiration and a guiding light in both research and virtually every clinic hour.

How much closer to the awe-inspiring quality of the human mind is the human mind which is believed to continuously *dream* itself into existence and into the awe-inspiring and the marvellous complexity of its own structure, its ever-changing qualities and its unreadably complex workings? How far closer to the truth of the human mind is the human mind in which the extraordinary inspiring strength of fragility is deeply revered and recognized to unendingly enrich the meaning of *being human*, this being the core of every session and of every analysis? What human mind is the human mind in which fragility is seen as a reluctantly tolerated flaw that analysts feel committed to work out into the disaster of firmness – into the "firmness" that would imply hammering certainties into the analysand instead of seeing fragility as a potentially inspired and inspiring oracle, revealing key qualities of the human mind that have not before been allowed to fully live in the course of the clinic hour as well as in both the transference and the counter-transference? How far closer to the awe-inspiring truth of the unreadable complexity of the human mind is the human mind tightly woven by the beauty of uncertainty and of mysteries, reading symptoms as evidence of what in us all remains unprepared to live the wonder of fragility and the privilege and the beauty of the experience of mystery?

How much of the core of the human mind has been rescued from the classical model by Bion's theory of dreams and his visionary model of the mind and brought back alive into the consulting room, as well as by Meltzer's visionary insights and findings branching Bion's theory of dreams in so many bright, new directions?

8 The Irreconcilable Conflict Between Two Minds – A New Note

If psychoanalysis has never been overwhelmed by the awe-inspiring qualities of the human mind, if it is not *constantly* shaken as to feel lost in sheer uncertainty as well as in both perplexity and wonder by the defeating complexity of the human mind as well as by its riveting beauty, if it is not drowned in the disconcerting and yet illuminating experience of uncertainty, if it not lost in the marvel of incomprehension before its unending enigmas and mysteries, if it has never been defeated by the creative strength of the unreadably complex dynamic of psychic reality, if it has never led analysts astray to wonder on what exact grounds can psychoanalysis claim any legitimacy to lecture history on the real marvel of the human mind, we may perhaps be better to Meltzer's late wise claim that we are *deeply* helpless before a patient – before *any* patient, before the human mind. Psychoanalysis may perhaps try to so-called *treat symptoms*.

For again, what human mind is the human mind that psychoanalysis has always lectured so proudly on? How exactly human is its dishearteningly poor human mind? What new light is psychoanalysis, in these puzzling conditions, prepared to shed on the meaning of *being human* as it most certainly should? On what exact grounds is it prepared to read into symptoms all that they may have to say not only and not even mainly about medical reading of the term *disease* but crucially about the unmeasured complexity of the human mind? Against what exact backdrop do symptoms speak to the analyst? In what voices and into what exact ears do they speak? Where exactly is psychoanalysis to find the *meaning* for what it alleges to read into them and even treat them? If this backdrop is the human mind, how reckless of psychoanalysis to so firmly believe it is equipped to successfully deal with every symptom? What exactly is it that we all call *an analysis*? How deeply is it supposed to go down into the unending enigma and even the mysteries crowding the human mind, and indeed, once again, *being* the core and the truth of the human mind? What new light should an analysis shed, in the eyes of both the analysand and the analyst, on the meaning of *being human?*

Note

1 The term *basic assumption* refers, of course, to the concept that Bion introduced and first studied in detail in his *Experiences in Groups* (1961 [1996]).

Chapter 21

The Myth of Interpretation and the Role of the Ineffable

1 An Odd Quote

> [1] The experience of the patient's communication and [the] psycho-analyst's interpretation is ineffable and essential. [2] The communication of this quality plays a vital part in any interpretation given to the psychotic patient. [3] The patient's reaction to the interpretation often depends more on this quality of the interpretation than on its verbal meaning. [4] Thanks to the nature of the psychotic transference, the fate of the meaning of the interpretation hangs on the tone of the interpretation.
>
> (Bion 1967, p. 122)

This chapter discusses Bion's four lines. In the attempt to make this discussion clear, I numbered the lines that I will next focus on in bold face and within square brackets.

Line [1] alone threatens to unseat much of the fundamental scaffolding of psychoanalysis. By itself alone, line [1] seems to blow away the fundamental basic assumption of psychoanalysis, that is, the belief that the group of both acknowledged and unacknowledged beliefs, principles, values, ideas and assumptions clustering around the concepts of knowledge, understanding, thinking and reason that Freud believed would gratifyingly equip us to research into the human mind, even to gradually near us to the truth of psychic reality, as well as guide us how to best direct every clinic hour.

In the light of [1], no analyst is ever equipped to put into readable words his experience of his patient's communication. The *OED* unfolds the word *ineffable* into *unutterable, indefinable, indescribable*. The

DOI: 10.4324/9781003375159-24

analyst's experience of the patient's communication, therefore, can never be described in any rationally readable language.

Line [1] also makes clear that the substance of any true interpretation is itself ineffable. Interpretations are not supposed to address the patient's communication but the analyst's experience of this communication. But by [1], this experience is ineffable. An interpretation is therefore not expected to address the immediate meaning of the patient's words and the syntax that has grouped these words together into a rationally intelligible piece. Therefore, no interpretation is supposed to address what is rationally intelligible. The object of *any* interpretation, therefore, is in itself ineffable.

In my tentative way of seeing it, the ineffable nature of the object of any interpretation invites seeing an interpretation as the analyst's *dreaming* the patient's communication. As it was said before, *dreams* and *dreaming* refer throughout this book to a key postulated psychical function performing two tasks: continuously converting the human mind into existence and leading us beyond the edge of the unknown, the unknowable and the unthinkable and guiding us through this realm towards the experience of the creation of meaning.

So in this tentative view, and in the light of [1], every interpretation should both be essentially rooted and worked out beyond the edge of the unknown, the unknowable and the unthinkable. This is just another instance of Bion's most crucial intuition that every relevant psychical phenomenon is rooted and essentially operates beyond that quite crucial edge.

Analysts are therefore expected to *dream* what is ineffable in his own experience of the patient's communication into new experiences of meaning. The analyst's experiences of meaning are then expected to be shared with the analysand in the form of interpretations. Nevertheless, what classical psychoanalysis understands by *interpretation* is certainly far from what Bion seems to mean by it. I briefly recall how Bion addressed an analyst who, in the course of a clinical seminar held in Brasilia, showed his concern about an interpretation he has suggested his patient believing it might not have been adequate:

> B. If you had been practising analysis as long as I have, you wouldn't bother about an inadequate interpretation – I have never given any other kind. . . . I would be rather bothered if you felt it was adequate. . . . The practise of analysis is an extremely difficult occupation which hardly provides space for dogmatic statements.

> (1987, pp. 43–44)

2 The Puzzle of Ineffability – A Brief Remark

Line [1] also claims that the analyst's interpretation too is ineffable. If the view that everything relevant in the human mind, and certainly every true interpretation, has essentially been worked out beyond the edge of the unknown, the unknowable and the unthinkable, we may perhaps be closer to distance ourselves from the view, so central in classical psychoanalysis, that both the meaning of the patient's communication and the analyst's interpretation are both supposed to be plainly read in the words and the complex task of the syntax critically assistant the life of meaning. And yet, I recall Wittgenstein's remark:

> 358. But isn't it our *meaning* it that gives sense to the sentence? . . . And meaning something lies within the domain of the mind. . . . After all, it is, as it were, a dream of our language.
>
> (Wittgenstein 2009, p. 120e)

Furthermore, I may perhaps be allowed to go briefly back to a few of Meltzer's lines called to assist the argument in this book already in the previous chapter:

> The patient does not know anything about whether they [the analyst's interpretations] are right or wrong, any more than you as analyst know whether they are right or wrong. . . . Things can be utterly wrong and fit the material; but that is just the intellectual content, and relates to our theories of emotional development . . . which are very flimsy and deal more or less just with the surface of mental phenomena.
>
> (Meltzer 2005, pp. 456–457)

Both the analyst's experience of the patient's communication and his own interpretation of this communication are believed to be ineffable. How are we to see this double claim translated into the language of classical psychoanalysis?

3 What, Then, Is an Interpretation?

Now I go back to Meltzer's view of the role of the internal characters in writing both the transference and counter-transference:

> We tend to think that the transference is directed toward the [analyst's] self. . . . I think that it is our internal objects that are the object of the transference. . . . [Furthermore] one's functioning in the

> counter-transference is . . . the functioning of our identifications with
> one's [internal] objects. . . . I think that the realization of this makes a
> very great difference.
>
> (Meltzer 1989, p. 5, cls. 1–2; unpublished)

An analysis, I believe, should gradually ripen into an awestruck and very
mysterious dialogue between internal characters – the analysand's and the
analyst's – in which the analyst is called to play an extremely sensitive
role. For he is expected to gradually entrust his own internal characters
with the analysand's clinical material so that the analyst's internal characters may confide to the analysand's internal characters, through the analyst, how the analyst's internal characters have converted the analysand's
ineffable into something creative. This is what I mean by an interpretation.
The analyst's experience of the analysand's communication is ineffable,
I would believe, because the truth of what has been confided to the analyst comes *directly* from the analysand's internal characters, not from the
analysand's self. In this light, an interpretation is a *dream dreamed* by the
analyst's internal characters and *directly* addressing the analysand's internal characters themselves. This is what I mean to understand in this book
by an interpretation.

In other, hopefully clearer words: an interpretation is a conversion into
the experience of meaning, operated by the analyst's internal characters,
of the analysand's internal characters projected into the analyst *directly
addressing the analyst's internal characters*, this being why every interpretation is believed to be rooted and essentially worked out beyond the
edge of the unknown, the unknowable and the unthinkable.

Also crucial in this *dreaming* process carried by the analyst is that the
analyst should be capable of *waiting* – giving himself the time he would
need to divest his links with his own internal characters from nightmaring
processes, among which stands, once again, the stupidity of smugness.

4 Interpretation as a Key New Step Into the Experience of Intimacy

We, therefore, are expected to be prepared to give ourselves the time
required for our own internal characters to quietly *see* what would seem
essential in the ineffable communication of his patient.

Every interpretation should be a new step in the unending path to the
mystery of things and a new step in the experience of intimacy for both the

analysand and the analyst. Nevertheless, the analyst's smugness as well as his nightmaring his own emotional conflicts too often may hamper the qualities of his internal characters as well as the qualities of his links to them. The more we entrust our internal characters with guiding the session which we ourselves are so helpless to carry into a new experience of intimacy, the more we seem to be invited not to allow doubts and questions to be degraded into the disaster of certainties but keep enriching our inspiration and ripen observation into *dreaming*.

How many *dreams* weave all that is ineffable? We should keep key point vividly present in every session, I would believe. How are we ever to be prepared to carefully read into all the unyielding enigmas pulsating within the ineffable if we do not trust our own internal characters to do this for us?

5 The Frightening Line [2] and the Meaning of Respect

Line [2] falls upon us as an unrelenting warning: "The communication of this quality plays a vital part in any interpretation given to the psychotic patient." For how exactly are we to communicate this quality to the analysand? Through what exact means? I will, for now, drop Bion's clause concerning the psychotic patients, believing that the communication of the quality described in [1] plays a vital part in *any* interpretation given to *any* analysand, whether or not he is psychotic. for this quality seems to fully embody what seems essential in the idea of *respect*. There is no experience of intimacy which does not spring from *dreaming* respect into a far deeper way of *hearing*, as well as into a deeper love for the truth. Furthermore, no analysis is ever possible if it does not ripen into a profound discovery and experience of respect.

But how then are we to convey to the analysand that our experience of his communication is both ineffable and yet essential? As I would tend to see it, there is no way to communicate this crucial quality to the analysand other than to entrust this key and sensitive task with our good internal characters to do it for us. In order to convey *the truth* of our experience of the analysand's communication in a way that it does carry conviction, we should perhaps not trust what we believe we know because we may not have any means to know it, but to carry it in the music of our own voice, this being crucially connected with what I believe is the essential of line [2]. For as I tend to see it, line [2] is about *respect* – the psychical meaning and the crucial *clinical* importance for both the analysand and the analyst of the experience of profound respect as an unending revelation, whether or not the analysand is psychotic. Moreover, I would venture the undocumented belief that the experience of respect may prove to have a special therapeutic effect on psychotics.

Here also, the line emphasizes, for both the analysand and the analyst, that analysis essentially runs beyond the edge of the unknown, the unknowable and the unthinkable. And it is about the human mind drowning us all in perplexity and yet in wonder. This line once again implies a degree of complexity that is believed in this book to demand relying on *dreaming functions* and *dreaming* for guidance in both research and clinical work.

6 Words as Musical Instruments

Line [3] seems, again, crucial: "The patient's reaction to the interpretation often depends more on this quality of the interpretation than on its verbal meaning."

By *this* quality of the interpretation, Bion evidently means the quality of the analyst's experience of the analysand's communication as well as of his own interpretation of being both ineffable. I recall Meltzer's belief that the core of interpretations are states of mind which are far more complex, both far deeper and inspiring than the translation of words and syntax into a form of meaning far closer to intellectual operations.

And indeed, soon Meltzer realized that Bion's illuminating insight seemed to be crucially at work in virtually *every* session of virtually *every* patient. Meltzer even gave Bion the authorship of his own extended understanding of Bion's early view:

> Bion's idea [is] that communication is only very partially linguistic and that the substance of it is musical, and operates by projective identification, by transmitting the mental state. And this is why it's very important to try to interpret as poetically as you can, and not in a dry and factual way; projective identification as a more primitive form of communication of states of mind.[1]

So no one seems to know anymore what exactly is the role of words in the course of any analysis, so complex and so crucial it seems to be. This, at least, seems to invite close consideration: words are the main carriers of the music of the voice of the analysand's internal characters as well as of the music of the voice of the analyst's internal characters and, therefore, of their thoughts and feelings.

It is in this light that Lima insightfully emphasized the importance of silence in analysis:

> This primary form of communication [projective identification] runs through . . . both the transference and the counter-transference transcending interpretation, being carried out by the music of the voice and the empathic quality of the silence – the most profound of all grammars.
>
> (Lima 2016, p. 29)

This, I believe, is the grammar ruling the dialogue between the analyst and his own internal characters in which the analyst withdraws from the centre stage in the session and waits for his own internal characters' guidance, handing them over the direction of the clinic hour. This silence is believed to create a new experience of intimacy between the analysand and the analyst.

Attention to the unending nuances of the music of the voices seems, therefore, crucial.

7 The Ineffable as a Key Guiding Light

Line [4] reads, "Thanks to the nature of the psychotic transference, the fate of the meaning of the interpretation hangs on the tone of the interpretation."

Bion's idea of *the fate of the meaning of the interpretation* should lie at the core of every session and at the front line of the analyst's main focus, inviting him, once again, to hand over the guidance of each single session to *dreaming functions* and his own internal characters.

This understanding is believed to inevitably change the qualities of the analyst's *hearing*. All these changes are believed to crucially enrich both the development of the transference and of the counter-transference.

8 The Ineffable as the Main Object of Psychoanalysis

Psychoanalysis has succeeded in bluffing its way, dodging the ineffable. Bion and, soon afterwards, Meltzer have, however, both brought the ineffable to the core of the clinic hour, entrusting it with crucially commanding the hour and extensively arguing, though in different languages and in different ways, that the hour – *every* hour – is about the ineffable and that psychoanalysis itself is fundamentally about the ineffable. The language of the internal characters is itself essentially ineffable. And yet, and to the best of my recollection, neither these groups of insights – Bion's or Meltzer's – have as yet been ripened into a theory or deeply woven into the texture of the analyst's way of closely following the clinic hour. The ineffable is viewed in this book not only to be the object of psychoanalysis but a unique source of inspiration. I am not aware that Bion has himself made much to grow his illuminating insight into a theory. I am also not aware that, in his hands, his own visionary finding has as yet filtered down to change in everyday consulting room. Meltzer alone, to the best of my awareness, has just begun to mature Bion's as well as his own view of the utmost importance of the ineffable into some draft of a theory. Nevertheless, Meltzer has this view rather more or less indistinctly spread throughout much of his written work as well as in the other forms of teaching in which he has excelled – analysis itself, lectures and supervisions.

Without the intuition of the ineffable pervading the sessions as it does pervade the human mind, how often the analysand has to go through the disheartening experience while lying on the couch, of listening to mother-analyst's prattling about the boring hour from the chair, giving him the unmusical bore of his uninterested voice, so neglectful and indifferent about the ineffable nature of the analysand's communication. The clinical consequences for the patient must be chilling. Being deaf to the ineffable, the analyst carries with him the unfailing seed of very soon forcing the evolution of the transference down into disaster. The scope of the emotional conflicts and unworked unconscious phantasies that the analysand would be anxious to project into the analyst at several different levels of his psychical experience soon begins to shrink into scraps of stories weaving the periphery of his adult life. Both the foetus' and the infant's parts of the patient personality must be keenly aware of how dull mother-analyst is, how unresponsive, how disheartening it must be to stretch his little arms towards the dull mother-analyst, the equivalent for the foetus to listen to her unmusical, indifferent voice. Such uninterested and incapable analyst will soon trigger the analysand's mistrust at deep levels of the transference, I would believe, inviting him to join mother-analyst in degrading analysis into yet another experience of unhope. How many parts of the analysand's emotional experience are met with the absence of passion coming from the chair? How many are hurtfully left outside the *unhearing* mother? How hurtful is the deep experience of disrespect coming, again, from the chair, projected into the patient by the analyst's swelling smugness as a defence against the ineffable and the overwhelming sensitivity of the human mind?

9 The Ineffable and the Mysterious – A Note

Bion's four lines that this chapter attempted to closely read adds a new voice to the belief that the human mind is tightly woven by awe-inspiring enigmas and mysteries. As repeatedly suggested previously, this odd web may essentially *be* the human mind itself. Being another foundational quality of the meaning of *being human*, the ineffable should silently escort the analyst all along each session, advising him. The analyst's awareness of the extent to which the ineffable seems the fundamental language of the human mind deeply changes the atmosphere in the consulting room and helps us shield the infinite sensitivity of the human mind from the unending assaults on it coming from all our destructive drives, particularly by the at times powerful drive never to think that we all seem so peopled by. Being keenly aware of the ineffable pervading the work of the internal characters – of the analysand's and our own – may assist us, remaining focused on the enigmas and mysteries that are tightly weaving the human mind and again shielding its infinite sensitivity from being destroyed by the cowardice and the hatred hidden behind the pride of knowledge and understanding.

Note

1 Personal communication.

Chapter 22

The Slippery Word
Understanding

1 Introduction

Soon in his earliest working days as psychoanalyst, Freud felt besieged by repeated therapeutic failures. Both the number and reach of these failures increasingly pressed him to rethink his earliest therapeutic method. At first, Freud showed himself unprepared to convert these difficulties into progress. The weight of evidence showing him how unconvincing his clinical approach proved to be increased his concern. Soon Freud decided to pause. He then thoroughly reassessed the therapeutic direction he had tentatively worked out. His first response amounted to a key insight: he decided to crucially shift his approach to clinical demands from the primary aim of curing, to the primary aim of understanding. His long letter to W. Fliess, dated the 21st September 1897, stands as an impressive witness to both the detail and extension of his awareness of the predicament that he then clearly saw himself in (cf. Freud 1985, pp. 264–266). Thoroughly, and yet quietly, Freud shared with his then close friend and confidant the fundamental details of the collapse of his first therapeutic model.

Both the strength and clarity of his description of how wrecked his model now lay right before his own eyes, witnesses to both Freud's courage to face the painful evidence and his loyalty to truth as his main guide.

Thirty years later, Freud faithfully shared with history a clear glimpse of how far this early shift of purpose eventually led him: "The only subject-matter of psycho-analysis is the mental processes of human beings" (1926, S.E. 20, p. 254). At least in sustained intention, the line firmly echoes Freud's early shift of purpose and direction. Though still early in the history of psychoanalysis, the line stands out mirroring Freud's early decision to privilege understanding as the key road to clinical hope. Now the

DOI: 10.4324/9781003375159-25

object of psychoanalysis is clearly laid down. This crucial shift of purpose ploughed the field in which psychoanalysis would soon begin to root and grow. Evidently, each of these conflicting ways to therapeutic confidence – focusing on curing or focusing on understanding – determined different models of mind. Freud's new model was now to be built on the assumption that the soundness of the former – the aim of curing – is contingent upon the soundness of the latter – that of understanding. By being unfaithful to Freud's new aim insisting on rushing to the easier gratifications of curing, analysts were soon promised to sadly meet a similar uninvited fate that Freud had himself met before. As Freud moved from the purpose of curing to the purpose of understanding, he soon found out that the more he attempted on the latter, the better the results of the former might possibly prove to be.

2 The Riddle of Understanding – A Preliminary Note

And yet Freud's apparently promising new direction of purpose eventually began to crack, weakening the impact of his own previously quoted line. What threatened both surprisingly walked into psychoanalysis coming from the meaning of the word *understanding*. Bion was first to extensively question the merits of *understanding* as a much revered tool in crucially assisting us in both research into the human mind and guiding us through virtually every clinic hour. Bion was first to argue that understanding may travel us to quite uninvited ends.

> I am reminded of Bion's comment to his analysand James Grotstein, after Grotstein responded to one of Bion's interpretations by saying, "I understand." Bion paused, and then calmly said, "Please, try not to understand. If you must, superstand, circumstand, parastand, but please try not to understand."
>
> (In: Schneider 2005, p. 1479)[1]

Bion's remark leads us puzzlingly back to the core of Freud's fundamental shift of purpose from the earliest aim of curing to the far more promising aim of understanding. Bion's kindly requesting Grotstein to try *not* to understand unexpectedly forces both the concept of *understanding* and its clinic and research roles into our perplexity. For the belief in the virtues of *understanding* to crucially guide us in both research into human mind and through most clinical hours joins the group of other beliefs, principles, values, ways of thinking and assumptions that analysts fight not to question. Like all the others, *understanding* too offers us a complex promise: the promise, that is, of soothing our anxiety of not knowing, of, indeed, never knowing, by clogging up the way eventually leading us to discover the privilege of being guided by the shining light of uncertainty, of *dreaming* our essentially uncertain ways in both research and clinical work, and to learn to entrust our internal characters with taking up the job instead of keep trusting our unmerited grip on what we are not prepared to have a grip on.

Wittgenstein's fragment 150 may help following Bion: "The grammar of the word 'know' is evidently closely related to the grammar of the words 'can', 'is able to'. But also closely related to that of the word 'understand'. (To have 'mastered' a technique)" (Wittgenstein 2009, p. 65e). Bion asks Grotstein to please try not to master anything concerning with the human mind.

3 Understanding as an Unsteady Compromise

Bion's fundamental intuition firmly stands behind his opposing *understanding* together with other factors central in both the fundamental basic assumption of psychoanalysis and much of the foundational structure of psychoanalysis encouraging the idea of keeping a soothing grip on the unending enigmas weaving the human mind. I may perhaps be allowed to once again recall Bion's key intuition that virtually all that is interesting in the human mind pulsates beyond the edge of the unknown, the unknowable and the unthinkable.

So Bion's kind plea to Grotstein invites apprehension concerning the merits of understanding that has earnestly been requested by analysts since Freud's shift of aims to play a key role in guiding us in both researching into the human mind and in every clinic hour. The unreadable complexity of the awestruck structure of the human mind, of its ever-changing qualities and of its defeatingly complex workings make vain the idea of ever coming to know or understand everything about the human mind, even *anything* about the human mind. It was this belief that has prompted and continue to swell the unfortunate gratifications of smugness.

In order, however, to ensure the survival of such vain idea, we must warp the awe-inspiring mystery of the human mind down into a mere object of knowledge, understanding and reason as it still lives degraded and yet happy today. The cluster of beliefs, values, principles and assumptions supporting this idea has been holding the human mind hostage, stripping it of its most awe-inspiring qualities. To force this view into the clinic hour may severely cripple both the analysand's and the analyst's experiences of the hour and *a fortiori* of the whole analysis itself. The creative strength of the unreadably complex dynamic of psychic reality alone – one of the most awestruck qualities of the human mind – blows away the semantic boundaries of the proud word *understanding* as a key piece within the fundamental conceptual frame of psychoanalysis. *Understanding* may indeed easily lure us, deceive us, even defeat us. The enticing attempt at compromising is never far. The slippery word *understanding* is a privileged attendant to this compromise. Hence, I believe, Bion's kind invitation to Grotstein not to understand anything really interesting about the human mind. He *could never understand* it, so complex, so awestruck, and so often so beautiful it certainly is.

4 The Riddle of Understanding – A New Note

So we are again called back to the question of the aim of psychoanalysis. This time, however, we were offered a relatively narrow door out of it: the subject-matter of psychoanalysis is *the mental processes of the human mind*, in Freud's own words. With what exact eyes, however, are we best supposed to very closely follow the dynamic of these processes? What processes are exactly those that we are expected to examine and what are those which have never yet been given a name? How equipped are we to very closely observe them at work and to extensively learn with them all that they lecture us on the unending enigmas weaving the human mind? How prepared are we to learn enough of them and enough from them? The measure of our illusion of understanding is given by the measure of our lack of passion. The latter faithfully speaks for the former. In other words, the lower the passion, the greater the understanding, and the greater the illusion that our understanding confirms us to be on the right track, speaking in the language of our pride and perhaps soon of our smugness.

Bion's greatest intuition – that all that is interesting in the human mind is believed to essentially pulsate beyond the edge of the unknown, the unknowable and the unthinkable – explodes the question of *understanding* as a key means to guide us in our groping way towards the truth of psychic reality.

5 The Courage to Try to Understand

I may perhaps be allowed to recall Niels Bohr's inaugural address to the Institute of Genetics at the University of Cologne, read the 21st of June 1962 – "Life and Light Revisited":

> I think that the feeling of wonder which the physicists had thirty years ago has taken a new turn. Life will always be a wonder but what changes is the balance between the feeling of wonder and the courage to try to understand.
>
> (In: Pais 1991, p. 444)

This continuous swaying between, on the one hand, the feeling of wonder and eventually the insight into a new vision and, on the other hand, the fear of change implying renouncing old certainties and venturing into still uncharted lands – this continuous swaying between both conflicting directions often tries us, sometimes defeats us into cowardice. This dramatic sway is believed to silently escort our days and hours through life like an unseen shadow. Deciding between one or the other speaks for our loyalty to passion and much of our resulting vision. The dilemma also lies vigilant in so many new pages of the psychoanalytic literature, but crucially, in the minutes of most clinic hours. The strength of passion may invite us, even compel us to try to understand beyond the limits of knowledge and, therefore, beyond the edges of our fear. The challenge tests us all at every turn of thought and life. The balance between both hinges on the strength of passion and the disloyalty to passion. In other words, it sways between gratitude to the qualities of mother's reverie and neglect and indifference to them.

Unfaithfulness to mother's reverie and unfaithfulness to the creative strength of passion may take the form of craving for answers not to deepen the experience of intimacy but to assuage persecutory feelings and hold back this frightening swaying so as to free us to enjoy the gratifications of mindlessness which promises us never to be tried again, and disquieted again, by the wonder of the enigmas and the mysteries peopling weaving the human mind, even *being* the human mind. Again, this swaying is believed to closely escort us throughout life, even if mostly not walking into our attention. The promise of absence of conflict is a faithful companion to cowardice. Cowardice before the trying experience of insight may easily wriggle its way into both our research into the human mind and into the clinical hour. Our responses to having to choose between seeing what, if seen, forces us into the disquiet of new perplexity and wonder or recoiling from emotional conflicts into ingratitude to the internal mother for the unsettling experience of the creation of meaning and, therefore, of the unparalleled experience of beginning to *dream* his own mind into existence.

The strength of a new intuition may disquiet us into renouncing beliefs and values and thoughts possibly determining many of our key choices in life. But the strength of passion is the one factor deciding us to closely follow behind the new unknown wonder, or its weakness, leading us to bow out of it into neglect and indifference. The core of our lives is believed to essentially hinge on our loyalty to the impact of wonder enkindled in us by the unsettling force of the mystery of mother's "beauty" as it is believed to wound us into life by what Meltzer called the *dazzle of the sunrise* (cf. Meltzer & Williams 1988, pp. 28–29).

6 Understanding and the Selected Fact

In *Learning from Experience* (1962, pp. 72–73), Bion introduced Poincaré's concept of *selected fact* and read, in Poincaré's description of the concept, the rough structure of the dynamic of Melanie Klein's PS↔D.

Bion proposed, however, two fundamentally different rereadings of Poincaré's concept, in 1962, p. 73, and 1992, p. 252: "The selected fact is the name of an emotional experience, the emotional experience of a sense of discovery of coherence" (Bion 1962, p. 73). In this previous chapter, however, I suggested converting Bion's reading of *selected fact* into the creation of a new passionate link to the world (cf. Chapters 7 and 17). I would now suggest an alternative to the usual meaning of *understanding* seeing it the name of the emotional experience of the creation of a new passionate link to the world.

This conversion of persecutory experiences into the marvellous emotional experience of the discovery of meaning and, therefore, in further *dreaming* our own mind into an ever enhanced existence is now seen as yet another alternative meaning for the idea of *understanding*. In other words, each single new step in *dreaming* our own mind into a more inspiring existence is the meaning I now propose for the term *understanding*. As often suggested before, the heart of this experience is the unsettling experience of the creation of meaning, this being now, in this new light, the epitome of understanding.

Bion's kindly suggesting Grotstein to try not to understand is a most inspiring voice favouring entrusting *dreaming* with the task of guiding us through the unending enigmas and mysteries weaving the human mind, or again, *being* the human mind. Bion's gentle plea to Grotstein also conveys to him how crucial it now seems to Bion peopling the human mind and the clinic hour with inspiring uncertainties as our best guiding light. But his gentle appeal also seems an invitation to us all to grope our uncertain ways along the untested hope of nearing the truth of psychic reality by trying to closely read the sense of mystery as the essential quality of the human mind being now better guided by the strength of passion.

7 "Understanding as Seeing the Beauty"

An illuminating instance of this profound shift of direction in seeing the human mind as well as the meaning of *being human* is Meltzer's insight into the psychical meaning of understanding: "Understanding and 'seeing the beauty' are indistinguishable" (Donald Meltzer 1987, p. 560). As psychical phenomena, *understanding* and *seeing the beauty* are indistinguishable. And it is in this sense that *understanding* is seen as a revelation. And yet it is exactly in this same sense that *understanding* is seen as a paradigmatic experience of intimacy.

This is exactly what I mean, in this book, by *understanding* in each single clinic hour as well as in researching into the human mind.

8 On "Understanding as Seeing the Beauty" and the Depth of the Transference and the Counter-transference – A Note

Meltzer's insight into the psychical meaning of understanding is believed to profoundly change the way we closely read both the transference and the counter-transference. We are now believed to *dream* both into new aesthetic experiences as distinctive evidence of having further ripening both. This experience, together with the experience of having created a new passionate link to the word, are believed to deepen the meaning of intimacy. Furthermore, seeing *understanding* as an essentially aesthetic experience is believed to ripen our listening into *hearing* both the analysand's many voices as well as the many voices of our own internal characters. The music of these internal characters' voices may soon be *heard* with a depth unknown to us before and indeed also unknown to the analysand in his going through *the concrete experience of a thinking mind in the room* as the main element of the setting. In this experience, when the analyst's *hearing* is converted into aesthetic experiences in both the analysand and the analyst, this is when the analysand may perhaps feel closer to the unique experience of *being heard* by the loving mother, the epitome of intimacy being, as always in this book, the unique emotional experience of further *dreaming* our own mind into existence which always implies the unsettling emotional experience of the creation of meaning. This is why changes of the quality of our *hearing* are believed to invite deeper levels of transference into the room.

The experience of the truth of "seeing the beauty" as the fundamental psychical meaning of understanding is believed to deeply change the atmosphere in the consulting room. Again, this view of *understanding* further illuminates the meaning of *being human*, adding a deep sense of kindness as a silent guiding light along virtually every clinical hour. Inevitably also, this way of experiencing things pulsating in the room deepens the truth of the analyst's interpretations as well as the music of the analyst' voice, which he couches them into.

Taking *understanding* and *seeing the beauty* to be psychically indistinguishable is a real gift.

Note

1 Grotstein 1990, personal communication, cited in Ogden 1997, p. 208.

Chapter 23

Knowledge as a Privileged Path to Intimacy

Plato seems to have no parallel in having enriched history with such illuminating and insightful questions. Among such hosts of illuminating others, this still stands today for both its simplicity and yet unyielding quality: *what is knowledge*? As so often both before and after, Plato gently asked Socrates to generously share with us all not only the question itself but his own puzzling thought about it:

> SOCRATES Well now, the point I have difficulty with, and cannot find an adequate grasp of in myself, is just this: what, exactly, knowledge really is? So can we put it into words? What do you all say? Which of us is going to be first to speak? . . . Why don't any of you say anything?
>
> Plato, *Theaetetus* 145c-146a[1]

1 "Why Don't Any of You Say Anything?"

Many contemporary philosophers seem to converge on that two and a half millennia of philosophical investigations around Socrates' key question, which still has not yet had much brighter light shed on it beyond what Plato has asked Socrates' *Theaetetus* to kindly offer history. Can we ever come to know what knowledge is? Can we *ever* find an answer to Socrates' question? How many different meanings may "I know" I have?

Puzzlingly, this much elusive word travels in so many of our thoughts everywhere we go carrying with it disconcertingly many different meanings and playing disconcertingly many different roles and functions. It seems pivotal in our relationship with ourselves and with the world. It is everywhere in the minutes of our days. We are constantly calling it back to all sorts of both reflected and unreflected purposes, both acknowledging

DOI: 10.4324/9781003375159-26

and unacknowledging how often we ask its assistance. And yet Socrates' question "Why don't any of you say anything?" can still be heard today being puzzlingly greeted basically by the same silence as Socrates was two and a half thousand years ago.

2 "What, Exactly, Knowledge Really Is"

Freud evidently revered knowledge. He infused it with promise, reassurance and pride. He heard it as his most respected oracle. Imprudently, Freud consulted knowledge as his most trusted guide all along the many unsafe and winding ways which he was the first ever to dare treading along. He went on even to offer knowledge of the role in the foundational structure of psychoanalysis. Unfortunately, however, Freud never gave much of his time and of his genius to closely investigate the view of knowledge that he inherited from the eighteenth-century scientific way of thinking.[2] Knowledge may be a friend and may be a foe. It may act as a master and as an executer. It may be invoked to crucially assist creation and to crucially assist destruction. Both forms speak of the meaning of *being human*.

In this chapter, I will take an odd angle of approach to Socrates' famously grudging question. This angle of approach endeavours to closely follow the question, what is the psychical meaning of knowledge? Or to put it in perhaps clearer words: what exactly is it that, at the level of psychic reality, we are in the habit of calling *knowledge*? To *know* is taken in this chapter as a name we give, at the conscious and colloquial level of speech, to a sequence of no one knows what processes and changes that have been worked out in either the structure or the qualities of one's psychic reality. What exact changes are, then, these?

3 "Now *I Know*"

As he first walked through the rooms of Jeu de Paume, in Paris, Bion felt both wonder and yet perplexed with what he unexpectedly found out while watching Monet's "Poppy Field":

> The painter paints a field of poppies. . . . You may see a reproduction of it – it doesn't mean a thing. If you walk into the Jeux de Paumes *(sic)* in Paris and see the painting itself, you think "I never saw a field of poppies until now; *now* I know what it looks like" – it is an emotional

experience, not a report on one. How does a great painter manage to use pigments and canvas to give countless people an idea of what a field of poppies looks like?

(Bion 1980, p. 13)

How should we exactly read Bion's claim: "*Now I know*"? What exactly does he mean by *I know*? Why *now*? What exactly is it that he *now* believes he *knows* something he did not know half an hour before having first watched Monet's painting? What exact transformations in his psychical world suddenly worked out while he was watching Monet's *Poppy Field*? What changes were these which Bion's *now* points so clearly to? Bion gave a strange name to these essentially psychical changes. He called them: *now I know*? What exact psychical changes give full substance to this odd name – *now I know*? To what exact extent does Bion's *now I know* participate in what Socrates meant by *knowledge* in his famous question *what, exactly, knowledge really is?* What exact kind of knowledge does Bion's *I know* refer to? Does he have any idea of what *exactly* he is talking about when he unreflectedly claims *now I know*? I certainly believe he does not. What exact qualities does this knowledge have? Again, the knowledge that I would believe best describes the one of Bion's *now I know* consists of the changes that his watching Monet's *Poppy Field* has worked out in either the structure or the qualities of his mind or in both. The statement *I know* is, therefore, now seen as a statement concerning the qualities of his own psychical world. Bion's claim is therefore translating psychic reality into epistemological language. If, however, Bion was asked what exact transformations were these that I am assuming were wrought in his own mind while watching Monet's great painting, he would probably not be able to offer any clear answer.

4 "Now I Know" – New Remarks

This chapter, therefore, tentatively argues that a key epistemological concept – *knowledge* – translates, at the level of conscious and colloquial language, an exceedingly complex cluster of psychical phenomena which essentially run beyond the edge of the unknown, the unknowable and the unthinkable. There are two claims in Bion's statement: "I never saw a field of poppies until now; *now* I know what it looks like." Neither claim is true, however. Nor is it true that Monet's painting has ever taught anyone how a field of poppies looks like. And it is equally evident that what Bion says he *now knows* has nothing or very little to do with a poppy field. Again, what exactly, then, is Bion talking about? What exactly is it that he claims to know although he has no means to know what exactly he believes he knows? Can we ever put it into words? Hardly, I would believe. For we now seem to hurt ourselves against a few barriers which we can neither ignore nor dodge. The transformations that seem to have occurred in Bion's psychical world while watching Monet's painting prompting him to claim *now I know* is believed to essentially run beyond the edge of the unknown, the unknowable and the unthinkable. As soon as we reach this elusive edge, we of course begin to lose our grip on language, being lost within the realm where nothing can be proved or disproved, where nothing is right or wrong and where we have a few privileged guiders along this uncharted and unchartable psychical world – where we meet the frightening experience of intimacy and the shining light of uncertainty for our best guides. We then lose sight of all the means feeding the illusion of the all-encompassing view of things, thus assuming that there are no enigmatic and mysterious elements or processes in the human mind, just like those believed, in this book, to have prompted Bion's *now I know*.

5 New Notes on the Meaning of Bion's "Now I Know"

This mysterious edge is not, however, the only barrier against which all our hopes to keep our grip on the language of facts, knowledge and understanding fall down in bits, leaving us once again lost in perplexity. For the creative strength of the unreadably complex dynamic of psychic reality is believed to *continuously dream* every psychical element into ever new, hopefully more creative elements. So in my tentative view, *now I know* is the name Bion unwittingly gave to an exceedingly complex psychical processes and changes worked out in either the structure or the qualities of his psychical world. Although this view can never be verified by any canonical means, the effects of these processes can be observed and discussed in any detail, even if, again, nothing can be either proved or disproved, and nothing can be converted into certainties. So Socrates' second question – "*So can we put it into words?*" – invites a puzzling answer.

So Bion's *dreaming* Monet's *Poppy Field* both while watching it and at any time afterwards is believed to endlessly convert it into new ideas, values, thoughts, even into new qualities of his own personality, as well as new qualities of thought. The changes operated on either the structure or the qualities of his own internal world by *dreaming* Monet's painting is believed to *be*, at the level of the psychical life, the meaning of Bion's short statement *I know*. These transformations are seen, in this chapter, to *be* both the psychical substance and life of Bion's *I know*. These transformations in both the structure and the qualities of the psychical world is exactly what, in this book, knowledge *is*.

Socrates' key question: *What, exactly, then, knowledge really is?*

6 On Knowing the Unknowable

The 2012 Nobel Prize in Physics was awarded jointly to S. Haroche and D. Wineland for the remarkable advancements they have both succeeded on research into the phenomenon of the superposition of states and the consequences for the understanding of quantum reality. In a long interview to both laureates conducted by Adam Smith, the highly gifted interviewer of the Nobel Foundation in the area of science, he asked both laureates, though very hesitatingly in the formulation of his question, carefully groping through each word he called to build his question, smiling away a fear to dare word the question whether they were both saying that it was possible that two opposite states of a particular [quantum] system could *really* exist simultaneously and even be simultaneously observed, the unuttered implication being, of course, that this would look like a blunt violation of the identity principle (also sometimes called *non*-identity principle)? Haroche quietly answered as follows:

> Superposition of states . . . cannot be observed but its effects can. It is possible to observe these superpositions in systems which become more and more complex. But the idea is that [in the quantum world] the system can be *at the same time* in two, or even in several [different] states at once, and this is very difficult to comprehend classically, but the deep meaning of it is that it can give rise to these strange interferences effects.
>
> (Haroche 2012)

I am neither prepared nor inclined to force any similarity whatsoever of the nature, the substance or the method of research between physics and psychic reality beyond this merely allusive and incidental point, common to both, in the immediate surface of the argument in this chapter: although we cannot directly observe any of these phenomena – either the superposition of quantum states or the detailed genesis of knowledge as an essentially psychical phenomenon – although, therefore, we cannot directly observe and, therefore, describe any of these phenomena, we can, in both cases, observe their effects and then try to read, in their effects, what we cannot otherwise read of their deep meaning. So Bion's "*now I know*" is the name of a revelation brought to him through *dreaming* Monet's *Poppy Field* into new qualities of his internal world the genesis of which, again, cannot possibly be directly observed, still less described, but its effects can both be observed and examined.

7 "What, Exactly, Knowledge Really Is?"

However, and again by the creative strength of the unreadably complex dynamic of psychic reality, Bion's *now I know* will itself endure continuous new changes, so hopefully, what we believed we knew at any given moment is no longer the same in the next moment. The group of psychical processes to which Bion, without having any idea in what they exactly consist of, calls "*I know*," is not always the same. At any given moment, we never know what we believe we know for we are believed to be continuously *dreaming* the very process leading to the claim *now I know* into different forms of it. This is an unending process, except if this most extraordinary and mysterious creative process is severely hindered by pathology, that is, by any nightmaring processes.

Opening yet another wide window over the immense complexity and the awestruck beauty of the human mind, I would briefly recall that perceptions are seen in this book to result from *dreaming* sensorial excitations into new psychical elements now endowed with a new life of their own in the mind. But in this new condition, perceptions are themselves continuously *dreamed* into ever new, hopefully more creative psychical elements. In this tentative light, we seem allowed to take a brief glimpse of the sea of complexities as times so removed by our inattentive eyes, implied in Bion's *now I know* what a poppy field looks like. It is in this sense that *knowledge* is a fundamentally creative psychical event.

If this view of knowledge invites any plausibility, knowledge should be seen as a celebration of mother's reverie and another voice of gratitude to the mother. If – again – knowledge can essentially be seen as a creative transformation of either some aspects of the structure, the qualities of the human mind, or of both, there is fundamental quality in every new step in knowing: a deepening of the experience of intimacy with what became known. The measure of the depth of knowledge is given by the depth of experience of intimacy with what *now I know*. The deeper the experience of intimacy, the less we can describe it, and yet the more visible its effects as consequences of all that changes in our internal world and our personality should become. Knowledge is believed to make us experience intimacy as a revelation.

The continuous discovery of the meaning of intimacy as a key guiding light to the meaning of grow, so often holding us in amazement and often in deeper perplexity, may also lead us, perhaps even compel us to re-examine the way in which we live our lives. This is how *knowledge* is treasured: as a privileged way to emotional experience of intimacy as a revelation.

8 Bion's Mysterious Little Word "Now"

What exactly is it that lives behind Bion's little mysterious word *now*? In my tentative understanding, this little *now* carries – though hiddenly – Bion's whole process of *dreaming* Monet's painting until it touches him as a revelation. The revelation is not, however, *directly* brought to him by the painting but by his *dreaming* the painting into all the unending purely psychical transformations. The revelation is therefore given to him by his *dreaming* the object, not from the object. This seems to be the strength and complexity of the life unprotrudingly pulsating behind Bion's enigmatic little word *now*. We have all to find our own unending way walking us from curiosity to the momentous emotional experience of intimacy and revelation. What most stirs us into *dreaming* our way from neglect and indifference to curiosity and to this momentous emotional experience is believed in this book to be the strength of passion. The deeper the passion, the less we can put it into words, and the less we are driven to do it, and the more it comes out in the quality of our *hearing* as well as in the music of our voice, the deeper our kindness.

Moreover, this emotional experience can itself be endlessly ripened into inspiration, as well as into an ever deeper insight into the meaning of things and, in particular, into the meaning of *being human*. This seems a very long and again frighteningly fragile way maturing curiosity into interest, and interest into fascination and awestruck experience, both hopefully being endlessly ripened into unending passion. This would seem the core of maturity, a key instance of which may take the crucial form of the experience of knowledge, within which all these qualities would then be supposed to live.

It is in this sense, then, that knowledge is seen in this chapter a particularly privileged way to the unsettling experience of intimacy as a revelation. This is also how *knowledge* is treasured: as a privileged way to intimacy.

No shade of control and power live in this sense of knowledge.

This tentative view implies that every piece of knowledge is an exceedingly complex psychical event. In light of this tentative understanding, this is why Socrates' key question may hardly find an answer couched into the language that Freud privileged as the language of psychoanalysis, that is, the language of direct observation, description, argument, of what is right and wrong, prove and disprove; the language of measure, of beginning and end, of parts and of whole, of whole encompassing knowledge of anything whatsoever related to the human mind; the language of logic, of reason, of argument.

In this book, *knowledge* is seen as a celebration of the unique privilege of mother's reverie and of the introjection of her qualities. It is a main road walking us to the unending discovery of the puzzling mystery of things.

This is what knowledge is about in this book.

Notes

1 Plato, *Theaetetus*. Trans. J. McDowell. Oxford: Clarendon Press, 1999.
2 And not from the nineteenth century scientific thought as it is sometimes inaccurately claimed.

Chapter 24

Passion and the Wonder of Unmeasure

1 Introduction

O'Shaughnessy's line stands as a warning to us all: "Each patient has a point beyond which he does not extend his K" (O'Shaughnessy 1981, p. 187). Her line carries an undertone of an ongoing drama: that patients and analysts are equally promised to watch, helplessly, the strength of passion inescapably ebbing away in themselves. And yet *passion* is believed in this book to be what most wounds us all into creativity. Furthermore, passion is also believed to be a key response to fascination and wonder, and it is what keeps the human mind shining with life. It is seen, in this book, a foundational emotion of the human mind, and equally central in our understanding of the meaning of *being human*.

Upsettingly, however, O'Shaughnessy's line condemns the patient – every patient – to such sombre fate, even while he is still enjoying the privilege of the analyst's diligent assistance.

Exactly the same drama, however, is seen, in the same eyes, to heavily weigh upon the analyst himself and possibly on every one of us all along the unrecognized sombre course of our lives. So O'Shaughnessy's line is now seen to overbrim its immediate area of focus – the patient – and spread a wide gloomy shade over the fate of us all.

2 On the Experience of Unmeasure – A Preliminary Note

I will now go back to O'Shaughnessy's flat claim that opened this chapter: "Each patient has a point beyond which he does not extend his K" (cf. above). Quite unwittingly, therefore, O'Shaughnessy's claim carries a drama which is here argued to upsettingly border on tragedy. And

DOI: 10.4324/9781003375159-27

yet O'Shaughnessy does not seem touched by the dramatic depth of her unstirred claim.

To stop extending one's K-link, to put it in O'Shaughnessy's words, is seen in this book as a major clinical event. It should draw the analyst's dedicated concern since it may result from repeatedly nightmaring the awestruck experience of mother's reverie and specially the unsettling experience of the creation of meaning as a foundational experience of the human mind and one of the most crucial pieces in the unending process of introjecting the qualities of mother's reverie. I would recall that the emotional experience of the creation of meaning is seen in this book a precious source of the discovery of intimacy and a key way in the experience of thought as a revelation.

Furthermore, to at times go through the experience of stop feeling lost in both perplexity and awe before the unending enigmas and mysteries tightly weaving the human mind, even *being* what is most crucial in the human mind may witness the ongoing nightmaring processes at work right before the unseeing analyst.

Surprisingly, however, O'Shaughnessy's line seems to take the limit of K-link as a plain fact she routinely meets, undisturbed, in her consulting room – a fate she believes that she cannot oppose, nor indeed seems to feel the urgency to oppose. Nor does she allow a word of concern about such sad fate. If, however, this is how an analysis should end, something may perhaps have to be re-examined. As often pointed out before, this book takes the creative strength of the unreadably complex dynamic of psychic reality and in particular the gradual growing vitality of passion as two of the most extraordinary qualities of the human mind and two of the most crucial purposes and hopes of any analysis for both the analysand and the analyst himself.

The previous chapter argued that knowledge is a privileged way leading us to the unending discovery of the mystery of intimacy. The mystery of intimacy is believed to be born from the marvel of introjecting mother's *dreaming* both her foetus' and infant's emotional experiences of being helplessly lost into the wonder of life and thought and, particularly, again, into the unsettling experience of the creation of meaning. As we introject the main qualities of mother's reverie, crucially including, of course, the overwhelming impact of her passion for her baby, may wound us into the discovery of passion as a key guiding light for life and our most inspired teacher of the wonderful discovery of unmeasure seen in this book as yet another of the most marvellous qualities of the human mind.

Psychoanalysis is about passion and its failure, not about symptoms. The epitome of pathology is seen in this book to be what in us severely damages our sweeping drive to keep making life and the world glittering with ever new insight and meaning and destroy the capacity for endowing things with the shining experience of awe and mystery. How then an analyst, who had never been stormed by passion and fascination for the discovery of the marvel of mental life and the awestruck mystery of things can ever be prepared to walk with his analysand along the long winding road back to passion, fascination and joy? How actively may analysts work on ending the analysand's K-link? How busy analysts can often be in promoting the analysand's neglect and indifference before the unending marvels of his own mental life, thus assisting him in screening away from his own eyes the disaster of living in neglect and indifference about the unending marvel of the human mind and in the desperate gratifications of smugness and the many disorders resulting from joining the group? How often has the analyst's own neglect and indifference before the marvel of his own mind showed the analysand the large way to compromise and to learn to gradually slip into the tragedy of living an unpassionate life, drowned in neglect and indifference?

3 On Passion and the Truth of Analysis

O'Shaughnessy's claim appears to burden the analysand with this gloomy promise, leaving the analyst's responsibility for the analysand to end his analysis on such poor key. He may have never succeeded to rebirthed his own possibly damaged passionate links to the world, nor, of course, the strength of his passionate drive to make life and the world glittering with creative insight and meaning. At the outset of his analysis, they may have both been left behind lost in bits scattered all along the many silenced, perhaps often hurtful disillusionments with his own analysis, with his analyst so incapable of passion. Perhaps the first, and in some ways more hurtful source of this continuous disillusionment comes right to the analysand from the analyst's dull, discoloured, unmusical voice, unmistakably speaking for his own dull, discoloured mind. One would expect analysis to come as a lasting rewarding experience of bringing back to life the analysand's shattered passionate drive to make life and the world again glittering with creative insight and meaning. O'Shaughnessy's line seems to leave the analyst's responsibility for such sad end of analysis entirely outside the stage of this drama. How vital and how profound is the analyst's own passionate response to the world as a key condition for the depth, even the truth of every analysis? What was the exact extent of the analyst's responsibility in watching, uncomprehending, his analysand gradually disbelieving life? How often the analyst himself lectures the analysand in both direct and indirect ways on how best should he wither away his own passionate response to life and the world by being himself so incapable of feeling lost in perplexity and wonder before the mysteries glittering with life within the human mind? How withdrawn from any state of mind nearing awe and passion are so many analysts? How deprived of passion, how taken by neglect and indifference before the disconcerting marvel of the human mind? When, in his own analysis, even in his own life has the analyst himself ended his own K-link, to keep it closer to O'Shaughnessy's words? Has he ever had it? Has the analyst ever been wounded by the strength of passion and the unsettling experience of the creation of meaning? If he has never been swept away by any of these foundational experiences of the human mind or has shied away from it in pain and cowardice, gradually degrading it into both neglect and indifference, how may he ever share it with his analysand? How could the strength of passion and his love for the shining light of uncertainty be possibly heard by the analysand's internal characters in the music of the analyst's voice? How would he share with his analysand his own experience of being drown in wonder and passion before the unending enigmas so tightly weaving the human mind? How can he possibly impart to his patient his profound thoughts on the meaning of *being human* and, therefore also, his deep sense of *respect* to him? How could all these emotional experiences ever enrich and crucially mould the qualities of his listening *dreaming* it into the depth of his *hearing*? How could the analyst ever succeed in profoundly transforming the dull music of his dull voice he couches his interpretations into? How would it ever be possible for the sweeping emotions of awe and wonder be heard in the atmosphere of his consulting room? When the patient's end of K, in O'Shaughnessy's words, comes from the chair rather than from the couch, how can the experience of intimacy as a privileged guiding light all through the sea of unknowns that most clinical hours are so full of still guide us in every session?

4 Destruction of the Delight in Dreaming

I hardly believe that an analysand can recover, in the course of his analysis, from the damage inflicted upon him by an analyst who has himself lost contact with his own experience of passion and awe about the unending marvels pulsating in the human mind, or has never been deeply touched by such crucial emotional experiences. How, then, can his lost feeling of awe for the creation of meaning ever be heard vibrating in and modulating the music of his voice all along the clinical hours? How deeply damaging for the analysand is the disheartening dullness of the analyst? What a lie is an analysis ruled by an analyst whose internal characters are no longer capable of sharing with the analysand the wounding beauty of introjecting the qualities of mother's reverie, the depth and the inspiring impact of his perplexity and his awe. How dishearteningly dull is an analyst who has never been touched by the unsettling experience of the creation of meaning as well as by the shining light of uncertainty. How can he share with the analysand the truth of his feeling drowned in both perplexity and wonder, drowned in the enigmas he is constantly meeting with as the clock gratifies him by ticking away the torture of yet another lifeless session? How offensive, really, is the analyst's smugness ringing in the analyst's untruthful voice lecturing patients and colleagues alike on the sweeping strength of K-link that they have never been touched by, resounding in the ear of those who have trusted him in the hope of seeing their own failing access to the unique experience of the discovery of thought and of the truth of intimacy redressing him back to life. How strikingly clear it may often sound in the analysand's ear the barren music of the analyst's voice who might have repeatedly nightmared his own passion for the inspiring unthinkability of the enigmas peopling the human mind. This might perhaps have led the analyst to dull away the possibility for the analysand to discover the delight in *dreaming* facts and feelings into the marvel of converting conscious and rational material into new *dreams*. One would expect analysts to attempt to closely read the evidence of nightmaring processes at work in themselves, leading them into the drama of neglect and indifference about the unending enigmas and marvels the human mind is teeming with. For such nightmaring processes will certainly be heard by the analysand's earliest ear in the music of their voices and in the untrue of the mother's feelings about her foetus and the infant. This being a key way by which the analyst may severely hinder the analysand's way back to passion, fascination and joy, a key evidence of which may surface in the clinic hour in the form of the analysand's curving his K-link down into lowering the values of everything and ending himself in the sadness of neglect and indifference instead of meeting in joy the passionate desire to keep growing his K-link unendingly, as well as the delight of the unmeasure.

And yet a coward silence travels, undisturbed, all through the psycho-analytical literature about all this and particularly about passion.

Neglect and indifference about all that would reasonably invite awe and a sense of wonder should, I think, be taken as evidence of an ongoing inner catastrophe being heard from the chair. I would tentatively see it as one of the most serious disorders one may come to face in the consulting room.

Puzzlingly, O'Shaughnessy's line itself sounds as an unruffled confirmation of this ongoing drama in psychoanalysis.

5 The Tragedy of Lowering the Passion

I now recall Meltzer's crucial remark made in the course of a supervision session:

> If she lowers the passion, she lowers the value of everything, and then abandonment is so much easier – to abandon this, to abandon that, if their value has been brought down. So I think that it is very important to bring out how it comes about that she is able to lower the value of the analysis, and then just vomit it out, lose the session, lose the babies.
>
> (Meltzer in: Monteiro 2019, pp. 57–58)

In these concrete circumstances, losing the babies is invoked as a metaphor for lowering the value of all that is more precious for her, that is, by suddenly growing neglectful and indifferent about what she should care more dearly and lovingly for, now suddenly abandoning them, after having lowered her passion and, therefore, the value of everything.

The key link between lowering the values "and then abandonment is so much easier" seems to lie in the roots of countless tragedies that travel so often so inconspicuously throughout the history of our internal life. Lowering of passion – perhaps any concrete instance of lowering the passion – would seem to speak of a disturbance, now re-emerging in the transference, of the unending process of introjecting the qualities of mother's reverie, particularly her boundless passion for her foetus and her baby. As suggested before, I have always implied in this book that introjecting the qualities of mother's reverie crucially involves keeping *dreaming* these qualities into ever new qualities of one's internal characters or of the personality or further ripen those already active, possibly including the qualities of the structure of our mind. Lowering the passion, Meltzer chillingly claims, implies lowering all values. Once this crucial link to mother's passion grows lastingly disturbed, our link to all the other values may as well be affected. This understanding sends a new light on the psychical genesis and meaning of values and the role of mother's passion and the capacity for introjecting it in the creation of values. The vitality of the creative strength of the unreadably complex dynamic of psychic reality, the sense of gratitude, of generosity, of loyalty, of faithfulness, of courage, of forbearance, dignity, tolerance – all these key values seem to crucially speak of this double role of passion but also as a celebration of gratitude. A deep sense of dignity is a critically important piece of the setting.

By lowering the passion, the vitality of the *dreaming functions* entrusted with continuously bringing our own mind into all its potentially unending qualities will, of course, also be disturbed. Hence Meltzer's urgency to investigate what exactly has disturbed the transference to the point of leading her to lower the passion.

What is the name of the severe symptom showing itself in the form of lowering the passion? How deeply concerned about this critically degrading form of mental life has psychoanalysis been? How extensively has psychoanalysis investigated into it? How often the phenomenology of such key deprivation seems to walk along the stage of the clinic hour right before the analyst's uncomprehending eyes? I am not aware that living untouched by passion, seen in this book as such an alarming condition, has ever been given a key place in the roster of mental disorders or, indeed, ever attracted the concern of psychoanalysis. Why, indeed, the silence about passion in the countless pages of the psychoanalytic literature, the countless hours in the conference rooms and, certainly far more upsetting, in the countless clinical hours? To the best of my recollection, the mental disaster consisting of allowing the dearth of passion to largely colour one's life has never yet been extensively researched into in psychoanalysis.

What condition is this that sees us quite unconcerned about values and yet going on living our lives neither disturbed nor even aware of this odd mental state? How seriously is this unfortunate disorder approached in everyday consulting room?

7 The Wonder of Unmeasure

As often suggested in this book before, the human mind is believed to continuously *dream* itself into its awestruck structure, its ever-changing qualities and its defeatingly complex workings. It has also been suggested that the creative strength of the unreadably complex dynamic of psychic reality is fundamentally governed by *dreaming functions*. This view makes the human mind unparalleled among all self-generating systems. It has often been suggested all along this book that the *dreaming functions* are believed to unendingly convert virtually every psychical element into ever new, hopefully more creative new psychical elements and even into ever new qualities of the personality. But how unendingly, exactly? What exactly is this "ever"? What exactly is the meaning of this disconcerting, defying little word "limits"? Where are the limits of the human mind and of the creative strength of the unreadably complex dynamic of psychic reality? Are these limits, indeed, anywhere? Where, exactly? What are the limits for the enhancing qualities of the human mind? Where exactly are the limits for the enhancement of the qualities of the structure of the human mind? Are there any final limits for the creative strength of the unreadably complex dynamic of psychic reality other than those generated by pathology? It has also been suggested in this book that limits may themselves be endlessly *dreamed* into ever new psychical elements, new ideas, perhaps more inspiring insights, deeper ways of *hearing*, perhaps emerging in the form of new voices of internal characters. I also believe, however, that behind the *dreaming* of limit into so many new qualities stands the strength of passion – of unending passion, as yet another voice of gratitude to mother's own passion and the mystery of her *dreaming* her foetus' and her infant's shattering emotional experiences into the experience of the creation of meaning as well as of their own thought.

What, however, are the limits of passion sparked by the experience of awe? What are the limits we are fated to meet with to our capacity for passion seen in this book as the main source of the compelling drive to endlessly *re-dream* the introjected qualities of mother's reverie and of awe and awe-inspiring new emotional experiences? Is there any limits to the experience of awe? Other than pathology, what else could these limits be? In what form may they emerge? What may determine them? Meltzer claimed that there are no limits to the enhancement of ever new qualities of the internal characters and, therefore also, of the personality (cf. 1973, p. 80). The human mind is therefore believed to *dream* all the limits that itself creates into new experiences of unmeasure. Stirred by passion, the creative strength of *dreaming functions* are therefore believed to challenge the idea of measure.

8 The Human Mind as the Celebration of Unmeasure

The idea of limits has tacitly been assumed to be inherent in mental processes. This undiscussed assumption is, however, tentatively seen in this book as yet another upshot of our nightmaring the idea of the human mind. For passion, stirring the cluster of the *dreaming functions* that are believed to govern the creative strength of the unreadably complex dynamic of psychic life, is believed to endow this cluster of psychical functions with the capacity for ever *dreaming* the experience of limit into new qualities of the mind. One of these new qualities is a brighter vision of passion.

Meltzer argues that a "successful analysis" ensures the analysand the capacity to endlessly enrich the qualities of his internal characters and endlessly create new ones (cf. 1973, pp. 74–80). One of these new qualities, I strongly believe, consists in endowing the role of passion in the human mind with a new vision and a new strength. *Dreaming* limits into the wonder of the experience of unmeasure is a privileged way into the unsettling mystery of the experience of intimacy.

One of the most fundamental responsibilities of psychoanalysis is to reveal to all of us yet another awe-inspiring quality of the human mind: of being the celebration of unmeasure.

Chapter 25

The Misfortune of Explanation

1 Introduction

The urge to explain things away often speaks of the paranoid-schizoid urge to distribute the burden of blame to "others" (cf. Meltzer 1986, p. 90). As, however, we move from paranoid-schizoid into depressive position, or to formulate it into a different language, as we allow our internal characters to ripen, and gradually, we ourselves become more capable of entrusting them with the task of enhancing the qualities of our personality, they may hopefully become better prepared to work out the conversion of split and persecutory elements into more integrated and creative others. This both crucial and unending converting process, believed in this book to enjoy the key hand of passion as a fundamental stirring factor and guide, allows us new insights into our ungrateful, omnipotent and egocentric demands on the internal mother, being deeply untouched by and neglectful of the qualities of her reverie and, in particular, uncaring of the treasure of mother's passion. Ingratitude seems both forced by split and persecutory elements. The urge to explain as a defence against paranoid-schizoid unconscious phantasies and experiences, as a defence against having nightmared insights and emotions that we have managed to remain unaware of, may, however, eventually be *dreamed* in the session into some new steps into the awestruck experience of intimacy as well as into the discovery of uncertainty as an unending source of inspiration. This defence is believed to go on all the time during the clinic hour. It may be of assistance if the analyst succeeds, in the session, to *dream* some of these nightmares elements through his way of *hearing* which may immediately recreate the experience of intimacy with the analysand by which we may restore the link between his own internal characters and those of the analyst's.

DOI: 10.4324/9781003375159-28

We may often feel the urge to explain things away more acutely. This may emerge when we meet what perhaps can least be explained, namely, the unending enigmas and mysteries continuously pulsating within the human mind, or more accurately, *being* themselves the essence of the human mind. The more we feel drowned in the sea of unknowns, unknowables and unthinkables that the human mind is believed to be woven by, the more we may tend to recoil from this unsettling experience finding refuge in explaining the world away.

But as we resist the drive, yet another extraordinary quality of the human mind may begin to emerge: as we keep *dreaming* split and persecutory elements into new hopefully more creative psychical elements, we may just be rewriting the edges of the unknown, the unknowable and the unthinkable a little farther away from what we have succeeded to have it.

I briefly recall Bion's crucial note concerning one of his two views of the *selected fact*:

> The selected fact is a discovery made by the patient . . . and is *the* tool by which he ensures the constant progression, the very essence of learning and therefore of growing. This is represented by the sequence: paranoid-schizoid position, selected fact (precipitating coherence of the elements of the paranoid-schizoid position) ushering in the depressive position, which then *instantaneously* reveals yet other vaster areas of hitherto unrelated elements belonging to domains of the paranoid-schizoid position which were previously unrevealed and unsuspected. . . . The *selected fact* then is an essential element in the process of discovery.
>
> (Bion 1992, p. 252; cf. Chapter 17 "The mysterious dynamic of selected fact")

By allowing *dreaming functions* to re-create our experiences of knowledge, understanding and thinking and re-drawing their edges beyond which all that is interesting in the human mind is believed to pulsate, we are led to redefine reality, perhaps moving closer to experiencing the mystery of things and, perhaps once again, to change the ways we live our lives.

2 The Drama of the Simplification of Enigmas

If the stupidity of smugness is ever allowed to become a third party in the room which I believe is indeed often the case, it may severely impair the analyst's ear by seriously disturbing the link between him and his own internal characters. The disturbance of these key links may make the analyst unprepared to closely follow the music of the analysand's many voices. Smugness is believed to prevent us from entrusting our own internal characters with the critically important task of governing the hour and closely following its key thread. We would not be prepared or indeed ever inclined to hand the ruling of the hour to our own internal characters. Trusting the internal characters' sensitivity and hopefully inspiring strength is an endless task both stirred and guided by the strength of passion and love once again in gratitude to mother's reverie. The analyst's inability to carefully follow the music of the analysand's many voices may seriously disturb the development of the transference to any promising depth. It is a permanent threat to the analysis. I believe that the analyst's smugness may invite the analysand to both carefully watch – and carefully choke – the truth of the transference at every one of its deepest levels. The earlier parts of the analysand's personality can never trust an unhearing mother, still less a compulsory lecturing mother. I do not believe the truth of the transference in which the analyst's smugness clogs up his ways to *hearing* the music of the analysand's voices at the earliest levels of his relationship with the mother.

Furthermore, smugness makes it impossible to touch, even remotely, the experience of the enigma and of the mystery, still less the sweeping fascination of hinting, even if only tangentially, that the core of the human mind pulsates with enigmas and mysteries forming, once again, all that is essential in the human mind. How could the analyst ever *hear* all the unending nuances of the analysand's many voices and, in particular, be touched by the foetus' and the infant's levels of transference if he himself has never had access to the experience of mystery?

I would believe that what ensures symptoms their value in assisting the analyst is what in them lends a voice to what in us all – analysands and analysts alike – is not ineffable. What in us remains unmoved by the unending discovery of the mystery of things, of what in us still remain untouched by passion is what symptoms lend a voice to. Symptoms as privileged harbingers of what in us cannot comprehend the unapprehensible, of what makes us unstirred by the unsettling experience of intimacy, by the gratitude for the shining light of uncertainty. This seems where mostly lie the key value of symptoms.

Explanations in psychoanalysis are believed to be assaults prompted by both envy and hatred on the awe-inspiring complexity of the beauty of the mystery of mother's inside here epitomized by mother's reverie. The core of the strategy commanding these destructive assaults that we use to call *explanations* seems to consist in forcing the "ineffable" into the condition of being describable and immediately understandable, thus forcing one of the most crucial qualities of communication between the foetus and the infant and their awed and *dreaming* mother under the easy grip of the explainer. The strategy enables the explainer to proudly share with his audience the wreck of the hated enigmas and mysteries.

These unfortunate "explanations" are believed to resort to the brutality of certainties seen here as nightmared insights and *dreams* degrading the preciousness of logic, of reason, of the beauty of an argument so often leading us to the marvellous experience of light.

The only creative "explanations" in psychoanalysis are believed to be those authored by one's internal characters creating new experiences of meaning in both the analysand and the analyst by which they further enhance the marvel of the experience of intimacy. These "explanations" are believed to create, in both the analysand and the analyst, new passionate links to the world.

Chapter 26

"Thinking With Passion Is the Unconscious Thing"[1]

1 Language as a Carrier of Dreams

The complexities that await us all on the other side of the fragile, continuously wavering line drawn between conscious and unconscious, threatens our capacity for always taming verbal thought into readability. What does much to put each word within context ensuring each of them its share of meaning is, I believe, a particularly important quality of the contact-barrier. Ensuring each word its own share of meaning seems to imply continuously preventing both syntax and semantics from growing disorderly. This is just yet another prodigy of the human mind that one's unfocused eye is unprepared to read continuously at work. As so many others, this extraordinary operative process is believed to be continuously carried out by the contact-barrier. Although I have carefully examined before Bion's theory of contact-barrier (cf. chapters 2, 3, 4, 6, 7, 8 and 15), I have not yet explicitly focused on any of the psychical enigmas inherent in the immensely complex psychical processes of language in which Bion's theory of contact-barrier seems to have the key hand in. And yet I believe that the contact-barrier is a key guardian of the possibility of language and an equally important factor in ensuring the possibility of its potentially unlimited development. The contact-barrier shows us the prodigy of gradually and yet unendingly endowing virtually each word with a life of its own, imparting each one with a complex soul, thus making semantics a realm of beautiful uncertainty and yet an inexhaustible source of inspiration and evocation.

So again the moment we attempt to cross the line both dividing and yet continuously connecting sense data and the psychical as we are continuously doing, our grip on words grows alarmingly elusive and uncertain while, at the same time, we surprisingly watch them maturing into their

DOI: 10.4324/9781003375159-29

new condition of marvellous sources of new thoughts. This extraordinary quality of the human mind makes it possible for us to lend words countless thoughts. I again return to Shelley, meeting in one of his lines already known to this book an evocative voice for what I was struggling to mean: "a single word even may be a spark of inextinguishable thought" (Shelley 1821, Harvard 10; Oxford p. 680). A single word even may be a spark of countless inextinguishable thoughts. The workings of the contact-barrier suggests that the idea of a dividing line separating conscious and unconscious should perhaps better be replaced by the idea of an interface continuously woven by the *dreaming functions* operating the contact-barrier, or as I often suggested before, *being* the contact-barrier.

Very soon, however, this interface drowns us all in unreadable complexities. In a way, the contact-barrier *is* the structure and the dynamic of this interface. As it was suggested before, however, soon the contact-barrier hands itself over to the creative strength of the unreadably complex dynamic of psychic reality, becoming a key piece of it, embedded in it, as it were, thus entrusting this extraordinary dynamic with its own continuous work. The contact-barrier may now, therefore, be seen as integral to this extremely powerful creative dynamic, already seen before as one of the most extraordinary qualities of the human mind.

The contact-barrier is therefore believed to crucially assist imparting meaning to grammar, or more precisely, to ask grammar to carefully help us reading into words and sentences many of the marvellous workings of the human mind.

I again return to Shelley though this time in his seeing poets as the "[authors of] the words which express what they understand not" (Shelley 1821a, Harvard p. 48; and Shelley 1821b, Oxford p. 701). Shelley's line hints at how words may be matured into autonomous entities, endowed with a life of their own, gifted with the creative power of making them into *dreaming* psychical elements, showing us what understanding is no longer capable of doing.

2 Words and Mother's Love

By continuously *dreaming* elements newly presented to the mind of whatever nature into new psychical elements, we see these new elements inviting words to name them. Not only words are, then, continuously summoned to play their full roles, but the rules of grammar are also invited to weave the words together into sentences so that the world of emotions, unconscious phantasies and thoughts that words soon begin to be peopled by, gradually emerge as key carriers of meaning, as endless harbingers of new meanings, even as ever new messengers. For as long as we keep *dreaming* these words and sentences into gifted harbingers of ever richer meaning, they become crucial in assisting us to keep making life and the world glittering with insight and meaning.

However, words and sentences cannot in themselves always do very much to carry meaning. Still less can we count on them alone to continuously create a rich, endlessly nuanced meaning, if they are not enriched by the music we so often ask words and sentences to carry in either spoken or written language. The music we may succeed in persuading words and sentences to "sing" is believed to be the great carrier of meaning.

So by continuously *dreaming* words into the life of meaning we of course count on them to continuously communicate so much of our psychical world. And it is an ongoing act of love and of gratitude for mother's reverie and for the sweeping emotional experience of creativity, the epitome of which is to continuously *dream* the human mind into its own existence. Words are also privileged carriers of joy. The endlessly nuanced music of their many voices are all telling ourselves and others one's intimate stories about our own experience of mother's love, thus inviting us once again back to Bion's insight: "When the mother loves her infant, what does she do it with? . . . my impression is that her love is expressed by reverie" (Bion 1962, pp. 35–36).

3 New Qualities of the Dreaming Functions

Endowing words with meaning and therefore also with an internal life of their own, speaks, sometimes remotely, some other times directly and intensely of one's own unparalleled experience of having been brought into psychical existence by mother's unbridled passion for her foetus and her baby.

Mother's passion is seen *the* heart of her reverie. For as long as we resist the enticing gratifications of closing up our commanding grip on the mysteries pulsating in mother's reverie, words may continue to shine as pieces of both love and joy.

To *hear* the music of words – be they listened to, read, or *heard* in both one's own and others' minds in their countlessly wavering many nuances – to *hear* in them these many voices is a concrete instance of *dreaming* what we listen in the experience of meaning. And it also is a vivid expression of gratitude to mother's reverie as well as a celebration of the experience of introjecting her qualities. What we *listen* should, in this light, constantly be *dreamed* into what we gradually *hear*. We therefore *hear* the meaning of what we listen to as we *dream* it. The conversion of what we listen into words celebrates mother's reverie in the unique music of meaning. The many nuanced voices coming from the couch as well as those coming along every session from our own internal characters tentatively reacting to the former are all believed to be telling stories and struggles of our emotional experiences and unconscious phantasies and uncountable thoughts. We are, however, expected to divest the many voices both coming from the couch and the chair of much of the rubble that our own listening to them wrapped them up in by *dreaming* them into both the analysand's and the analyst's experience meaning. In other words, we have to continuously convert our listening into *hearing* (cf. Chapter 21 "What is *hearing*?").

How far, however, what we *hear* nears the core of the meaning of what the analysand has communicated to us, no one seems prepared to say. For the meaning of whatever the analysand is struggling to communicate to us, as well as of what we communicate to him in the form of a tentative interpretation, are both believed to speak of emotional experiences pulsating beyond the edge of the unknown, the unknowable and the unthinkable. Furthermore, the analyst's experience of what the analysand communicates to him, as well as the analysand's experience of what he has been offered as a tentative interpretation are also believed to be ineffable (cf. Bion 1967, p. 122; cf. Chapter 23). So here again we are lost in both perplexity and wonder, craving for the assistance of the shining light of uncertainty to guide us in the course of the clinic hour.

Nevertheless, we may still strive to closely follow Wordsworth's word as another guiding voice: "Poetry does not have to invoke a god to sanction its working: its truth . . . [is] carried live into the heart by passion" (cf. Heaney 1995, p. xviii).

4 Mother's Reverie – A Note

Bion's concept of mother's reverie is usually taken as referring to mother's capacity for dreaming her baby's too frightening and disruptive emotional experiences for him to be prepared to convert by himself alone into new, hopefully creative psychical elements. The mother is expected to do this all the time for him, formulating most of these experiences back into the foetus and the baby into a language that he can now work out by himself into new elements of both the structure and the qualities of his own mind. The emphasis has, however, always been laid on rescuing the infant from the impending threat of psychical chaos for not being able to convert his object of overwhelming emotions and terrifying experiences into new qualities of their budding self. In this chapter, however, I will focus on the creative side of mother's reverie as well as on the infant's capacity for converting it into the continuous prodigy of creating a human mind – of endlessly moulding his own mind into existence. This must be an unparalleled and yet endless experience for every one of us, even if we are puzzlingly unable to recognize it.

What exactly, however, is the cluster of psychical processes pulsating within the name of *mother's reverie*? As the process of *mother's reverie* goes on, a deluge of feelings, emotions, unconscious phantasies and thoughts pulsating in mother's mind travel into the foetus and the baby inevitably crowding their minds. The way the mother carries her foetus as she moves – her sweet and dancing and gracious movements are hued by her passion for her baby and her feeling in awe with him. All the qualities of the way she moves must tell her foetus how passionate and in awe she feels about him. The qualities of the way she moves must leave a profound imprinting in his mind and already let him "learn by experience" what it really means *being contained*. Just like mother's tense and anxious and harsh way of carrying her foetus tells him how desperate or frightened or in hate she is, all this being as projected into him. Exactly the same should be said concerning the infinitely nuanced music of her voice. What a host of mother's qualities travel into the foetus and the infant as she *dreams* her baby's unthinkable frights? How is he going to gradually discover the experience of unmeasure without mother's close assistance to dream for him the disruptive strength of her own passion and her potentially unsettling feelings of awe and fascination for him into some creative new psychical elements, even including some new psychical functions. What is the fate of all that pulsates within the mysterious term *mother's reverie* traveling into baby through the music of her voice, the unendingly nuanced light in her eyes, as well as the sweetness or harshness of her movements? What is the fate, in her foetus' and her baby's minds, of the deluge of feelings, emotions, unconscious phantasies and thoughts coming from the mother no one would ever be equipped even to remotely guess?

> But a breaking point can be reached and the sense of continuity lost. In normal circumstances the mother nurses the baby back into existence to the point where discontinuity can once more be tolerated and used for growth purposes. Over and over again the baby dies out and is reborn. Faith is nourished by this repeated resurrection.
>
> (Eigen 1985, p. 329 (pp. 26–27))

As suggested in Chapter 7 – "Mother's reverie and the mystery of introjection" – many of the foetus' and the baby's experiences of dying out and being reborn are gradually strung together by the emotional experience that we used to describe in conceptual language, *hope*. More precisely, the mother is believed to *dream* most of the infant's experiences that he himself is unprepared to convert into new psychical elements into new, hopefully creative experiences. Furthermore, as the mother *dreams* many of these potentially disruptive experiences of her baby's into new psychical elements, not only does she rescue him from the promise of emotional and thought catastrophe – this being where the main point of Bion's concept of mother's reverie is mostly focused on – but she begins to grow some sort *of* new *psychical functions* in her baby, however embryonic, and therefore, even some sort of nascent personality potentially gifted with the capacity for *dreaming* some of his own disruptive experiences into new experiences of the creation of meaning.

But as the mother *dreams* her foetus' and infant's too-trying troubles into budding new qualities, no matter how, a host of mother's feelings, emotions and thoughts are believed to travel into her baby, even to storm into him. The very core of all mother's emotions and qualities that travel into her baby and indeed both stir and govern her *reverie* is her passion and her awe for her baby – her passion, awe and joy for bringing a new mind into the dazzling light of existence. This is seen in this book to be a sweeping experience carrying the enigma of joy into her baby.

As it echoes the marvel of mother's *dreaming* both her foetus' and the infant's own terrifying experiences, even if they are overwhelming emotions, whatever their sources and whatever their natures, into the experience of meaning in the infant, the mother opens for them the mysterious way of introjecting her qualities and, therefore, of growing their capacity for *dreaming* as the epitome of *thinking*.

This makes it possible to see another instance of how to trace back the source and the psychical substance of such a fundamental concept, in this case of concept of hope. If this tentative view invites any plausibility, we can see mother's reverie may eventually surface in the form of a key concept or, in other terms, how a key concept speaks back of its fundamental psychical substance.

This seems how the unsettling emotional experience of the creation of meaning may itself begin to play the key role of container. In the experience of hope, we may *hear* the music of mother's voice in her "speaking" to her foetus and her infant.

5 Mother's Reverie – Another Note

And yet as we succeed in being repeatedly reborn, we are once again back to Bion's line perhaps now seeing a little better how deeply infused is mother's passion into what we tend to call her *love* for her baby: "When the mother loves her infant, what does she do it with? . . . my impression is that her love is expressed by reverie" (Bion 1962, pp. 35–36). How countless feelings, emotions, unconscious phantasies and thoughts intensely pulsate in mother's love for her foetus and her infant? How immensely complex psychical processes live within this little word *love*?

How immensely complex, then, is the introjection of mother's countless feelings and thoughts and qualities disorderly pulsating within her emotions and her thought and her reverie?

How much of mother's love crucially leaves, though so often unseen, within the experience of hope? How often do words echo in this infinitely complex experience of mother's reverie and, therefore, of the strength of her passion and of her shining joy? How much this little word *hope* has to recount to us all of mother's love for her foetus and her infant. How important, I believe, it is to better understand this exceedingly complex cluster of emotions which we use to call *hope* to carefully learn all we can about this other little word *love* – mother's love for her baby, her love being swept into life by the strength of passion, fascination, awe and joy.

How crucially present in the prodigy of the genesis of hope. It furthermore seems evident that as mother's reverie may rescue the baby from imminent mental disaster rescuing him back into the mystery of mental life, it also crucially reveals to the baby the way for him to keep *dreaming* his own mind into an awestruck structure and qualities, leading him, even if at times too abruptly, through the marvellous world pulsating with life and wonder beyond the edge of the unknown, the unknowable and the unthinkable.

How could we *ever* expect to insight, even remotely, into the depth of gratitude and of awe we owe the mother for her reverie? How deeply the experience of hope speaks of her foetus' and of her infant's experience of the mystery of mental life.

What a tragedy that must have ravaged us to the point of leading us to destroy our capacity for passion and fascination. I would take this as perhaps the most fundamental clinical problem challenging and constantly defeating – psychoanalysis.

6 Words as Inspired Harbingers of Unseen Meaning – A Note

We may, at any rate, always hope to have words gradually matured into inspired harbingers of unseen meaning, inviting us not to focus our more immediately observing eyes on their unspeaking surface but rather on their unseen *dreamed* meaning as well as on the *dreams* themselves that they may carry into us, coming from no one knows how many sources but travelling mostly in their music. This seems why Meltzer draws our attention to what he believed, already in his later workings years, that "the music of the voice is the important thing, which is that of your internal objects, which you share with your patients" (1998, p. 202). Meltzer's understanding makes analysis a deeply engaging dialogue between internal characters. Much the same, I would believe, may be said of a love relationship as well as of the connections between creative work and all those who closely follow it. This is also why analysis is to some crucial extent outside the realm of right and wrong.

> The patient does not know anything about whether they [his interpretations] are right or wrong, any more than you as analyst know whether they are right or wrong. Either they fit the material or they don't fit the material. Things can be utterly wrong and fit the material; but that is just the intellectual content, and relates to our theories of emotional development and so on, which are very flimsy and deal more or less just with the surface of mental phenomena.
>
> (Meltzer 2005, p. 457)

The complexity of the genesis of meaning and of the role it plays in mental life goes immeasurably beyond all that we can read in the realm of right and wrong.

We may invite words to flow into the structure of grammar, finding their own ways into sentences, even if sometimes their inspiring strength pressures us to *dream* the grammar so as to persuade it to accommodate inspiring changes in its own previous structure, sharing with us the delight of watching the current sense of sentences repeatedly emerging. If, however, words begin to shine to us as inspiring harbingers of the passion stirring mother's reverie, they may allow us to read into them the prodigy of the creation of meaning. It may also allow us to tentatively read into them how deeply this experience speaks of the meaning of mother's love.

7 The Strengths of Passion and the Myth of Boundaries

Words can be endlessly enriched in at least two different ways. One can endlessly enrich their meaning and endlessly enrich their inspiring strength. Both these ways of enhancing the psychical qualities of words, regardless of what each word in particular may concretely be, are believed to be ruled by the creative strength of the unreadably complex dynamic of psychic reality. The endless enrichment of both the meaning and the inspiring strength of words is a major piece of evidence of the endless enrichment of the work of the contact-barrier crucial to continuously maturing both the *conscious mind* and the *unconscious mind* that the contact-barrier is believed to both continuously create and govern (again, cf. Chapters 2, 3, 4, 6, 7, 8, 9, 13, 14 and 15). This is also crucial to keep making life and the world glittering with insight and meaning. But what best brings this key quality into full life and guides its potentially endless strength is once again believed to be passion for the mother and to the experience of converting her reverie into *dreaming* his own mind into life.

In other words, the strength of passion is believed to be both the more immediate drive and the main guiding light of the creative strength of the mind. The creative capacity of the human mind is believed not only to challenge the concept of limit but to ultimately dissolve it away into an irrelevant abstraction. Chapter 26 – "Passion and the wonder of unmeasure" – examined yet another awe-inspiring quality of the human mind – the capacity, that is, for continuously creating the unmeasure. This quality too plays a key role in deepening the meaning of *being human*.

8 Loyalty to Passion and the Meaning of Being Human – A Note

And yet Bion keeps warping language down into many pages that constantly defeat readability. He again and again walks us all along an odd, uncertain edge between intuition, evocation, perplexity and incomprehension. Words are often seen running out of his own grip, this seeming at times the realm he may feel closer to, even deeper into. Unintelligibly, however, never stopped him. He never gives up worrying language into even insane oracular pieces. Dilemma recurs in his hand over and over again. Even so, he keeps forcing language to speak out for his own vision however awkwardly. And yet I believe he still remains fully loyal to what this book believes, once again, was his most illuminating vision: that psychical life essentially pulsates beyond the edge of the unknown, the unknowable and the unthinkable. This is where Bion's direction of research most crucially focus. This also is where Bion's direction of research invites us to go with him, even to lose our direction, or *any* direction. He, therefore, pushes the boundaries of language aside, surprising us by constantly disbelieving the pseudo wisdom of limits as well as the rhetoric of right and wrong. The idea of all-encompassing view of the human mind had, of course, been blown away into the dust of limits and rules. The dynamic of psychical life, both raised and crucially directed by unbridled passion, repeatedly teaches us that behind our submission to compromising with limits and restraints breathes the cowardice before the wounding strength of passion, the awestruck experience of mother's reverie, as well as the unsettling impact of the beauty of the mother called by Meltzer the impact of the *dazzle of the sunrise* lying in the core of Meltzer's *theory of aesthetic conflict* (Meltzer & Williams 1988, pp. 28–29). To have no limits in *dreaming* the human mind itself into ever new qualities, ever new *dreaming functions*, ever new qualities of the personality, ever new ways of feeling, ever new ways of thinking, is perhaps the most distinctive quality of the meaning of *being human*. I would believe that we should ask the unique quality of *being human* to give us a hand in guiding us through every clinic hour.

Bion's loyalty to his own far-reaching intuition opened a wide way for Meltzer's vision of the critical role of passion in mental life, in giving the creative strength of the unconscious the commanding voice in psychical life, and here again in the history of psychoanalysis, in reshaping anew the meaning of *being human*.

9 The Rider and the Horse

In his XXXI New Introductory Lecture to Psychoanalysis, Freud called back on to the stage the image of the rider and the horse to more vividly represent the general ties linking the ego and the id (1933a, S.E. 22, p. 77). In Freud's image, the ego prided itself to command the powerful energy of the unthinking horse directing it wherever the ego wished the horse to take it. Only too often, however, does the proud rider see himself suddenly incapable of persuading the horse to obey its command, being itself often forcefully driven to where the horse wished to go, just ignoring the ego's wishes and protests. Meltzer, however, turned Freud's image on its head, seeing the ego the frightened horse, opposing each new insight and idea coming from the internal characters' passion and vision, recoiling before change and still more before the creative strength of the unreadably complex dynamic of psychic reality. The frightened ego assaults, in despair, the internal characters' voices that point us the many ways leading us into inner maturity. The quivering ego finds refuge in the cowardice of the groups, struggling to be listened to as the authorized voice of reason and common sense. And indeed, Freud has always infused into the ego a host of reassuring virtues, seeing it as the flag and the voice of reason, the last guarding of men's fate. In the last of his New Introductory Lectures of Psychoanalysis – Lecture XXXV – Freud made his voice more clearly heard than ever before or after on a way of thinking that soon became not only foundational of psychoanalysis but *the* most important element in the fundamental structure of psychoanalysis. This voice of Freud's can perhaps best be listened to as he neared the end of this famous lecture:

> Our best hope for the future is that intellect – the scientific spirit, reason – may in the process of time establish a dictatorship in the mental life of man. The nature of reason is a guarantee that afterwards it will not fail to give man's emotional impulses and what is determined by them the position they deserve. But the common compulsion exercised by such a dominance of reason will prove to be the strongest bond among men and lead the way to further unions. Whatever, like

religion's prohibition against thought, opposes such a development, is a danger for the future of mankind.

(1933a, S.E. 22, pp. 171–172)

These lines string together countless pieces of evidence of the same fundamental way of thinking scattered virtually throughout his entire work. This is the same voice which, five years later, we easily recognize as coming from the same source: "We have arrived at a general acquaintance with the psychical apparatus, with the parts, organs and agencies of which it is composed, with the forces operating in it and with the functions allotted to its parts" (Freud, S. (1940 [1938]), S.E. 23, p. 183). Ten years before Freud had already endorsed the ego with these qualities, so consistent with both previous quotes: "The ego represents what may be called reason and common sense, in contrast with the id, which contains the passions" (Freud 1923, S.E. 19, p. 25). What human mind is, then, on the one hand, warped to obey Freud's vision, but on the other is believed to pulsate with life well beyond the edge of the unknown, the unknowable and the unthinkable; that generates *dreaming functions* which are believed to continuously create and govern the creative strength of the unreadably complex dynamic of psychic reality; that is believed to wound us with the impact of beauty and the creative power of passion and that the *dazzle of the sunrise* which we may watch everywhere in life and the wonder of passion are seen as the core of the human mind; that thinking with passion is the only way of being faithful to the prodigy of thinking; that the keen sense of unmeasure lies in the heart of joy, making it shining out as a key light of the human mind; that research into will soon drown us into perplexity and wonder.

What human mind is, then, the psychoanalytic human mind? Which of these human minds is the one psychoanalysis proudly alleges to investigate, cure and lecture the world on?

So as he turned Freud's image of the rider and the horse on its head, Meltzer saw the frightened and recoiling ego to really embody Freud's view of resistance and of compulsion to repeat. It is the ego that is now seen as the fierce guardian of the status quo, of what in us shy at the unknowable, the unknowable and the unthinkable, that is taken aback before the unbridled strength of passion, that guides us into the lifeless humiliation of the groups.

And yet closely following Bion, soon Meltzer entrusted the helm of creative thought with the unconscious and the internal characters utterly changing things in virtually every clinic hour, providing both the analysand and the analyst himself with a very different experience of analysis.

10 On the Rhetoric of Right and Wrong and the Voice of Passion – A New Note

Jim Allison, awarded the 2018 Nobel Prize in Medicine and Physiology, had already been awarded the Lascker Foundation Prize. When he received the latter, he made it clear why he had decided not to be a doctor but rather a scientist: for he would not stand the responsibility of always being supposed to be right. While doctors are indeed always supposed to be right, scientists were always supposed to be wrong. So scientists feel free to launch themselves into research and carefully look into their problems and their conjectures freed from the choking threat of having to be right. Answers never interested him. Evidently, Freud's genius straddled both qualities: of being a doctor as well as a scientist. He indeed has never given up the call of a doctor in him. However, as a scientist, he had never seen himself to challenge the eighteenth-century scientific frame of thought.[2] We really had to wait for Bion, but particularly for Meltzer, to move away from the urge to be right for the urge to be passionate. Loyalty to our own passion may compel us to live in the privileged light of uncertainty. Loyalty to passion may soon reveal the rhetoric of right or wrong to be both a bore and a paranoid-schizoid factor disturbing the strength of passion and of the depth of our gratitude and awe for mother's reverie.

Deprived of the shining light of passion, if we deeply involve ourselves in either clinic or research, we are always believed to be essentially wrong. The courage we summon to assist us in standing before our internal or external enemies pale in the face of the courage we need to stand before the unsettling strength of passion as well as of the experience of intimacy. Shunning both these constant experiences, we are believed to threaten the truth of analysis and, possibly also, the truth of the way we live our lives.

11 "Thinking With Passion Is the Unconscious Thing"

Psychoanalysis has always been alarmingly silent about *passion, fascination* and *awe*. And yet these are all foundational experiences of the human mind and crucial in illuminating the meaning of *being human*. We had to wait for Meltzer to first watch these emotions being unearthed from the sadly poor conceptual frame of psychoanalysis and moved to the core of research. Meltzer was also first to argue, furthermore, that analysis ultimately turns around the vitality, the truth and the fate of these emotions in both the analysand and the analyst. In my tentative understanding, this lack of passion and awe before the unending prodigies of the human mind is the gloomiest and most unfortunate side of psychoanalysis. It continuously wounds the human mind as well as the unique privilege of being allowed to very closely follow its endless marvels. This seems to be why Meltzer's insight that thinking with passion is the unconscious thing is so crucial.

How could we ever get a glimpse of the meaning and the reach of mother's reverie and of the experience of introjecting the deluge of emotional experiences storming into her baby by which the mother makes it possible for her foetus, her infant, and indeed for us all throughout life to endlessly *dream* it into the unique prodigy of creating a human mind? How could we ever go through that experience if we do not passionately follow our own unconscious deeply passionate experience of it? How could we come any near the *meaning* of the creative strength of the unreadably complex dynamic of psychic reality if, again, we do not somehow *read it* in ourselves, going through the emotional turmoil it throws us into? And the same about the sweeping experience of intimacy, the unsettling experience of the creation of meaning through introjecting mother's reverie, the intuition of the mystery of things pulsating in the human mind being, in Meltzer's claim, the deepest meaning of knowledge. Thinking with passion is the truest way of thinking in psychoanalysis and the truest way of thinking outside it. This view would burden analysts with the trying responsibility of watching themselves particularly closely along the clinic hour, reading the parts of their personality that seem incapable of thinking with passion, of experiencing the awestruck mysteries tightly weaving the human mind, the frightening marvel of intimacy, the inspiring power of uncertainty, and of closely *hearing* the shining light of unmeasure gradually emerging in the couch as well as in the chair, as the analysis ripens.

The creative strength of passion wounds us into the turmoil of creativity, and therefore, to risk seeing what we do not.

I do not know of any way of thinking about the human mind which is not grippingly passionate.

Notes

1 Donald Meltzer 1998, p. 202.
2 And not, I believe, the nineteenth century as it is sometimes inadequately said.

Chapter 27

The Inspiring Light of Perplexity and the Emerging Experience of Mystery

A Note

We all owe Bion the discovery of uncertainty in psychoanalysis, and to Meltzer to have ripened this discovery into a key guiding light through both research and all along virtually every single clinic hour. Meltzer has, furthermore, ripened uncertainty into a precious source of inspiration in both these areas.

The discovery of the preciousness of uncertainty in psychoanalysis is believed to profoundly shift its history. Many crucial points of evidence arguing for the crucial importance of this puzzling and yet highly promising shift have already been discussed in this book. And yet I am not even remotely equipped to follow the eyes of the still unwritten history of how far into the future the discovery of uncertainty in psychoanalysis will ultimately reshape it. In Bion's hands, soon the discovery of uncertainty came to walk its way into his own way of thinking and reveal its surprisingly inspiring strength both in closely following the course of virtually every clinic hour and in best guiding him all along his researching efforts into the human mind. Soon uncertainty became the fundamental syntax of much of Bion's language. Closely following Bion's as well as Meltzer's, the language of psychoanalysis has been maturing so as to best equip us to grope through the unending enigmas and mysteries tightly weaving the human mind, or once again more precisely, even *being* the core of the human mind. This odd syntax is believed to assist us in taking a few deeper steps into the unreadable complexities of the human mind and, crucially, to learn to trust the far wiser voices of our good internal characters by *hearing*, in the unending changing music of their voices, the much they so often have to tell us, even to reveal to us and, in particular, its awe-inspiring beauty, never recognized before. Most of this book does not exactly come from the words themselves through which Bion has shared with history so many of

DOI: 10.4324/9781003375159-30

his so revealing thoughts, but from the inspiring depth of his own experience of perplexity and continuously feeling lost before the immense much he could not see of the unreadable complexity and awe-inspiring beauty of the human mind. Soon his deep experience of perplexity ripened into his feeling lost and indeed uncomprehending before the sea of enigmas and mysteries tightly texturing the awestruck complexity of the human mind. His feeling so often lost in both perplexity and yet in wonder leaves us in little doubt of how profoundly Bion came to disbelieve the merits of knowledge, understanding, thinking and reason to alone guide our steps towards the truth of psychic reality and, therefore also, all along the clinic hour. Bion being so often lost in perplexity being *in itself* so deeply inspiring and fundamental for us all.

It was, however, for Meltzer to ripen the treasure of Bion's discovery of uncertainty as well as his courage never to resort to the soothing and yet degrading device of certainties, into the awestruck experience of the beauty and the defeating complexity of the human mind.

But Meltzer is believed in this book to have gone even more deeply in ripening Bion's visionary model of the mind. The deeper and truer our feeling lost in both perplexity and wonder, the deeper and truer our *hearing*, rather than listening to both analysand and ourselves, and the deeper and truer we become to the sense of mystery of the human mind.

As both Bion's and Meltzer's ways of thinking begin to filter down to both every clinic hour as well as our groping steps along research, I believe we grow more and more sensitive to the key importance of the music of the voices in the room, flowing from the couch to the chair as well as from the chair to the couch, teaching us to convert the canonical way of *listening*, so deeply infiltrated by the myths of knowledge, understanding, thinking and the disaster of certainty and the stupidity of smugness, as both Bion's and Meltzer's ways of thinking begin to filter down to our own view of clinical work and direction of research into the far more demanding and sensitive way of *hearing* is believed to show us to ripen the clinical work into the experience of intimacy in Meltzer's sense of intimacy as the place in the psychic world where thoughts are created. And the more passionately we *hear* both the music of the analysand's internal characters as well as the one coming from our own internal characters' voices, the more we are believed in this book to deepen our insight into the mystery of things.

Conclusion

I am immensely privileged to have worked with Donald Meltzer in supervision for 13 years, meeting him in Oxford every month and twice monthly for the last few years.

The last time I worked with him, Meltzer was already fatally ill. As I entered the room, on that last sad morning, I immediately realized that it might perhaps be too demanding for him to closely follow and comment on yet another particularly long clinical report. And yet Meltzer still asked me to read for him a draft of an essay on his claustrum theory that I was writing at that time. Two other colleagues had joined us that morning. I edged my chair so as to even touch his. I kept reading my drafted essay very slowly, making sustained pauses at the end of each paragraph.

Meltzer's breathing was already so difficult that a heavy sense of gloom dominated the atmosphere in the room. Exhausted, his eyes closed, Meltzer was making an evident effort to closely follow my reading. At a certain moment of my reading, one of the colleagues attending this last meeting commented: "But after all, you cannot be beyond the breaking point." At that moment, Meltzer's voice suddenly erupted through such atmosphere in such a strenuous and astonishingly powerful clamour: "NOOO!! You *always* have to be *beyond* the breaking point!!"

DOI: 10.4324/9781003375159-31

Bibliography

Aguayo, J. (2013). "Bion's Caesura: From Public Lecture to Published Text". In: *Growth and Turbulence in the Container/Contained*. Ed. H. B. Levine and L. J. Brown. London: Routledge, 1975–1977.

Aquinas, T. (1990). *Somme Théologique*. Coord. A. Raulin and Trans. A.-M. Roguet and J.-H. de Nicolas. Comm. ns. I, tomes I–IV. Paris: Éditions du Cerf, 2–26.

Aristotle. (1984). "De Anima". In: *The Complete Works of Aristotle – The Revised Oxford Translation*. Ed. J. Barnes, vol. I. Princeton: Princeton University Press, 1991.

Aristotle. (1990). "Sleep.- Dreams". cf. D. Gallop. In: *Aristotle on Sleep and Dream*, Text Trans. and Intro. Peterborough, ON: Broadviesw Press, 1991.

Aristotle. (1991). "On Memory". Ed. and Trans. J. I. Beare. In: *The Complete Works of Aristotle – The Revised Oxford Translation*. Ed. J. Barnes, vol. I. Princeton: Princeton University Press.

Bion, W. (1961). *Experiences in Groups*. London: Routledge.

Bion, W. (1962). *Learning from Experience*. London: Karnac, 1990.

Bion, W. (1962a). "A Theory of Thinking". In: *Second Thoughts*. London: Karnac, 1990.

Bion, W. (1965). *Transformations*. London: Karnac Books, 1991.

Bion, W. (1967). "Notes on Memory and Desire". In: *Los Angeles Seminars and Supervision*. Ed. J. Aguayo and B. Marlin. London: Karnac, 2013. (see below)[1]

Bion, W. (1970). *Attention & Interpretation*. London: Karnac Books.

Bion, W. (1978). *Four Discussions with Wilfred Bion*. Pertshire: Clunie Press.

Bion, W. (1980). *Bion in New York and Sao Paulo*. Pertshire: Clunie Press.

Bion, W. (1987). *Clinical Seminars and Four Papers*. Abington: Fleetwood Press.

Bion, W. (1990). *Brazilian Lectures 1973–1974*. London: Karnac Books.

Bion, W. (1992). *Cogitations*. Ed. Francesca Bion. London: Karnac Books, 2006.

Bion, W. (1997). *Taming Wild Thoughts*. Ed. Francesca Bion. London: Karnac Books.

Bion, W. (2005). *The Tavistock Seminars*. Ed. Francesca Bion. London: Karnac Books.

Bion, W. (2013). *Los Angeles Seminars and Supervision*. Ed. J. Aguayo and B. Marlin. London: Karnac Books.

Bloom, H. (1999). *Shakespeare – The Invention of the Human*. London: Fourth Estate.

Brenner, S. (2002). "Interview to Peter Sylwn of the Nobel Foundation". *Nobelprize.org*.

Breuer, J. (1895). "Studies on Hysteria III – Theoretical". *S.E.*, II, 181–251.

Carroll, L. (1897). "Through the Looking-Glass". In: *The Annotated Alice*. Ed. M. Gardner. New York: W. W. Norton, 2000.

Cavell, S. (1987). "The Avoidance of Love: A Reading of *King Lear*". In: *Disowning Knowledge – In Six Plays of Shakespeare*. Cambridge: Cambridge University Press.

De Masi, F. (2000). "The Unconscious and Psychosis: Some Considerations on the Psycho-Analytic Theory of Psychosis". *International Journal of Psychoanalysis*, 5.

De Masi, F. (2009). *Vulnerability to Psychosis*. London: Karnac Books.

Eigen, M. (1985). "Towards Bion's Starting Point: Between Catastrophe and Faith". *International Journal of Psychoanalysis*, 1985–1966, 321–330.

Freud, S. (1895). "Project for a Scientific Psychology". *S.E.*, 1.

Freud, S. (1900a). "Interpretation of Dreams". *S.E.*, 4.

Freud, S. (1900b). "Interpretation of Dreams". *S.E.*, 5.

Freud, S. (1911). "Formulations on the Two Principles of Mental Functioning". *S.E.*, 12.

Freud, S. (1915a). "The Unconscious". *S.E.*, 14.

Freud, S. (1915b). "Instincts and Their Vicissitudes". *S.E.*, 14.

Freud, S. (1920). "Beyond the Pleasure Principle". *S.E.*, 18.

Freud, S. (1923). "The Ego and the Id". *S.E.*, 19.

Freud, S. (1926). "The Question of Lay Analysis". *S.E.*, 20.

Freud, S. (1930). "Civilization and Its Discontents". *S.E.*, 21.

Freud, S. (1933a). "The Dissection of the Psychical Personality". *New Introductory Lectures on Psycho-Analysis. S.E.*, Lecture XXXI, 22.

Freud, S. (1933b). "The Question of a Weltanschauung". *New Introductory Lectures on Psycho-Analysis. S.E.*, Lecture XXXV, 22.

Freud, S. (1938a). "Splitting of the Ego in the Process of Defence". *S.E.*, 23.

Freud, S. (1938b). "Some Elementary Lessons in Psycho-Analysis". *S.E.*, 23.

Freud, S. (1940 [1938]). "An Outline of Psycho-Analysis". *S.E.*, 23.

Freud, S. (1985). *The Complete Letters of Sigmund Freud to Wilhelm Fliess, 1887–1904*. Trans. and Ed. J. M. Masson. Cambridge: Harvard University Press.

Gardner, M. (2000). *The Annotated Alice*. New York: W. W. Norton.

Gombrich, E. H. (1986). *Kokoschka in His Time*. London: Tate Gallery Publications.

Gomes, A. (2014). "Kant on Perception: Naïve Realism, Non-Conceptualism, and the B-Deduction". *Philosophical Quaterly*, 64. 1–19th Century Scientific Frame of Thought.

Guthrie, W. C. (1971). *The Sophists*. Cambridge: Cambridge University Press, 1991.

Haroche, S.; Wineland, D. J. (2012). Interview to Adam Smith: Nobel Foundation. In: Nobelprize.org.

Heaney, S. (1995). *The Redress of Poetry – Oxford Lectures*. London: Faber and Faber.

Isaacs, S. (1943a). "The Nature and Function of Phantasy". In: *The Freud-Klein Controversies 1941–1945*. Ed. P. King and R. Steiner. London: Tavistock, Routledge, 1991, 265–321.

Isaacs, S. (1943b). "The Nature and Function of Phantasy". *International Journal of Psychoanalysis*, 1948, 29, no. 2.

Isaacs, S. (1952). "The Nature and Function of Phantasy". In: *Developments in Psycho-Analysis*. Ed. M. Klein et al. London: Karnac Books and The Institute of Psycho-Analysis. First published in *International Journal of Psychoanalysis*, 1948, 29, 73–97.

Kahn, C. (1979). *The Art of Heraclitus: An Edition of the Fragments with Translation and Commentary*. Cambridge: Cambridge University Press, 1989.

Kant, I. (1992). "The Jaesche Logic". Ed. G. B. Jaesche, 1800. In: *The Cambridge Edition of the Works of Immanuel Kant*. Trans. and Ed. J. M. Young. Cambridge: Cambridge University Press.

Kant, I. (1996). *Critique of Pure Reason*. Trans. ns. W. S. Pluhar. Indiapolis and Cambridge: Hackett Publishing Company.

Kant, I. (1997). *Critique of Pure Reason*. Eds. and Trans. P. Guyer and A. W. Wood. Cambridge: Cambridge University Press.

Keats, J. (1970). *Complete Poems*. Ed. and Notes Miriam Allot. New York: Longman.

Keats, J. (1990). *Letters of John Keats*. Ed. R. Gittings. Oxford: Oxford University Press.

Klein, M. (1930). "The Importance of Symbol-Formation in the Development of the Ego". In: *The Writings of Melanie Klein*, vol. I. London: The Hogarth Press, 1975.

Klein, M. (1931). "A Contribution to the Theory of Intellectual Inhibition". In: *The Writings of Melanie Klein*, vol. I. London: The Hogarth Press, 1975.

Klein, M. (1933). "The Early Development of Conscience in the Child". In: *The Writings of Melanie Klein*, vol. I. London: The Hogarth Press, 1975.

Klein, M. (1935). "A Contribution to the Psychogenesis of Manic-Depressive States". In: *The Writings of Melanie Klein*, vol. I. London: The Hogarth Press, 1985 (1975).

Klein, M. (1946). "Notes on Some Schizoid Mechanisms". In: *The Writings of Melanie Klein*, vol. III. London: The Hogarth Press, 1987 (1975).

Klein, M. (1958). "On the Development of Mental Functioning". In: *The Writings of Melanie Klein*, vol. III. London: The Hogarth Press, 1975.

Klein, M. (MS und.). "Notes re Terms 'Internal Objects', 'Inner Objects', etc., 'Good' and 'Bad' Objects, etc." MS., Melanie Klein Trust, Wellcome Library, D16, udt.

Lima, M. C. S. (2015). "Thinking with Passion". An Interview Conducted by J. S. Monteiro. In: *Theaching Meltzer*. Ed. Meg Harris Williams. London: Karnac, 143–156.

Lima, M. C. S. (2016). *Em que sítio da minha cabeça levo a Maria do Carmo?* (*In What Place of My Head Do I Take Maria Do Carmo?*). Lisboa: VSE, 2017.

Meltzer, D. (1973). *Sexual States of Mind*. Perthshire: Clunie Press, 1979.

Meltzer, D. (1978a). "A Note on Introjective Processes". In: *Sincerity and Other Works*. London: Karnac Books, 1994.

Meltzer, D. (1978b). *The Kleinian Development III: The Clinical Significance of the Work of Bion*. Perthshire: Clunie Press.

Meltzer, D. (1978c). *Introduction to the Collected Papers of Roger Money-Kyrle*. Ed. D. Meltzer. Perthshire: Clunie Press.

Meltzer, D. (1985). "The Urge to Assimilate New Ideas Are Experiences Equivalent to Falling in Love". Interview to J. S. Monteiro. *Revista Portuguesa de Psicanálise*. Lisboa, 2022.

Meltzer, D. (1986). *Studies in Extended Metapsychology*. Perthshire: Clunie Press.

Meltzer, D. (1987). "Concerning the Distinction Between Conflicts of Desire and Paradoxes of Thought". In: *Sincerity and Other Works*. Ed. A. Hahn. London: Karnac Books, 1994.

Meltzer, D. (1988). "Concerning the Stupidity of Evil". In: *Sincerity and Other Works*. Ed. A. Hahn. London: Karnac Books, 1994.

Meltzer, D. (1989). "Models of the Mind: The Development of Psychoanalysis from Freud to Melanie Klein to Wilfred Bion". Read in Munich. Unpublished.

Meltzer, D. (1992). *The Claustrum: An Investigation of Claustrophobic Phenomena*. Perthshire: Clunie Press.

Meltzer, D. (1996). "On the Claustrum". Lecture held at the UKC Centre for Psychoanalytic Studies – Tenth Anniversary Guest, June. Unedited and unpublished. By Courtesy of R. Willoughby.

Meltzer, D. (1997). "Interview by Marc du Ry". In: *The Klein-Lacan Dialogues*. Ed. B. Bourgoyne and M. Sullivan. London: Rebus Press, 177–185.

Meltzer, D. (1998). "I've Been Done Its Way!". Interview Given to C. M. Smith. *Journal of Melanie Klein and Object Relations*, 16, no. 2, June. Reprinted In: S. F. Cassese, *Introduction to the Work of Donald Meltzer*. London: Karnac, Appendix 1.

Meltzer, D. (2005). "Creativity and the Counter-Transference". In: *The Vale of Soulmaking*. Ed. Meg Harris Williams. London: Karnac Books, 175ff.

Meltzer, D., and M. Williams. (1988). *The Apprehension of Beauty – The Role of Aesthetic Conflict in Development, Violence and Art*. Prethshire: Clunie Press.

Miller, L. et al. (1997). *Closely Observed Infants*. London: Duckword, 1989.

Milton, J. (1990). "Paradise Lost". In: *John Milton*. Ed. S. Gorgel and J. Goldberg. The Oxford Authors. Oxford: Oxford University Press.

Monteiro, J. S. (2019). *Long-Term Psychoanalytic Supervision with Donald Meltzer: The Tragedy of Triumph*. London: Routledge.

O'Driscoll, D. (2008). *Stepping Stones – Interviews with Seamus Heaney*. London: Faber and Faber.

O'Shaughnessy, E. (1981). "W. R. Bion's Theory of Thinking and New Techniques in Child Analysis". In: *Melanie Klein Today*. Ed. E. B. Spillius, vol. 2. London: Routledge, 1988, 177–190.

Ogden, T. (2003). "On Not Being Able to Dream". *International Journal of Psychoanalysis*, 84, no. 1.

Ogden, T. H. (1997). *Reverie and Interpretation: Sensing Something Human*. Northvale, NJ: Jason Aronson.

Pais, A. (1991). *Niels Bohr's Times in Physics, Philosophy and Politics*. Oxford: Clarendon Press.

Plato. (1987). "Republic". Trans. P. Shorey. In: *The Complete Dialogues of Plato*. Notes Ed. Hamilton and H. Cairns. Princeton: Princeton University Press.

Plato. (1997). "Theaetetus". In: *Plato – Complete Works*. Ed., Intr. and notes J. M. Cooper. Indianapolis: Hackett Publishing Company.

Plato. (1999). *Theaetetus*. Trans. J. McDowell. Oxford: Clarendon Press.

Poincaré, H. (1908). "Science et Methode". In: *Philosophia Scientiae Archives – Centre d'Études et de Recherche Henri Poincaré*. Paris: Éditions Kimé, 1999.

Poincaré, H. (u.d.). *Science and Method*. New York: Dover Publication.

Riviere, J. (1952). "General Introduction". In: *Developments in Psycho-Analysis*. Ed. M. Klein et al. London: Karnac Books and The Institute of Psycho-Analysis, 1989.

Robinson, T. M. (1987). *Heraclitus: Fragments*. Text Trans. Comm. Toronto: University of Toronto Press.

Scalzone, F., and G. Zontini. (2001). "The Dream's Navel Between Chaos and Thought". *International Journal of Psychoanalysis*, 82, no. 2.

Schneider, J. A. (2005). "Reply to Dr. Alexander". *International Journal of Psychoanalysis*, 86, no. 5.

Schneider, J. A. (2010). "From Freud's Dream-Work to Bion's Work of Dreaming: The Changing Conception of Dreaming in Psycho-Analytic Theory". *International Journal of Psychoanalysis*, 91–93.

Shakespeare. (1997). *King Lear*. Ed. A. R. Foakes and Arden Shakespeare. Walton-on-Thames: Thomas Nelson and Sons.

Shakespeare. (2000). *King Lear*. Ed. S. Well. Oxford: Oxford University Press.

Shakespeare. (2006). *Hamlet*. Ed. A. Thomson and N. Taylor. London: Arden Shakespeare.

Shelley, P. B. (1821a). "Defence of Poetry". In: *English Essays: Sidney to Macaulay*, vol. 27. The Harvard Classics, 1909–1914.

Shelley, P. B. (1821b). "Defence of Poetry". In: *Percy Bysshe Shelley – The Major Works*. Oxford: Oxford University Press, 2003.

Sidney, P. (1593). *The Countess of Pembroke's Arcadia*. Ed. and Trans. M. Evans. London: Peguin Classics, 1987.

Sidney, P. (1987). *The Countess of Pembroke's Arcadia*. London: Peguin Classics. In: *Psychoanalytic Quarterly*, 85, no. 2.

Stänicke, E. et al. (2020). "The Epistemological Stance of Psychoanalysis: Revisiting the Kantian Legacy". *Contemporary Psychoanalysis*, 89, no. 2.

Steiner, J. (2016). *Illusion, Disillusion, and Irony in Psychoanalysis*. In: *Psychoanal. Q.* 85-2, p. 434.

Van Gogh, V. (1999). *The Complete Letters of Vincent Van Gogh*, vol. I–III. London: Thames & Hudson.

Wittgenstein, L. (2009). *Philosophical Investigations*. Trans. G. E. M. Anscombe, P. M. S. Hacker, and Joaquim Schulte and Ed. P. M. S. Hacker and J. Schulte, rev. 4th ed. Oxford: Wiley-Blackwell.

Note

1 The first edition listed – Bion 2013, ed. J. Aguayo and Malin – is the only one to my knowledge that offers the four Discussants' responses in full, as well as an introduction, even though this is a very brief introduction.

Index